O9-ABH-626

OXFORD

Jack Russell — p. 84

EX LIBRIS

TSM

OXFORD

JAN MORRIS

OXFORD UNIVERSITY PRESS

OXFORD LONDON NEW YORK

Oxford University Press, Walton Street, Oxford OX2 6DP

OXFORD LONDON GLASGOW
NEW YORK TORONTO MELBOURNE WELLINGTON
IBADAN NAIROBI DAR ES SALAAM CAPE TOWN
KUALA LUMPUR SINGAPORE JAKARTA HONG KONG TOKYO
DELHI BOMBAY CALCUTTA MADRAS KARACHI

First published October 1965
by Faber and Faber Limited
Second impression November 1965
New Edition 1968
Revised edition published by
Oxford University Press and
first issued as an Oxford
Paperback 1978

© *1965 and 1978 by Jan Morris*

All rights reserved. No part of this publication may be reproduced,
stored in a retrieval system, or transmitted, in any form or by any means,
electronic, mechanical, photocopying, recording, or otherwise, without
the prior permission of Oxford University Press

This book is sold subject to the condition that it shall not, by way of
trade or otherwise, be lent, re-sold, hired out, or otherwise circulated
without the publisher's prior consent in any form of binding or cover
other than that in which it is published and without a similar condition
including this condition being imposed on the subsequent purchaser

British Library Cataloguing in Publication Data
Morris, Jan
  Oxford—Revised ed.
  1. Oxford—Description
  I. Title
  914.25′74′04857   DA690.098   77–30693
  ISBN 0–19–211571–5
  ISBN 0–19–285074–1 Pbk

Printed in Great Britain by
Butler & Tanner Ltd
Frome, Somerset

For
SUSAN MORRIS
born in Oxford

Acknowledgements

I owe my especial thanks to the Master and Fellows of University College, who most kindly and unexpectedly offered me membership of their common room during the time I was working on this book, enhancing the pleasure of an already agreeable chore.

So many other people have helped me with the work, in its original edition and in revisions, that I hope they will accept the book itself as a token of my gratitude, forgiving its faults and claiming its merits as their own.

Contents

Illustrations

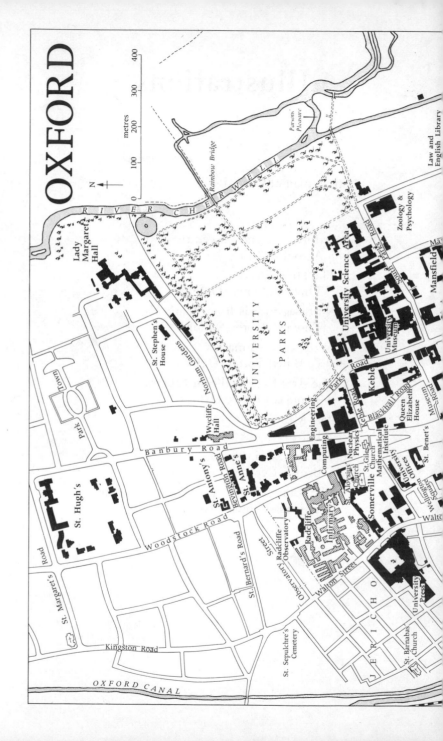

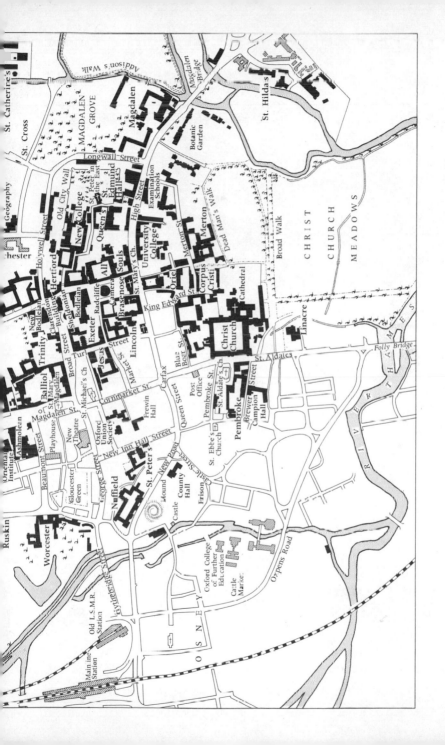

ONE

Slap in the middle of England stands the city of Oxford, on an ancient crossroads beside the Thames. Its origins are obscure but its fame is universal, and it forms a national paradigm—in whose structure, sometimes shadowy, sometimes splendidly sunlit, we may explore the history, the character and the condition of the English.

1. Piebald

Fifty years ago, if you stood beneath the western escarpment of the Chiltern Hills, you could sometimes see the smoke of London drifting through the Goring Gap. The hills here form an outerwork of Middle England—by which I mean the agricultural basin that lies like a no man's land between the capital and the industrial regions of Birmingham and Coventry. The Chilterns, the Berkshire Downs and the Cotswolds ring this patch of pastoral country protectively, and seem to keep the world at bay: and though London is not so smoky as she used to be, still anyone standing today on the countryside of the Chilterns is likely to feel that some great black energy is contained by the hills and beechwoods, and that by suggestive contrast the landscapes behind are delectably sweet and peaceful.

Through this soft central country runs the River Thames. It rises near Cirencester (a chipped and supine figure of Father Thames, rescued from the ruins of the Crystal Palace, stands sentinel at its source); meanders placidly across Oxfordshire and Berkshire; disappears between the Chilterns and the Downs; and is finally set upon by London to be turned into 'liquid 'istory' and spewed grimily into the sea. The Thames sets the style of Middle England, so undramatic, so gentle, so eminently a region for weekend anglers with folding stools, Sunday newspapers and patient wives in floral frocks. The progress of the river is slow and orderly—it passes through 62 locks between source and sea. Its manner is sedate: 89 bridges cross the stream, by my count on the map, and you can walk along its towpath all the way to London, except at moments when, for infuriating reasons of lost convenience, the path suddenly springs from one bank to the other without bridge or ferry-boat. It used to be a great highway, for the war galleys of the Danes as for the coal barges of the English, but nowadays almost its only craft are launches, skiffs, punts, comical electrical canoes and graceful old-school pleasure steamers with raked white funnels like royal yachts.

Very little ugliness mars these rural reaches of the Thames. The river passes calmly between rich woods and lush meadow-lands, through handsome market towns and villages with graceful bridges, and most people think of it in terms of warm evenings in cushioned boats, gnats, beers on the lawns of riverside pubs and hilarious contretempts at mooring places. In retrospect it always seems to be summer on the Thames, and a fine day at that. The meteorological records for these parts assure us that July 4, 1862, was 'cool and rather wet': but on that day Lewis Carroll first told the tale of *Alice in Wonderland* to four people in a Thames gig, rowing upstream for a picnic tea, and to the ends of their lives all four remembered the afternoon as a dream of cloudless English sunshine.

When the Thames is half-way to its mouth the River Cherwell joins it from the north, at a point where the counties of Oxfordshire, Berkshire and Buckinghamshire more or less meet. This is the very middle of Middle England, almost as far from the sea as you can be in these islands. It is pleasant country, but mouldy, as though the damp has got in. Once heavily forested, now it is mostly meadow-land, interspersed with low wooded hills and threaded by the flood-fields, soggy but fertile, that line the rivers themselves. Its villages, by and large, win no prizes from tourist associations. Its country houses, though fine, are often in bad repair, standing as they do just outside the fructifying range of London's commuters. Its rectories have often been sold to the laity, and are decorously done up by local solicitors, or camped in by blithe Bohemians with uncountable children. There is nothing spectacular to this stretch of country—no downland above the river, no magnificent gorge, not even a white chalk horse on a hill face. It is standard England rural scenery: just, as exiles from London like to say with a sniff— just *country*.

The junction of Thames and Cherwell is equidistant from the three main sea inlets of southern England—Thames Estuary, Bristol Channel, Solent. If you placed a cross on a map of the southern country, its arms would meet somewhere here. The site is thus almost allegorically central, and is an ancient and important crossroads. Here the main road from Birmingham to the south coast crosses the Thames, at a point where the shallow gravel bottom has always made an easy ford. A mile or two away a big lateral road passes on its way from London to South Wales. The railway from London to Worcester runs nearby, and there are lines northward to Coventry and Birmingham, north-eastward to Bedford. Here, too, the Thames is linked with the English canal system, spreading fan-like through the Black Country into Yorkshire. Five bridges cross the Thames at this place, and in the winter most of those condescending old pleasure steamers come here to hibernate. It is a fulcrum: a hub where the industrial energies of England, rampaging across this pastoral country from factories to ports, distributors to markets, meet with a roar of exhausts in an environment of moist green languor.

Around the crossroads stands the middle-sized city of Oxford. It is a municipal and parliamentary borough, so the gazetteer tells us, a county town, the seat of a university and of an episcopal see, with a population in 1978 of about 115,000 and factories for the production of cars, agricultural implements, printed goods and marmalade. Since 1963 it has boasted a Lord Mayor, instead of a plain Mayor, a distinction which it shares with 18 other English cities and which means, pomp apart, nothing whatsoever. Its rateable value is about £19m—rather more than Ipswich, the book says, a little less than Guildford. Its soil is mostly clay, its mean temperature is 50·1° Fahrenheit, and it suffers 172 rainy days in an average year.

Keats thought this city the finest in the world. Ramsay Mac-Donald called its University 'a painted lady, from which Labour has nothing to expect'. When the young men of its University debating society declared, in 1933, that they would on no account fight for their King and Country, all Europe took notice. In Oxford Disraeli coined the phrase 'on the side of the angels', Robert Burton wrote *The Anatomy of Melancholy* and Lawrence of Arabia propelled himself through an underground stream in a canoe. The mathematical devices $<$, $>$ and ∞ were all invented here, and here for the first time penicillin was given to a patient. Richard the Lion-Heart was born in Oxford, Boyle evolved his Law here, Kenneth Grahame is buried in an Oxford graveyard, part of the Authorized Version and part of the New English Bible were translated in the city. In Oxford the Wesleys launched Methodism, Keble and his

No!

?

friends the Oxford Movement, Buchman Moral Rearmament. Here
Dr. Spooner announced as the next hymn *Kinquering Congs Their
Tikles Tate*. Roger Bannister ran the first four-minute mile on an
Oxford track, and in this city also, in 1876, Marshall Jones Brooks
jumped the first recorded six foot high jump.

Among those educated at the University of Oxford have been Dr.
Johnson, Charley's Aunt, Sir Walter Raleigh, Pope Alexander V,
Earl Haig, Richard Burton the explorer, Richard Burton the actor,
Evelyn Waugh, Tom Brown, Shelley, 22 English Prime Ministers
out of 46, 10 Viceroys of India out of 20, Washington's great grandfather, the Duke of Windsor, the first Prime Minister of Ceylon,
Beau Nash, Beau Brummel and several hundred bishops. President
Kennedy's administration contained 16 Oxford graduates. King
James I once said that if he were not a king he would like to be
an Oxford man. Gibbon thought his months in Oxford the most
idle and unprofitable of his whole life. 'I was a modest, good-
humoured boy,' Max Beerbohm wrote. 'It is Oxford that has made
me insufferable.'

The pirate Henry Morgan went to sea in a ship named for this
city. There is an Oxford in New Zealand and an Oxford in Canada,
and there are 21 Oxfords in the United States, besides a Mount
Oxford, two Lake Oxfords and Oxford County, Maine, whose capital is South Paris. The city has given its name to Oxford bags,
Oxford marmalade, Oxford grey, Oxford shoes, the Oxford Group,
the Oxford Movement and the Oxford accent. Oxford pickles are,
so the Massachusetts advertisements say, the Pride of New England.
In Oxford there are at least six First Folios, the best collection of
Raphael drawings in existence, Dr. Johnson's teapot, the claw of
a dodo, Uccello's *Hunt in A Forest*, Moore of Corunna's shroud
straps, a mint Stradivarius, Holman Hunt's *Light of the World*, an
incomparable assembly of astrolabes and one of the most splended
concentrations of Gothic architecture in Europe.

The science of modern geology was nurtured in Oxford, and so
was the MG sports car. The solitary sycamore in Oxford's High
Street has been called, quite plausibly, one of the most important
trees in Europe; the Sheldonian Theatre has been described, imper-
tinently, as the most splendid room in Europe; upon the top of Tom
Tower in Oxford Sir Christopher Wren prudently declined to deposit an astronomical observatory—he said the telescopes would

see above

wobble. Hitler, it is said, wanted Oxford as his English capital. Charles II held his last Parliament in the city. The only English Pope was boy-vicar of an Oxford church.

The climate is enervating, the water is hard, the central altitude is 208 feet above sea level: few cities have been more loved, loathed and celebrated.

Of course the Trojans founded it, abetted if you believe all the legends by Merlin the wizard, Apollo, and Memphric, King of the Britons, of whom 'no good thing is remembered but only that he begat an honest son and heir, and built this noble city'. We are assured that the situation of the place was 'agreeable to the principles laid down by the ancient philosophers', and that its first scholars migrated here from the immemorial universities of Cricklade and Lechlade—institutions specializing respectively, I need hardly say, in the study of Greek and of medicine.

The most tangible of these misty founding fathers was King Alfred, whose status as first patron of Oxford University was for several centuries a local article of faith. In 1381 University College, one of the constituent colleges of the University, forged some deeds to prove its foundation by Alfred, and used them to win a lawsuit; nearly 400 years later the Court of King's Bench confirmed the lie, when the college found itself awkwardly governed by two Masters at the same time, and claimed the intervention of the Crown as a Royal Foundation. The Alfredian legend, as Oxford antiquarians affectionately call it, gave much pleasure in its time. All the old guidebooks loyally record it. In the late eighteenth century the young Lord Eldon, being examined for an Oxford degree in Hebrew and history, was asked simply what was the Hebrew for the place of a skull, and who founded University College: Golgotha, replied the hopeful peer, and King Alfred—and got his degree. In the 1850s they proposed to erect a monstrous monument to King Alfred on a pedestal in the middle of Broad Street, and in nineteenth-century Oxford images of the king were all over the place—in niches, on medallions, above the main gateway of University College, even in a painting at Brasenose College sagely described in the catalogue as 'Portrait of King Alfred in Fancy Dress'. In 1872 University College solemnly celebrated its own millennium with elaborate toasts to its great founder—'whose memory will dwell like honey', so the chronicler Camden prophesied, 'in the mouths of both clerics and people'.

The myth died hard, with a chuckle and a blush. The historian E. A. Freeman, excusing himself from the millenary banquet, sent along two old burnt cakes by messenger, and gradually the legend disintegrated. They decided not to erect that monument in Broad Street. They forgot the whereabouts of that portrait in fancy dress. The figure of Alfred above University College gateway ended its days as a bump in the Master's rock garden, and if you look in the senior common room now you may see a pale silhouette of faded wood above the fireplace, all that remains of another Aluredian effigy. There is still a medallion of the king in the college dining-hall, with his crown very straight on the top of his head, but today the only proper bust of Alfred I know in Oxford stands in the parish hall of the University Church, forlornly surveying the play projects and blazing crayons of Sunday school.

Each year on October 19 the Lord Mayor of Oxford, the Sheriff, the Proctors of the University, the Chief Constable of the city and the canons of diocese assemble in Oxford Cathedral to honour the memory of another early benefactor—St. Frideswide, an indistinct divine who is the patron saint of the place. Begowned, befurred, cassocked, epauletted and even bewigged, the dignitaries process through the cathedral to the verses of *Jerusalem, My Happy Home*, arriving eventually at the saintly shrine—where, still singing away, they are intended to recall the holy life of the virgin, her royal birth as daughter to King Didanus of Oxford, the miracle by which her importunate princely suitor was struck blind by lightning at a moment of excess, the further miracle by which she magnanimously cured him, her retreat with its holy well among the water-meadows and the great priory she founded upon the very site of the cathedral. St. Frideswide was the first of the properly local celebrities, and in Oxford you can hardly escape her presence (a herd of pedigree cows is named after her).

When I was at that service some years ago I noticed that one of the most venerable of the canons at the shrine showed signs of irritable impatience. He scowled, muttered audibly to himself, hitched his hood, twitched his surplice, nudged his companions and occasionally glared frowardly around the congregation. It was true that *Jerusalem, My Happy Home* did seem more than usually protracted that day, with so much civic weight to slow it down. I watched that clergyman closely, though, and after a time I came to the conclusion that he was not annoyed by the music, only by the occasion. He didn't dislike the hymn-tune. He had doubts about the saint.

More reliable origins are harder to trace. Near the city centre they once found the grave of an Early Iron Age chieftain—the ceremonial trench that had carried his blood disappeared ominously beneath the walls of the Examination Schools. Very early Oxford, though, seems to have been a little-frequented swamp. The Romans, remembering the disaster of the Caudine Forks, distrusted sites like this, where their troops could be trapped between rivers. Their roads passed nearby, and not so long ago farmers used to hear the ghostly rumble of their wagon wheels across the neighbouring marsh of Otmoor, but they never settled at the ford. In Wychwood Forest, 10 miles west, foraging gourmets may still find edible snails said to be descended from the commissariat of the legions, but never a *Helix pomatia* crawls through the greeneries of Oxford herself.

It was evidently the Saxons who founded this city, though they seem to have built their town to a Roman model, with a planned grid of streets. Why they called it Oxenford has been an issue for happy pedantry ever since. Was it a ford over the River Ocks (there is still such a tributary, a few miles downstream), or the River Ouse, or the River Usk? Or was it, as wilder theorists used to postulate, named after the cry of the holy Frideswide as she withdrew from the city on a cow—'Ox, go forth'? Saxon coins supposedly minted in the city do not greatly help, for they abbreviate the name of the place in 28 different ways, ranging from Oxenfo to a bald O, besides lettering it indiscriminately backwards, jumbled or upside down: but the city arms display a hefty bull stepping across some wavy water, and most etymologists now accept what the rest of us thought all along, that this was a ford where the oxen crossed.

The original Oxford was pre-eminently a river city—part port, part market, part fortress. She stood on the frontier between the kingdoms of Mercia and Wessex, and became a favourite venue for gemots and royal conferences—a kind of Saxon convention centre. The Normans also recognized her central significance, and built a castle by the river. Henry I chose her for his great palace of Beaumont, where the Lion-Heart was born, and for several centuries

Oxford served almost as a second capital, convenient, comfortable, safe, and set in one of England's richest regions. She became a thriving mediaeval borough, a centre of the Cotswold wool industry, with confident trade guilds and royal charters; and some time in the twelfth century she also became a meeting place of scholars.

Nobody really knows how the University of Oxford began, and nobody can put a date to it. Some think its first scholars were English refugees from the University of Paris, thrown out with all other foreign students during a fit of French xenophobia in 1167. Others suggest it may have been an offshoot of the local monasteries, or perhaps of the collegiate church that stood within the castle walls. Whatever its origins, colonies of masters and students appeared here in the Middle Ages, gradually evolving their own guilds and privileges, establishing themselves in halls of residence, coalescing by the end of the twelfth century into a full-blown *Universitas Magistrorum et Scholarium*.

It grew explosively, often in controversy and sometimes in violence—'massacres', says Jas. J. Moore's *Historical Handbook*, 1871, 'have been somewhat frequent in the city'. Oxford's first students were often poor, dirty and obstreperous, and the city understandably resented their arrival. There were bloody battles between Town and Gown, quarrels between northerners and southerners, assaults upon the Jews, lawsuits, petitions, papal interdictions. Through it all learning fitfully flourished. The teaching friars introduced new currents of thought from Europe; men like Roger Bacon and John Wycliffe studied and taught in Oxford; by the time of the Renaissance the little city had become one of the intellectual centres of the Western world—on a par with Paris, Bologna, Padua and Salamanca (and Cambridge, itself founded by an exodus of Oxford scholars).

By then the University had also evolved its present general shape—a group of independent colleges, that is, each a kind of little university, loosely federated to form a nebulous but influential unity. This ramshackle construction became an anvil of England, where successive national issues were hammered out, and national attitudes repeatedly forged. The Reformation was mirrored in Oxford by martyrdoms in both causes—on the one side a Cranmer, on the other a Campion. In the English Civil War Charles I had his court in Oxford, and Cromwell besieged the city. The seventeenth-century resurgence of English science had its birth in Oxford, and the eighteenth century, here as in the kingdom at large, was notable for idleness, corruption, remarkable men and beautiful buildings. Nineteenth-century Oxford was infused with such colossal controversial energy that almost every street retains some vestige of the age, and the texture of England, even today, bears the imprint of the city's Victorian vigour. Twentieth-century Oxford has reflected, perhaps more clearly than any other city, the changes that have transformed the life of England—the spread of industry, the decline of a ruling class, the end of Empire, the impact of urban values, the legacy of two crippling wars, the faltering of religion.

In Oxford you may see it all—century by century, or face by face. She is an England in miniature: an essence of England, drawn from the wood.

The hills around Oxford never reach 600 feet, but standing as they do above that damp river landscape they seem higher than they are. Up there on Shotover, Elsfield or Boar's Hill you feel indefinably elated, as the wind off the Downs ruffles your hair, and a smell of hay and woodland hangs upon the morning. For a moment, if the day is right, your very perceptions are sharpened. Hardy's Jude the Obscure, when he first passed this way, caught his first sight of Oxford at a distance of some 30 miles through an intervening slab of high ground. Matthew Arnold's Scholar Gypsy, looking down on Oxford from Cumnor ridge on a snowy night, could easily identify the lights of Christ Church hall, two and a half miles away. Romantics sometimes say that nothing higher stands between the ridge of Shotover and the Ural Mountains, on the other side of Europe, and there used to be an old man at the village of Wootton who claimed that from Boar's Hill he once saw a ship sailing up the Bristol Channel, 70 miles west.

In this state of exalted expectancy you may look down upon the city, encouched in its amphitheatre below. As likely as not, in this country of cloud and change, at first you will see nothing in particular. The river valley is plunged in shadow, and all looks rather dismal. Then as you wait, perhaps with a shiver in the wind, a patch of sunshine breaks through the clouds, and sweeps westward up the Thames. Over the opposite hills it goes, like a scythe among the trees, and across the dull suburbs of the city. A factory is momentarily illuminated, the humdrum pattern of a housing estate, a mass of red-brick terraces, the glass geometry of a school, until the beam lands at last upon the ancient centre of Oxford. Instantly something like a vision shines out of the valley. The towers, spires and pinnacles of the city, honey-gold and tightly packed, leap suddenly from the shadows as though they are floodlit. All is sudden etched intricacy—chiselled, elaborate, vertical—a cluster of golden objects picked out in theatrical silhouette.

It only lasts a moment, before the sunshine peters out, or scuds away upstream beyond the railway lines: but it leaves you with a shame-faced mystical feeling—as though you have enjoyed a moment of second sight, or have looked, like that old man of Wootton, smack through the horizon. A minute later all is dark down there again, and the city has dissolved among the shadows. Oxford is a place that comes in flashes—sometimes lovely, sometimes dispiriting: and in just such a mood of changeable emotions, in which ecstasy and disillusion chase each other through the narrative, should we venture down that hillside, take a red bus into town, and explore this piebald prodigy closer.

TWO

The temper of this jumbled place is at once testy, ironic and tolerant. Its celebrated University, a thing of baffling complexity, is embedded in a city rich in its own pride and history. The climate is lowering, but the emotions of Oxford are always intensified—by the momentum of her central situation, by the fierce and sometimes silly independence of her institutions, by social diversity and a gift for pleasure.

2. Rich Mixture

Sometimes, very early on a June morning, when the mist is still floating among the spires, I take my breakfast at George's Café, in the covered market of Oxford: for there, settling myself over a mug of coffee, I can enjoy the complexity of this city at its most agreeable. Oxford is a very jumbled place. At George's in June there are often a few young couples eating bacon-and-eggs after dancing all night, their long dresses crumpled, their black ties askew, their faces expressing an awful determination to keep awake and amused for just half an hour longer. Polite Oxford market-men grab a cup of tea between truck-loads—stocky round-faced men, inclined to the rubicund, with accents rustically curled at the edges. Despondent women look in with Paisley scarves on their heads, on their way to scrub floors or clean office desks. Dashing young labourers ask for toast with dripping on it. Pakistani bus conductors look cold and fragile, towering blonde hitch-hikers carry rucksacks and talk German, cadaverous men of intellectual bearing appear to be collecting sociological evidence, or perhaps escaping poetic insomnia. It is a very lively café on such a morning. The coffee is strong, the breakfast is enormous, and at first taste this cosmopolitan diversity, so abundant for a town of medium size, seems only stimulating. It is a metropolitan sort of sensation, for a smallish provincial city on the upper Thames.

Later you may come to feel that the mixture is a little too rich. Oxford is chiefly famous for her University, but she is not at all one of your discreet and sylvan groves of scholarship. She is a vivacious shambles. Her University is not, like the Sorbonne, almost indistinguishable in the mêlée; nor is it deposited neatly, like Heidelberg's, in some romantic old corner beneath a castle wall, or lapped in resolute good taste, like Princeton, or prettily sheltered, like Harvard Yard, within its own protective campus. It neither dominates the city, nor is swamped by it. The very centre of Oxford is the crossroads called Carfax—*Quatre Voies*—and around it the original walled city still stands, the mediaeval pattern of its streets almost intact. Higgledy-piggledy among this antique mass stand the old buildings of the University, some inside the walls, some outside, and the whole is cemented forcibly together by slabs of industry and suburbia. There is no dissecting Town from Gown. Every now and then somebody proposes to create twin cities in Oxford, vulgar commerce in one half, fastidious scholarship in the other: but it would be like perforating a man down the middle, and inviting him to split.

The mixture is brought to scalding-point by a constant heat of motion, as the traffic floods, rubs or lurches its way through these streets. Oxford is an edgy and exhausting place. Long ago most of the bustle was on the river, and the Thames bargees were rumbustious familiars of the city. When Robert Burton found the melancholy too much for him, he used to go down to Folly Bridge to hear the bargemen swearing—'at which he would set his hands at his side, and laugh most profusely'. Thomas Warton, too, later the Poet Laureate, used to distress his friend Dr. Johnson by smoking and drinking with these rough characters; and in 1839 the chaplain of the Boatmen's Floating Chapel, reporting to his committee on progress in 'bringing these poor wanderers to a sense of the value of their souls', had to admit that 'several still persisted in their irreligious habits'.

There are still one or two last stalwarts of the monkey-boats in Oxford, loose-limbed, gypsy-like men, who live in small houses near the canal, in the red-brick quarter called Jericho. They are last witnesses to the days when the Thames was the chief thoroughfare of the city—when wool came by barge for the Oxford weavers, and manuscripts for the Bodleian Library, and wines for the Oxford colleges, and arms for the garrison in the Civil War—not to speak of the *Rarities* and *Curiosities* of the Tradescant Museum, shipped to Oxford in 1683, and including among their lading bills A Babylonian Vest, A Turkish Tooth-Brush, and A Copper Letter-case an Inch long, Taken in the Isle of Ree with a Letter in it, which was Swallowed by a Woman, and Found.

Oxford is still one of the headquarters of the Thames Water Authority, the managing body of the river, and its Oxford offices are nice old rambling buildings, with boathouses and repair yards, down by Osney Lock. The catchment area of the Thames sprawls over 15 counties, and the Oxford lengthsmen of the Authority spend their days tramping along a score of tributaries, looking for fallen trees or pollution—100 miles a month is their statutory patrol, and there are two or three families in which the job has become hereditary, and whose names are known up and down the river. The Thames Authority has a pronounced sense of style, and on ceremonial occasions you may sometimes see its officials chugging along the river in dazzlingly polished old-fashioned motor launches, wearing nautical jackets and yachting caps.

There are bits and pieces of the Thames all over Oxford, runnels and reaches and backwaters—'more in number than your eyelashes', Keats said—and beneath the very centre of the city runs the Trill Mill stream, a gloomy underground waterway in which was discovered, one day in the 1920s, a rotted Victorian punt with two Victorian skeletons in it. The ferryman is the oldest of Oxford figures—the ferry across the Cherwell at Marston was in continuous use from the thirteenth century until the 1970s—and the professional river fisherman crops up in every mediaeval archive of the city. The early inhabitants of Oxford must have considered themselves river people, like Mississippi mudlarks, and the very names of the western districts—Osney, Binsey, Hinksey—recall old island settlements in the swamp.

But the Thames itself, now tamed and channelled, feels as though it long ago went into an enjoyable retirement. Its lock-houses are like little pleasure villas, with trim gardens and white notice boards. Its old watermen's pubs seem to have turned their backs on it, and cater half-heartedly for the lubber trade. It is 112 miles to London by river, compared with 56 miles by road, and though in 1824 six Guards officers rowed it in $15\frac{3}{4}$ hours, nowadays only the most leisurely forms of traffic can afford to use it. The only proper ships to be seen upon its waters are the fine old pleasure boats of the Salters fleet, based at Folly Bridge. They were mostly built in Oxford, though the *Mary Stuart* was once the *Kagerplass*, built in Germany and sailed here from Holland under her own power. All are diesel-powered now, the biggest is 115 feet long, and several of them remember the nineteenth century.

They sail, however, in domesticated waters. The Thames speed limit is nine knots, you can be fined £500 for flaunting a Union Jack on its stream, and any ill-treatment of the swans should be reported to the Vintners' Swan Marker, the Dyers' Swan Marker, Her Majesty's Swan Keeper, or failing all (the notices conclude bathetically) to Any Police Officer. In Oxford the Thames is often called the Isis, even on maps—an eighteenth-century literary name said to be derived from the tail end of the Latin Thamesis; and this decorous eponym well fits its present condition, so fastidiously removed from the cussing and whoring of the bargees.

Superannuated, too, is the Oxford Canal, which was intended to revive the commercial life of the river by linking it with the Potteries and the booming industrial north. It was completed in 1790, connecting the Thames with the Trent and the Mersey, and began life stylishly. The original offices of its Company of Proprietors are now the home of the Master of St. Peter's College; they were designed by the engineer of the canal itself, and a fine neo-classical house they make, white and elegant, beside the mediaeval alley called Bulwark Lane. This was one of the first of the English canals, a precursor of the industrial revolution so soon to break upon the kingdom; but the railways soon humiliated it, the traffic petered out, the wharves were sold, and today it ends abruptly at a brick dam beside Hythe Bridge, on the way to the railway station.

Only occasionally does a coal barge, driven off its normal route by floods or canal-works, steal past Jericho in the night, with a thumping of its engines and a tug at the hearts of those high-and-dry watermen. For the rest, it is only messing about in boats. Isis Lock, where the canal connects with the Thames, has long been a favourite place for suicides—its steep sides rule out a change of mind. Otters have sometimes been seen mooching about in the waters of the canal, and James Elroy Flecker once wrote a morbid poem about it:

> *Do you see the great telephone poles down in the*
> *water, how every line is distinct?*
> *If a body fell into the canal it would rest*
> *entangled in those wires for ever, beneath earth and air.*

Past the lethargic waters of the canal go the trains that ruined it. They came to Oxford late. Brunel chose his route from London

to Bristol partly because it would be easy to run a branch from Did-
cot to Oxford, but the University colossally distrusted the notion.
It would, so the greybeards thought, place awful distractions in the
way of undergraduates—distracted enough already, in an Oxford
then full of wine-houses and loose women, with a stage-coach service that only took six hours to London (the first trains, it later
turned out, took seven). It would disturb the metabolism of the
place, vulgarize the learned setting, and bring hordes of common
strangers into the city. The idea of building a railway station
adjacent to Magdalen Bridge was therefore abandoned.

Defeated, too, was a plan to build in Oxford the main workshops
for the whole Great Western Railway. This project aroused one of
Oxford's nineteenth-century *causes célèbres*—a hammer-and-tongs
battle between Town and Gown. 'Not a moment must be lost,' cried
one citizen in an anti-University manifesto. 'Unless we wish to see
ourselves over-ridden and trampled upon by a party, whose actions
have always obstructed the progress of our City, we must bestir ourselves and fight tooth and nail!' But they were trampled on anyway,
and the works went to Swindon instead. Even the railway was kept
out until 1844, delayed to the last by an imaginative opportunist
who built himself a house of brown paper in the line of the track,
and demanded substantial compensation for its removal. The nonagenarian President Routh of Magdalen College, who wore a wig and
remembered Dr. Johnson, flatly declined ever to recognize its existence, and as late as 1886, so difficult was Victorian Oxford to mollify,
a writer in the *Oxford Magazine* was complaining that the avoidance
of natural obstacles by the route of the railway was 'detrimental to
the geological education of passengers'.

When the trains did come they came full blast, and for years
Oxford was a fierce arena of the railway mania, as ephemeral systems
like the Oxford, Aylesbury and Metropolitan Junction sprang into
existence and were swiftly stifled, as tiny lines to places like Brill,
Fairford and Witney were hopefully laid, and the ruthless battle
of the gauges—broad against narrow—swirled all about the Midlands. Today the western edge of Oxford is swathed in all the paraphernalia of the railways: not just the tracks, and the bridges, and
the signal-boxes, but all those mysteriously inescapable appendages
that spring up like thistles along the lines—gravel pits, and
allotments, and ponds, and little black wooden huts.

The present railway station, built in the 1960s, replaced a wooden structure which had been scheduled for demolition for nearly a century, but was immortalized by the fact that on its No. 2 Platform, on the very first page of Beerbohm's *Zuleika Dobson*, Zuleika stepped off the Paddington train to be met by the Warden of Judas. A hundred yards away the London and North Western Railway, bringing in a line from the north, erected a station not only putting into practice for the first time the principles of construction evolved for Paxton's Crystal Palace, but actually using some discarded woodwork from the entrance to the 1851 Great Exhibition—the first of the world fairs. It was an exciting building in its time, all glass and iron ribs: the London, Midland and Scottish took it over, and it is now a tyre depot, painted yellow and plastered with advertisements—old tyres are piled desolately along its platforms, salesmen smoke in its booking office, and only an occasional string of coal trucks, finding nowhere else to go, is shunted contemptuously beneath its rusted cantilevers for the night.

Now the pace and the tumult are all on the roads. Oxford is elongated for her population—some six miles long, but seldom more than a mile wide. This shape was dictated in the first place by the shape of the gravel bank she was built upon, and it makes her look rather like a spiral nebula, with a hub at the centre where the roads cross, and gaseous extrusions thrown off. It is as though the whole place is violently revolving: and to most of Oxford's visitors that is precisely what it feels like.

The ring roads that surround the city are almost never silent, but a heaving mass of traffic still squeezes its way, like dentifrice through a nozzle, over the two old road bridges in the centre of the place—Magdalen Bridge over the Cherwell, Folly Bridge over the Thames. The traffic of Oxford is an international curse. In 1938 19,200 bicycles crossed Magdalen Bridge in an average day, making it the busiest place for bicycles in the world, and even then somebody worked out that the effect of the passing traffic on the façade of University College was 'equal to the force of a blow given to each square yard of the structure by a ton weight falling from the height of one foot every day of the year'.

Today some of it is siphoned off by the motorways, but still if you stand beside the Headington roundabout on a weekday afternoon all England seems to be roaring by on wheels. There are trucks with bold northern names on their tailboards, like Bolton, Huddersfield or Runcorn; and padded limousines from London, heavy pomaded men sunk in their recesses with cigars and spring-binders; and streams of jerky little family cars, woolly tigers dangling at the rear; and brewers' trucks polished like old silver; and bright tourist coaches on their way to Stratford, their windows flashing with bracelets and jewelled spectacles; and big red double-decker buses, of course, and undergraduate sports cars with deafening engines and flying hair; and very upright black Rolls-Royces that once belonged to dowagers and are now driven by bearded commercial artists; and nurses in crash helmets on motor scooters, and clergymen in shirt-sleeves with large sticky families, and arrogant salesmen with cotton dresses on rows of hangers, and visitors to Britain in Volkswagen buses with slogans and maps of Africa on their doors, and sometimes a proper bigwig of State or diplomacy, in a big black car with a flag on the front, so enormously grand, so suggestively screened, that he seems to be passing in a veil of significance, like an archbishop beneath an embroidered canopy.

Everyone comes this way, sooner or later. It used to be one of the great coaching centres of England, in the days when 30 or 40 stage-coaches lumbered into Oxford each day, with names like *Defiance*, *Magnet* or *Tantivy*, destinations as remote as Cambridge and Aberystwyth, and guards to play old bugle calls as they swept over Magdalen Bridge. As early as 1786 wagoners were being fined in Oxford for obstruction, and today the centre of the city is almost never at rest. Late at night the hot-dog vans are still ablaze with strip lighting in High Street, smelling horribly of fat and sausages, while the motor-cycle Galahads roar home to the eastern suburbs; and even when the traffic dies at last, in the still of the small hours, somebody always seems to be talking, with an echo of words and laughter among old walls. If it isn't academics in dinner-jackets walking off the port, discussing Hegelian derivatives at the tops of their voices, it is probably a couple of Irishmen, cheerfully swapping scurrilities outside the Old Tom public house.

In the middle a tremulous civic balance must be maintained. Oxford is a place of awkward confrontations, and it has taken several centuries to evolve today's relationships between the City and that monstrous cuckoo in its nest, the University.

Until 1950 Oxford sent three members to Parliament in London—one from the City, two from the University: the latter were elected by the vote of all living Oxford graduates, wherever they lived, and at one time or another included in their roster Peel, Gladstone and A. P. Herbert. Until 1974 the University was still powerfully represented upon the City Council, and provided the Lord Mayor and the Sheriff alternately with the Conservative and Labour Parties.

Now all is normalized, and the University has no more municipal authority than the Thames Water Authority or British Rail, but academics are often elected to the council as private citizens. The scholarly content of the administration is always high, its sewage disposal committee may be presided over by an eminent mediaeval historian or the current *enfant terrible* of ferrous metallography, and the general standard of debate is, if not more entertaining, at least more grammatical than in most municipal assemblies.

Oxford's is not an easy equilibrium, even now. Her various energies chafe each other, setting up magnetic fields and making sparks fly. In the past these frictions have often flashed into violence. Now they only create a certain electric feeling in the air, like the brooding excitement of a thunder-storm that refuses to burst. In such an English city there are countless hidden tensions of taste, interest and aspiration—kept in check by the discipline of an advanced and subtle civilization, but still themselves a source of energy. The Socialist councillor with his strong views on steel and his encyclopedic knowledge of association football may walk off arm in arm with the University alderman who lives in a Cotswold manor house and collects cloisonné enamels of the later Tang period: but jovially though their voices ring, as they walk down the ornate staircases of the Town Hall, between the sculpted griffins and the Rolls of Honour—bravely though they put a face on it, *au fond* they have about as much in common as A.C. and D.C.

This suggestion of half-hostile fields, or of neutrons bouncing off one another, strikes me most sharply at the annual junket called St. Giles's Fair, which is a survivor of the great country fairs of mediaeval England, and which falls upon Oxford like a feverish

dream on the Monday and Tuesday after the first Sunday in Sep-
tember (though if the Feast of St. Giles falls on a Monday, Ward
Lock's guide helpfully reminds me, the fair is held on the *following*
Monday and Tuesday). It is an inexorable sort of festivity—in Sep-
tember 1914 they tried to cancel it, but the Home Secretary himself
admitted that he was powerless to do so. The whole wide street of
St. Giles is closed for it. For these two days of the year the University Parks and Christ Church meadows, the two main open
spaces of the city, are closed to the public. Traffic is diverted, business is disrupted, the night is gaudy with neon, and all among the
plane trees there proliferate the side shows, caravans and pulsing
generators of the showmen.

It is the most boisterous of Oxford traditions, the profits of which
go partly to the city and partly to the college of St. John's, the local
landowner; and it brings together in an atmosphere of unnatural
intensity every type and kind of Oxford citizen. The academics go
with their burbling children, eating iced lollipops and arguing the
toss with indulgent showmen in piping cultured accents. The factory families go, trailing balloons and sweet papers, and hugging
flowery vases they have won at shooting galleries. The farmers go,
stumping stoically through the hubbub with kind wives in blue hats.
The aldermen go—in 1950 Alderman Smewin officially complained
to the City Council that there had been only one set of Galloping
Horses to ride on. The parish clergy go, from a sense of boyish duty,
and the weedy louts go, to stand around in bow-legged moronic
cliques, licking candy floss, and the shop-girls go, to let their skirts
fly on the Big Dipper. Every degree is represented there, from the
exquisite patrician to the grubbiest slut in carpet slippers: and
flushed from their normal habitats like this, thrown together
between the Bingo stalls and the Man-Eating Rat, they always seem
to me larger, finer or more awful than life. George's Café feels geni-
ally blended: but St. Giles's Fair is like a city with its masks torn
off, seen with a flushed or psychedelic clarity.

Oxford, however, is old, and experienced at the game. By Wednesday morning all those stalls and roundabouts have miraculously
disappeared, and the scholars, the charge-hands, the oafs and the
parsons are restored to their blurred and unalarming selves.

3. Town and Country

Oxford had already seen five centuries of borough life', the historian J. R. Green once wrote, 'before a student appeared within its streets.' The City came first, and still feels older. On the north-western flank of Oxford, between the river and the railway line, there lies a large slab of pasture-land called Port Meadow. It has never been ploughed. Ponies and cows graze on it, fleets of ducks and geese launch themselves from its banks, plume-thistles and ragwort infest its grass, abandoned cars litter its outskirts, lapwings, curlews, herons and gulls frequent it.

On a winter day it is a melancholy but evocative spot, when the damp mists lie low over its expanse, the towers of Oxford stand like vague giants in the distance, the river looks like cold tea and only the muffled rumble of a passing train breaks the silence. It was an airfield in the first world war, and a small memorial near its northern edge records the spot where two of the earliest British aeroplane pilots were killed in a crash. In the second war exhausted survivors of the retreat from Dunkirk set up their tents on its grass to get their breath back. Port Meadow feels very old indeed, as though the ghosts of a hundred centuries pace it; and when some years ago pieces of Minoan pottery were found on an adjacent allotment, it scarcely seemed surprising (though in fact they got there *via* an archaeologist's dustbin).

This great meadow has always belonged to the Freemen of Oxford, of whom there are about 130—some hereditary, some admitted as apprentices to other Freemen. The Freemen meet in assembly every now and then, wearing neckties specially designed for them in Macclesfield, and they are very conscious of their rights (which include, or so they like to claim, all fishing rights on the Thames within the city limits). Whenever somebody has tried to nibble a corner off Port Meadow the Freemen have been up in arms.

Charles I was only grudgingly allowed the hay crop for his army when he was quartered here during the Civil War, and the claims of the City Council to ownership have been angrily disputed for 140 years.

It is almost as though the empty liberty of the place has some sacred origin, to be defended instinctively, like an Ashanti stool; and once a year the Sheriff of Oxford, as Curator of Port Meadow and of the City Fisheries, sets a seal upon this organic possession by impounding all the grazing animals, and releasing them only upon payment of a statutory £3 fine. He does not announce the date of this ancient coup in advance, in case unscrupulous owners whisk their animals away for the day: but secretly, early one morning, with his posse of Freemen around him, he precariously mounts a horse at the edge of the meadow, and aided by numbers of stout young women on ponies, rounds up those creatures, every one, and pens them in his corral.

In such a setting, for such a purpose, no ceremonial could better express the knobbly continuity of Oxford. The very snort of a horse on the morning air sounds feudal in those queer circumstances; and it did not even detract from the comic solemnity of the ritual when one recent Sheriff of Oxford, having spent a lifetime in the Royal Air Force, decided to deviate from tradition, and do the job from a hovering helicopter.

The rural strain is strong in Oxford. 'Stop For Country Buses', says a sign endearingly plumb in the middle of High Street, and from almost every upper window, even at the end of central city streets, the Oxford country shows. Oxford is full of green spits and patches, unexpected meadows, creepers and damp stains. This is partly because of the city's skinny shape, and partly because it is set in a particularly stubborn sort of countryside. The very faces of the Oxford country people—often flaccid, nearly always mild—seem to denote an inexhaustible capacity for staying put. Oxfordshire yields are low, and Oxford farm wages have been notoriously among the meanest in England, yet the impact of industry and the automobile took generations to disrupt the dazed traditionalism of the countryside.

There is a fungus-feeling to it even now. Within a few miles of Oxford they still net freshwater crayfish, poach swans and catch moorhens for the pot (though no longer, I think, by snaring them on baited eel-hooks). All kinds of yokel traditions curiously survive. Here they have a tug-of-war across a river; there they roast a pig at Michaelmas. On the first Monday in July the hay rights of the local water-meadows are auctioned in the Grapes Inn at Yarnton in one of the very last survivals of English feudal tenure. The fields are divided into their original mediaeval strips, with names like William of Bladon, Gilbert and Watery Molly, lots are drawn with antique cherrywood balls, and the auction takes place in an atmosphere curiously compounded of levity and reverence—as if those farmers, sitting over their beers in the smoke-room beside the big main road, would like to laugh the whole process out of existence, but are held in some mystic thrall.

This ethos inevitably penetrates the city, too, and makes the grass roots still feel close. My favourite name in all the Oxford chronicles is that of Abbot Hokenotton of Oseney: but almost as Chaucerian are those to be found in the roster of North Hinksey Women's Institute, whose members have included Annie Bunce, Ellen Kettle, Eliza Beer, Clara Trotman, A. Haggie and Margaret Grundy. On Wednesday especially, when the cattle market is held down at the Oxpens, the country comes into Oxford. Above the cattle pens the squat old castle tower surveys the scene like a beery Lord Lieutenant. Red stout men in long mackintoshes exchange ribaldry with auctioneers. Jolly Jews down from London sell hats, frocks, shoes and old picture frames (they have been coming to Oxford for at least a century, and visit several different market towns each week). There is a mooing, barking, snorting and busking on the air—gumboots everywhere, pigs in trucks, smells of manure, fish and cabbages. I once looked through the market gate to see four young elephants being led down the street to a circus tent across the way: nobody seemed in the least surprised, and the farmers around me eyed those animals with a purely professional scrutiny, as if to estimate how many pounds of prime beef they might reasonably be expected to yield.

This is the capital of Oxfordshire, and the county lobby is still influential. The county government sits in a ramble of buildings near the prison, some Victorian, some contemporary. The local government reforms of 1974 paradoxically revived its old ascendancy over the city—they used to call the Oxford Freemen 'a pack

of Blenheim spaniels', and the city arms are still born by the ele-
phant of the Knollys, Earls of Banbury, and the beaver of the Nor-
rises, Lords of Rycote. The classic English country figures still
circulate in Oxford. The comfortable yeoman farmer is always
about, parking his Range Rover in St. Giles while he goes to the
bank and his daughter has her hair done; and occasionally you
may even see an old-school country gentleman, in heavy tweeds,
reluctantly trailing his wife through the millinery department of
Debenham's, or testily inquiring at the newsagent why his copy of
The Field didn't turn up last week. Country forces are inescapable
still in such an English borough: country families like the Marl-
boroughs or the Harcourts, still playing from their great country
houses a kind of Anglo-Irish role in the affairs of the region; country
institutions like the Heythrop Hunt or the Agricultural Show; or
simply country economics, in a part of England where agriculture
remains a major industry, and there is no other city within 40 miles.

Even that prince of countrymen, the gypsy, sometimes ambles
in. Matthew Arnold's Scholar Gypsy had his historical prototype—
a 'Lad in the University', so Joseph Glanvill recorded in 1661,
joined a company of vagabonds, and 'among those extravagant
people, by the insinuating subtlety of his carriage, he quickly got
so much of their love and esteem, as that they discovered to him
their *Mystery*'. The Oxford country is a familiar stage in the English
gypsy circuit—now followed, too, by several kinds of mumper and
itinerant labourer. Some live in caravans, with trucks to tow them,
some in shacks apparently made of old rags and perambulators.
Many switched directly from horse-coping to car-dealing, and will
make you an offer for your spare wheel as sharply as ever they surreptitiously looked your grey mare in the teeth. The most prosperous of all have entered the affluent society themselves, and are
sometimes to be seen sitting outside their caravans in gravel pits
beside the ring roads, with Sunday afternoon's television plugged
into the battery.

In the covered market, not far from George's, there is a well-
known game shop. Its window-shelves are loaded in the season with
grouse, partridge, ptarmigan, venison, wild geese, ornamental
pheasants, squadgy coloured ducks, hares with glazed open eyes,
and mounds of lesser game-birds tossed together so lavishly that
they look like one big coagulation of beaks and bright feathers. Into

this place there sometimes saunters a worldly young gentleman who wishes to inquire if there is any market at present for pigeon. His is a perennial Oxford figure. He brings a breath of the woods with him, wears a yellow spotted kerchief at his throat, and has been specializing in pigeon ever since My Lord Abbot Hokenotton clamped down on the red deer.

How near the surface of the city this bucolic level lies you may see from the map. Oxford has grown enormously in the last half-century, and in doing so she has swallowed up half a dozen villages that lay, a generation or two ago, well out in the country. They show as tight irregular blobs on the city map, looking recognizably older and more gnarled, even in the Ordnance Survey, than the suburban estates now surrounding them. They have proper country-sounding names—Hinksey, Binsey, Headington, Marston, Wolvercote, Iffley—and in each you may recognize the village street still, the fine old village church, the pub on the corner and the tang of local character. Immemorial footpaths meander among their buildings, like the long quiet lane which you can still follow all the way from St. Clement's, among the suburban houses of Headington, across the northern by-pass to the once-holy well of Barton. Industry came very late to Oxford, with the Motor rather than the Steam Age, and these buried villages remain more vivid entities than the country communities long ago absorbed by London, Birmingham or Bristol. Some of them really were villages within living memory, and in others the village atmosphere is nostalgically maintained by fêtes, wistaria and petitions of protest.

Some have preserved traces of their antique functions. The paper mill of Wolvercote, now owned by the Oxford University Press, has been the chief local employer since 1690. The hamlet of Binsey, all on its own beside the Thames, still feels like the fishing village it used to be, with its cluster of cottages and the yacht sails loitering up and down its river. Headington Quarry is built around, beside and inside the abandoned quarries—all bumps and indentations, like a volcanic plateau—from which half the Oxford colleges bought their stone. It used to be a rugged sort of community, with a name for violence and bad drains, several disreputable ale-houses (Joan's, Widow Coxe's and Mother Gurdon's), and a reputation among its neighbours so black that elsewhere in these parts the children used to sing obscurely but with rude intent: 'Who's ate all the bread and cheese? Us too, Quarry hogs.'

At Iffley one of the most exquisite Norman churches in England stands in a hush above the river—with a long low rectory on one side, and an old country house on another, and an owlish stump of a dead tree, and a big yew, and a patch of shaggy walled graveyard so green, silent and mole-heaped that you might still be far out in some distant rural backwater. The churchyard at Headington Quarry looks out upon a little dingle, where ponies graze among the brambles. The church at Old Marston is famous for its bell-ringing, and has a delightful modern bell-loft of polished oak. In a lane at Old Headington stands Oxford's first Quaker meeting house, with tombstones in its garden and an air of happily faded piety. The bell-ringer at Cowley is given a shilling on St. Thomas's Day under the terms of a seventeenth-century shepherd's will. There is a village green at Wolvercote, and the old church school at Iffley has a thatched roof.

It was in a garden at Headington, on Boxing Day 1899, that the musicologist Cecil Sharp first saw a morris dance, then all but extinct. A local labourer called William Kimber, out of work because of bad weather, mustered up a team to dance upon the lawn, and Sharp saw them through the window. The interest it aroused in him possibly saved the dance from oblivion, and certainly led to the revival of things folksy throughout the English-speaking world. It was only a few years ago that the last of the Kimber family retired from the flourishing Headington morris group, often to be seen in ribbons and cross-garters contributing to local jollities; the man in the garden that Boxing Day is commemorated in William Kimber Crescent at Headington Quarry; and in the garden itself, now part of the group of houses called Horwood Close, his disciples still perform.

In a dingy upstairs office above a garage in Longwall Mr. William Morris arranged the transformation of Oxford. He was a small bicycle manufacturer who, one day in 1913, put together a motorcar, and until he died in 1963 you could still visit his original office, miraculously preserved in its pristine state. It was not preserved by order, or even by intent: but Morris had long since become Lord Nuffield, his works had moved to the eastern suburb of Cowley, and somehow or other his old room was left just as it was. Nobody liked to touch it, and though Nuffield sometimes used to say that he really must go through his things there, somehow he never did.

You could therefore open its brown door and walk straight into the 1920s. There was an old diary on the desk, sprinkled with not very interesting engagements in exceedingly careful handwriting. There was a blotter entirely free of doodles, a writing pad ornately printed, a bottle of very stale medicine (four times daily before meals). The walls, painted dark brown and yellow, were decorated with cigarette advertisements, each illustrating some harmlessly amorous situation, in which girls with cloche hats and fur wraps were being courted by young men with ginger moustaches holding De Reszke cigarettes—*The Light of his Life* was the caption of one, *The Burning Question* another. Heavy brocade curtains hung at the window, the lampshade was ponderously fringed, and you would suppose the occupant of this drab tasteless room to have been a mediocrity indeed. By 1936 his car factories were easily the largest outside the United States, and today they turn out, when they are not on strike, a car every 50 seconds.

Before Lord Nuffield created this great Oxford industry, almost single-handed, this city was a kind of elfin workshop, full of respectful craftsmen tapping away in back-alleys. It seemed, as an observer wrote in 1907, 'prevented, as if by fate, from ever attaining the position of a great industrial or commercial centre'. Some of the craft feeling survives. The weavers' looms no longer clack in Magdalen Grove, but the city is still rich in tiny upstairs enterprises, engineering firms or foundries, so that quite modest Oxford burghers may disconcertingly introduce themselves as directors of steel companies, or invite you to step into the kitchen for a costs-and-delivery estimate. There are some 25 men in England, I am told, qualified to build a first-class racing shell, and seven or eight of them work beside the river at Oxford, in boatyards smelling deliciously of wood, glue and varnish, and cluttered with the exquisite skeletons of boats. Oxford boatbuilders are properly proud of their workmanship. I once congratulated a firm on the superb wooden punt they had just spent a winter making for me. 'Ah,' they said, 'we pride ourselves on doing things the proper way here, no skimping things, no fooling about with fibre-glass in *this* yard'—and even as they said the words, I realized too late that a fibre-glass punt was just the very thing I wanted.

They used to make steam-rollers in Oxford. They still make harpsichords. Frank Cooper's Oxford marmalade is made in Wantage now, and is American-controlled, but Oxford and marmalade will always go together, and for generations of homesick addicts the very name of the place has conjured up visions of noble English breakfasts with kippers and the morning mail. Mr. Frank Cooper first started making it in his shop at 83 High Street in the 1870s. Some say he got the recipe from his wife, others that he was given it by a rash customer across the counter; certainly his descendants stuck closely to marmalade ever after, except for the one who took up railway engineering, helped to build the Moscow underground, and was awarded the Order of Lenin.

And chief of all the Oxford craft industries is printing. This was one of the earliest printing centres in Europe, and beautiful books have been printed in Oxford ever since. It was the Alden Press, then off the Botley Road, which printed, with infinite care, irritation and interruption, T. E. Lawrence's *Seven Pillars of Wisdom*, and the machines of the Oxford University Press, grandiosely housed in classical buildings in Walton Street, are among the most famous in the world. They are owned by the Chancellor, Masters and Scholars of the University, and they print anything from a visiting card to an encyclopedia. In particular they print more Bibles, in more languages, than anyone else, and their technicians are uniquely knowledgeable about the problems of printing fast on thin India paper. Together with the Cambridge University Press and Her Majesty's Printers, the Press enjoys a monopoly right to print the Authorized Version of the Bible and the Book of Common Prayer. It has long been a boast of the Oxford University Press that anyone who finds a misprint in one of its editions of the Authorized Version is entitled to a guinea reward: every now and then they have to pay up, though more often it is discovered that hopeful applicants are referring to the Revised Version, the New English Version, or even the Bible in Arabic.

The Press is a much-respected Oxford institution. The quarter of Oxford called Jericho—perhaps the original of Hardy's Beersheeba, where Jude the Obscure found his lodgings—was created for its work-people, the first industrial community in the city and

there is a strong sense of guild to its organization. Careful enthusiastic craftsmen clamber over its great machines, the job of Printer to
the University is one of the plums of the profession, and when one
of the chief readers died some years ago people seriously doubted
whether a successor could be found who also knew 55 languages.

For years it was Oxford's chief employer,but the emergence of
the car industry dwarfed it: first Morris Motors, now part of British
Leyland, then the adjacent Pressed Steel Company, which began
as a half-American company making car bodies in a new way, but
is now all-British too. Cowley lies three or four miles from the centre
of Oxford, connected with it by a long ugly ribbon of houses and
shops, given cohesion only by the factories themselves, and by the
brave new shopping centre recently built, all plazas and plate glass,
to keep local shoppers out of the congested city centre. This is one
of the great car manufactories of Europe. The twin plants are neither
smoky nor spectacular, and seem a world away from the noble simplicity of Volkswagen's mile-long assembly hall; but they do ema-
nate a certain sense of power—the smell of paint baking in the paint
shops, the armies of new cars lined up in the yards outside, the
thump of the big power presses, the works policemen at the gates,
the floods of cars and bicycles pouring home at the end of the shift,
the rambling Pressed Steel die-yard, looking like an enormous junk
heap, where dies of old models are permanently stored, the railway
wagons in their sidings, the test cars scurrying off into the country,
the half-finished cars rumbling by on transporters, the car bodies
lurching from their conveyor hoists through the closed bridge above
the ring road, the crowd and the clamour and the colour of it all.
You could live in Oxford for years without once glimpsing these
plants: but their presence on the fringe of the city, away over Magdalen Bridge, has created modern Oxford. 'Welcome to Oxford',
a notice at the railway station used to say, 'the Home of Pressed
Steel': and it is true that since the arrival of the industries the city's
population has almost doubled.

They are important plants by any standards, and the cars they
have produced since 1913 are an index to English progress—or decline: the bull-nosed Morris of the 1920s, a British equivalent of
the Model T Ford; the Morris Cowleys of the 1930s, which first
began to tap a middle-class market; the vastly successful Morris
Minor, which Morris himself despised, but which became a very

symbol of the post-war years; the lumpish series of the 1950s, which had Italian-designed bodies and reflected British uncertainties about the national style and purpose; the series initiated by Alec Issigonis's Mini-Minor, which brought a transient new bite to British motoring, and were the first really original cars Morris ever produced. Of all Oxford's products, from mathematical symbols to sugarless marmalade, none have been so familiar to so many millions of people as her cars, and few have more profoundly affected the English manner of living.

The city's welcome to these prodigious newcomers has sometimes been reserved, and often wry. In 1948 one city development plan proposed that the Cowley plants should be removed somewhere else, lock, stock and radiator, and certainly the whole character of the place has been altered by their arrival—vulgarized in some ways, as the cheap chain stores spring up on each other's heels, enlivened in others, as an altogether new strain of citizen fertilizes the Oxford stock. The high wages of the car industry have lured workers to Oxford from all over Britain—the largest proportion, oddly enough, from the comfortable south-west—and in boomtimes the demand is so great that coach-loads of night workers are brought to Cowley each week from Portsmouth, 70 miles away on the coast. The old paternal flavour of Oxford has been broken down by the arrival of the militant trade unions, and even the country villages find their ways jolted and their ideas shuffled, as the Cowley workers buy their cottages or build their bungalows. The population as a whole, once dependent upon the University and thus half destitute every Long Vacation, is now among the most prosperous in Britain, and Oxford is said to save more money than any English city of comparable size. She is economically vulnerable still, because some 25,000 of her workers are now employed by one industry: but wherever you go in her streets today you will see the booming supermarkets, electrical shops and car showrooms that are the particular symbols of industrial affluence.

Yet country ways fight back. Cars are only assembled in Cowley, from parts actually made in Birmingham, Coventry, South Wales or East Anglia, and this constant convergence at the plant of a million little bits and pieces, from entire car bodies to finicky dashboard ornaments put together by dear old pensioners beneath coloured postcards of Bognor Regis—this rather fiddly kind of process has inspired one eminent authority to call the whole complex, even now, just another Oxford cottage industry. These great motor plants, which stand on the very edge of the countryside, still preserve remnants of pastoral simplicity—reminders of the slower, older Oxford they have themselves shattered. The piece-workers on the assembly line, who work at ferocious speeds for exceedingly high pay, still have time to greet the visitor with unhurried courtesy, and even the official guide is quite likely to interrupt his panegyrics with a sad thought about the inhumanity of the industrial life—a train of sentiment not often pursued, I suspect, in Detroit, Tokyo or Düsseldorf.

Over all hangs the consequence of the City. The Town Hall at Oxford is full of unexpected things, from ancient firearms to a vast allegorical hunting scene of silver, dedicated to a dead Mayor and now gleaming eerily, all writhing silver hounds, doomed silver fox and formidable silver huntsmen, beneath a glass case in a dark basement of the building. There is a collection of plate in a mediaeval cellar. There is a door marked Radio-Active, which is something to do with civil defence. There is a magnificently florid fireplace, such as Cecils or Palmerstons would happily warm their buttocks at—proof of the enormous confidence with which the City Council, cheerfully knocking down the comely Cotswold town hall that stood here before, built this vast neo-Jacobean edifice in 1897 (at the student rag which its opening provoked F. E. Smith, later Lord Chancellor of England, was arrested for assaulting a policeman).

Best of all the Town Hall contains the archives of the city, all its deeds and rolls and charters, impeccably kept in a dry vault, and testimony to the proud consistency of an English borough. A retired servant of the municipality shows them to you, and he knows them backwards, from King John's royal charter, sealed and taped on yellow parchment in 1199, to the six folio volumes, drably labelled Emergency, which record all those multitudinous fatigues of fire watching, milk distributing, evacuee minding, Red Cross volunteering, allotment gardening and Keeping Cheerful by which the English won their second world war. Oxford is not among the most ancient of cities, but she has never been bombed or burnt, and her records are particularly complete. They give a stalwart impression of yeoman confidence—nothing fancy, they seem to say, carefully dusting themselves off, only sensible, steady Midlands progress. There is nothing fiery to the Oxford temperament. Without its University this city would scarcely be celebrated, but one can imagine it a pleasant enough sort of place, with a prosperous parish church and a local industry, and a nice little Georgian town hall.

It is full of Authority, only waiting to have its helmet knocked off by high-spirited undergraduates. All the panoply of municipal pride is upheld here with chains, maces and protocol. Oxford is stiff with law courts—county courts, city courts, coroner's courts, chancellor's courts. The magistrates have a discreet new courthouse off St. Aldate's, but the Crown Courts sit more full-bloodedly, in a sham castle in New Road, and the Judge is always given a pair of hand-embroidered gloves from Woodstock as a memento of his visit. Until 1965 he also used to take over the house called the Judge's House in St. Giles, whose occupant, under the terms of his lease, had to vacate the place for the session: now he has an official flat in a country mansion up the road at Wheatley.

Oxford is one of the oldest prison towns in England. Until 1771 there was a famous lock-up above the north gate of the city, beside the present church of St. Michael. It was called Bocardo, supposedly after a kind of syllogism from which there is no escape, and was chiefly for University prisoners, who are sometimes to be seen in old engravings lowering collection boxes on long strings for the charity of passers-by below. The present prison is more severely removed from philanthropy, in the grim purlieus of the castle. It is a small but awful place, filled with the jangling of keys, the scraping of padlocks, the tramp of feet and the voices of warders echoing against old stone walls. It has been a prison since the thirteenth century, with its gallows then as now, and its courthouse unkindly close beside the gate.

In prison history it is chiefly famous for a ferocious outbreak of gaol fever. This was a common prison hazard until modern times, but there can have been few more disastrous visitations than the epidemic which struck here during the Assize session of 1577. It lasted for 40 days, killed the Lord Chief Baron, the High Sheriff, the Under Sheriff, two Judges, the Clerk of Assize, the Coroner and 300 more, and has immortalized the session as the Black Assize. 'The malady developed itself from the stench of the prisoners', so a notice near the prison tells us, 'during the Trial of one Rowland

Jenkes, a saucy foul-mouthed Bookseller, for scandalous words uttered against the Queen.' Today the prisoners of Oxford are mostly short-term convicts, though sometimes a transient murderer appears, and in 1964 one of the Great Train Robbers, whose hide-away was a farmhouse 10 miles east of Oxford, was locked up here in what was hopefully called Maximum Security. A little white-washed yard beside the castle tower is where hanged men used to be buried, and in the base of the tower itself (a lugubrious structure of rubble and rickety platforms) the young offenders perform the most distasteful of their chores, scrubbing their tin chamber pots.

In Oxford Authority can do almost anything to you, or for you. It can issue you a temporary passport, a birth certificate or a yellow fever inoculation; it can find you a job, a house or at a pinch a bed in the maternity ward; it can knock down your home, promise you a room in an old folks' home, recruit you for the Greenjackets' Brigade or lock you up for ever. In such an English regional capital, you realize how strong-armed a system democracy can be, and how unobtrusively pervasive are the powers of the State. Nearly all this machinery of Government is contained within the old circuit of the city walls—hardly more than a mile round, but packed solid. From the top of Carfax Tower—the remains of an ancient church—you may see all its emblems. There is the tower of St. Michael's, a fortress tower, erected by Saxons or Normans to protect the northern entrance to the city. There is the City Church of All Saints, where for many generations the Lord Mayor and his aldermen periodically attended service: it is converted now into a college library, but remains a somewhat aldermanic presence itself, in which eminent ironmongers are remembered still, and managers of waterworks. To the south is the exuberant façade of the Town Hall, with the City Police headquarters beyond. To the west are the County buildings, the castellated Crown Court, and that grey rubble tower above the prison. And wherever you look, in all four corners, there stand the venerable churches of the place, each in its parish—St. Giles's and St. Michael's, St. Aldate's and St. Mary Magdalene, St. Peter le Bailey and St. Peter at the East Gate—to remind us that the form, order and standards of this city are based upon the Christian discipline.

On Ascension Day, to press this point home, they beat the bounds of St. Michael's—establishing once again the parish limits, and emphasizing the old pre-eminence of the Church. This is an antic occasion, but moving. Led by the vicar, a little raggle-taggle group of choirboys and parishioners parades through the city centre, now and then pausing at immemorially ordained spots to thrash a wall with canes and shout 'Mark! Mark! Mark!' (in the old days they used to thrash the choirboys, too, to impress the boundaries on them once and for all). The route they pursue is involved, but the vicar and his crew are not perturbed. Once they scramble over a 12-foot wall, once they march deadpan clean through Woolworth's, and once they beat a wall in a banana store in the market. They follow the line to the bitter end, thrashing as they go, as 15 generations of parsons and giggling choristers have loyally done before them.

4. *Universitas Oxoniensis*

Into this intricate jigsaw we must now fit the most complex piece of all, *Universitas Oxoniensis*—the Chancellor, Masters and Scholars of the University of Oxford, in this city assembled.

A fairly farcical charade of its character is regularly performed at the degree-giving ceremony, itself a function so involved that visitors are given a printed guide to what is going on, 10 pages long and not much help. It takes place in the Sheldonian Theatre, which was, when the young Christopher Wren built it, as functionally daring as the London and North Western railway station two centuries later, or a geodetic dome today. Designed like a classical amphitheatre, its ceiling is painted to represent a vast canopy, being rolled back by obliging *putti* to reveal a patch of blue Oxford sky above—'Future ages must confess they owe,' said a contemporary poet of its artist, 'To Streater more than Michael Angelo.' Curiously shaped (externally its front does not seem to fit its sides), erratically decorated with sphinxes and fasces, with a handsome gilded organ and very nasty modern chairs, this oddly delightful building is just the setting for a peculiar but endearing function.

Mediaeval dream-like figures people it on degree-giving day: black beadles with silver wands or huge brass badges on their arms, scurrying scholars in scarlet gowns or rabbit fur, students in white bow ties, the Vice-Chancellor grave upon an elevated throne, the two Proctors, intendants of University discipline, with the tassels of their mortar-boards hanging indolently over their eyes. The ceremony goes at a cracking pace. In come the lines of happy graduates, marshalled by a testy verger in a black gown, and a Latin incantation is read at them at breakneck speed, and sometimes they bow, and sometimes the Proctors remove their mortar-boards, on and off, on and off, and then in a sudden brisk convulsion the Proctors spring from their seats and march up and down the hall, in case some dissenter wishes to register a protest by plucking their gowns, and there are further Latin admonitions, and then the candidates, kneeling before the Vice-Chancellor, are touched gently on the head with a Bible, bumpity-bump, bumpity-bump, and up they get again, and the verger gestures them towards the door, and out they all troop to the yard outside, pink-cheeked and pleased as Punch. The beadles, the Proctors, the Doctors and the Vice-Chancellor fade away like so many wraiths: and the new Bachelors of Arts are left in the sunshine beside the theatre, discussing with proud parents the best place to go for tea.

I have grossly simplified the form of it, for it proceeds, in fact, through several complicated stages, and sometimes seems to double back upon itself; but then this University has never set out to make itself clear. It possesses, indeed, a natural gift for publicity. As long ago as 1664 the University published a long history of itself specifically 'for the honour of the University in forreigne countries', and after so many centuries of practice, nowadays it slides easily into the habits of self-advertisement—like landing at garden parties in helicopters, being visited by foreign Prime Ministers, cantankerously contributing to television debates or simply pursuing its own affairs with a maximum of colourful ritual.

This talent does not, however, extend to clarity of exposition. Everybody has some mental image of Oxford University, but very few people can break it down into logical detail—'there is no person or body in Oxford', it was authoritatively observed in 1931, 'competent to declare what the functions of the University are'. The University Statutes are republished every year, and run to 700 pages, but are likely to leave you more hazed than in command of things. Until 1969 half of them were in Latin. One regulated the carrying of bows and arrows by students; and if you wished to know, for example, whether an undergraduate might own a car, you had to look under *De Moribus Conformandis*, paragraph 14, *De Vehiculis*, Add. p. 7, ante 320. (1838). Corp. Stat. p. 145. (1636). Add. p. 420. (1851). Add. p. 1964. (1960), to discover that he might not, except that 'cum consensu Praefecti Domus suae aut ejus vicem gerentis, a Procuratoribus concessa sit'. Even the University buildings often mystify the stranger, for there is no central campus, no helpful symmetry or logic of design, and the antique doorway marked *Schola*

Linguarum turns out to be, if you pluck up the effrontery to enter it, rather a comfortable lavatory.

This obscurantism is inherent to the nature of the thing, for Oxford University is a rambling kind of semi-private democracy, put together in bits and pieces down the ages. In its wider sense this University is a federation of its constituent colleges: 34 in all, some for men, some for women, some for both. The colleges are themselves private corporations, with their own royal charters, and in theory they are perfectly autonomous—they can choose their own students and make their own rules. It is the University as a whole, however, that awards degrees, and in practice it is the University that arranges curricula, accepts State aid and sets up commissions of inquiry. When people speak of the University—they seldom say Varsity nowadays, though one or two old-school retailers still have a weakness for the word—they generally mean this whole nebulous conglomeration of colleges, buildings, customs and traditions.

In a narrower sense the University is the central authority established to bind together the federation, with the libraries, museums, laboratories and lecture staffs which it administers for all the colleges. The government of Oxford University includes no outsiders—no politicians, no businessmen, no honoured benefactors. It is drawn exclusively from its own teachers and researchers. Its nominal head is the Chancellor, elected for life as an honorific, but its executive head is the Vice-Chancellor, appointed for a four-year term in rotation from among the colleges. Its effective legislature is a body called Congregation, in which some 2,000 of the graduates working at the University have a right to vote. (There is also a wider body called Convocation, which consists of all Oxford graduates everywhere who have paid the necessary dues, but it only votes on two specific issues, the choice of a Chancellor and a Professor of Poetry, when fervent Oxonians assemble from every quarter, generally not to get a man in so much as to keep another out.)

Congregation elects 18 members to the Hebdomadal Council, which really does meet once a week in term, and with the General Board of the Faculties forms a kind of core for the innumerable boards and committees that actually run the University—Boards of Curators, Boards of Electors, Boards of Faculties, Boards of Delegates, Boards of Visitors—Committees for Appointments, for Dispensations, for Comparative Philology, for the Administration of the Beit Fund, for the Computer Laboratory—the Craven Committee, the Referees as to College Contributions for University Purposes, the Management Committee for the Iffley Road Running Ground—the Trustees of the Higher Studies Fund, the Advisory Council for Ornithology, the Ruskin Trust. There is a small professional secretariat, headed by the Registrar. There is a finance section, called the University Chest because its curators used to keep the cash in an iron-studded box—they still have one in their headquarters in Wellington Square: nowadays they get almost three-quarters of their funds from the State. There is also a little police force, four men strong, whose members are nicknamed Bulldogs, and wear bowler hats on duty: they are responsible to the Proctors, who are elected annually in rotation from the colleges, whose names have been recorded since 1267, who get £2,752 for their year's pains, plus a free copy of any book published by the University Press during their term of office, and who wear a small black tippet on their gowns for the rest of their lives.

If you think all this confusing, bear in mind that we have not discussed the colleges themselves, each with its own constitution, and that even so I have spared you the functions of the Bellman, the High Steward and the Summoner of Preachers. I have not explained the difference between the Assessors and the Assessor of the Chancellor's Court, and I have perhaps not made it clear that though the initiation of a statute is normally the prerogative of the Hebdomadal Council, nevertheless members of that Council, who are, you will remember, elected by Congregation, may oppose the statute when it comes before Congregation—which may initiate a resolution, by the way, if at least six members support it, and if not less than 40 members vote in its favour the Hebdomadal Council is obliged to submit back to Congregation a decree putting it into effect.

Nobody knows *everything* about Oxford University. A lifetime would be too short. Much of it does not mean what it appears to mean, much of it shifts its meaning from year to year, and some of it has been totally meaningless for several centuries: for 600 years every Oxford graduate was required to swear that he would never on any account be reconciled with somebody called Henry the son of Simeon, who had murdered an Oxford man in 1242, and who was, even after so long in an unmarked grave, not to be touched with a punt pole.

This labyrinthine structure *moves*—not very fast, but with a ponderous and inexorable momentum, like a grand elderly Cunarder. One of these days they are sure to modernize its tangled mechanism—subdue the autonomy of the colleges, perhaps, appoint a permanent President, and make it all more clear-cut and professional. It is hard, however, to break so old a cycle, and over the years a vast amount of wisdom has gone into the evolution of this University. The Hebdomadal Council meets in a long room at the back of the Clarendon Building, in Broad Street, and I know of no other chamber, not even the Admiralty Board Room, that seems so infused with solemn experience. Oracular old portraits look down in supervision. Beside the window stands an ancient voting machine, a box into which generations of learned doctors plunged their wrinkled hands to deposit their voting tokens in secrecy—left for yes, right for no. There are works of legal reference on the table, and the windows look out across the gravel yard to the Bodleian Library, where another three million volumes are available for consultation if the need arises. It is true that I have only seen this chamber empty, and have thus been able to people it with my own infallible sages: but it will be a brave reformer, all the same, who disturbs its dusty gravity at last, and fixes it up with ball-point pens.

Certainly this University, so obscurely organized, is recognized as one of the half-dozen most important in the world, and long ago outstripped most of its mediaeval peers—Padua provincial, Bologna undistinguished, Salamanca humiliated, Salerno dead. Thanks to the island immunity of the English, it has advanced almost imperceptibly from mediaevalism to modernity (Matthew Arnold said it was still 'whispering the last enchantments of the Middle Ages', but Max Beerbohm thought he must have been referring to the railway station). Its present preoccupations range from the fabric of the Divinity School, one of the best fifteenth-century buildings in England, to the accelerator of the Nuclear Physics laboratory, whose attendants can be summoned to the Professorial presence by a blurp on the radios in their pockets.

The very first University building still stands, so gradual has been the development of it all. It is a chamber attached to the fabric of St. Mary's, the University Church, in High Street. Downstairs was an assembly room, upstairs a library, but in the late fifteenth century they slapped big windows on it to make it uniform with the rest of the church, and from the outside it merely looks like an aisle of St. Mary's. In fact it retains exactly its original form. It has been in its time an archives, an ammunition depot, a type-depository, a book-store, a school, a fire station and a lecture hall. Now there is a little crypt chapel downstairs, attended by three or four crumbly statues removed from the spire above, and a parish hall upstairs. Any sense of historic significance has long evaporated, I fear, but there is one sign of its grand origins: that last surviving bust of old King Alfred, all among the Free Expression, beneath whose plinth an inscription gamely sticks to its story, like a last royal retainer beside an exiled dictator. *Aelfredus Legum Anglia Academiae Oxon Conditor*, it says—'Alfred, Founder of the Laws of England and the University of Oxford.'

From this secluded start, seven centuries ago, the University burst in expanding splendours. Halls of residence were established, monastic institutions came to Oxford, schools were built, the college system was born, and by the early seventeenth century the headquarters of the University was the great quadrangle of the Schools, which is now part of the Bodleian Library, and which represents in its very shape the pattern of mediaeval scholarship. The gateway from Catte Street is only opened two or three times a year, on ceremonial occasions (though you may not park your car in front of it, because it is the only entrance big enough for fire engines). If, however, you stand inside, you may see from the names still painted above the quadrangle doors how the mediaeval curriculum ran. Immediately around you, right and left, are the eight rooms of the Faculty of Arts, in which the student pursued a basic course of grammar, logic, rhetoric, music, arithmetic, geometry, astronomy, Greek, Hebrew, history and philosophy. He then moved to the other side of the quadrangle for his superior education, choosing either the Faculty of Medicine, on the left, or the Faculty of Law, on the right, or, most ambitious of all, the great doorway that would lead him into the splendours of the School of Divinity. It took seven years to graduate from the lower faculties to the upper; and today the Oxford Bachelor of Arts must wait seven years from his matriculation before, handing over his £5 fee, he becomes a Master of Arts without further ado.

Year by year, endowment by endowment, this structure was elaborated, and successive phases of New Learning left their mark upon the University—widening its interests, bifurcating its faculties, until by the late nineteenth century it could properly claim to represent virtually every intellectual interest. It is not, by international standards, a large university—some 11,500 students, with about 1,350 permanent staff. Its reputation varies among the faculties and the generations, so that sometimes it is pre-eminent in philosophy, sometimes in classical studies, sometimes in experimental physics. A phenomenal range of knowledge and inquiry, though, is concentrated within its confines. Its 16 faculties support professorial chairs in subjects as diverse as Race Relations, the Interpretation of Holy Scriptures and Ancient Icelandic Literature. It has its own publishing house, said to be the biggest in the world after Her Majesty's Stationery Office, its associated teaching hospital, its own experimental farm, its Radiation Protection Officer, pocket diary, computer laboratory, paper mill, Exploration Council for the sponsoring of overseas adventure, park, theatre, cathedral and cricket field—one of the only two in England where the public may watch first-class cricket free.

I open the lists at random, and find that on one single Wednesday an Oxford undergraduate was offered lectures on the Political Ideas of St. Augustine, Topics in Contract, Chemical Microbiology, Induction and Probability, the Morphology of Greek Dialects, Speculative Systems of History, the interpretation of Sir Gawain and the Green Knight, La Rochefoucauld, Turkish Prosody, the Energetics of Simple Molecules, Gas Dynamics, the Place of Man in Soviet Affairs, Schubert's Songs, Animal Husbandry and Analytical Topology—plus a couple of dozen more. In the evening the insatiable student could enjoy a Cabinet Minister at the University Labour Club, a Welsh Nationalist leader at the University Liberal Club, a talk about West African architecture at the University Archaeological Society, jazz at the University Jazz Club, Büchner's *Wozzeck* at the University Playhouse or *The Maid of the Mountains* at the New Theatre. And on the same day, I see from a list compiled by the Committee for Advanced Studies, individual students were investigating, among several hundred other subjects, the language of Tamil inscriptions, the mechanism of the menschutkin reaction, the interaction of economic and technical factors in the design of industrial plants, and the attitude of Robert Whytt (1714–66) towards the problem of the seat of the Soul.

Every day of every University term all this immensely varied activity is pulsating away in this city, and some of the cleverest men in Europe are teaching or learning or thinking hard. The University itself, by and large, offers neither hospitality nor corporate living—the prerogative of the colleges: but it constitutes a kind of huge umbrella, sheltering all the separate institutions of the place, pulling all their energies loosely together, and sometimes gilding them with a fancy touch of ornament. 'Mr. Vice-Chancellor', the University *Gazette* announces once a year, 'invites Heads of Houses, Doctors of Divinity, Civil Law, Medicine, Music, Letters and Science, the Proctors, the Assessor, the Public Orator, the Professor of Poetry and the Registrar to partake of Lord Crewe's Benefaction to the University.' A spiritual homily? A distribution of textbooks? A contribution to faculty expenses? Certainly not: peaches and cream with champagne, willed to the University *in perpetuum* by a seventeenth-century bishop, and best eaten, if you don't want to spill cream on your doctoral robes, by balancing the bowl on top of the champagne glass, and alternating sips with mouthfuls.

Two archetypal figures dominate this University—the Don and the Undergraduate. The don's title, rather out of fashion nowadays, is derived, like that of a Spanish grandee, from the Latin *dominus*, or master of a house, and his generic species may roughly be taken to include all who teach at this place. The undergraduate, who cherished until recently a profound antipathy to being called a *student*, or still worse an *undergrad*, is referred to on college notice boards as a gentleman, and in University publications as being in *statu pupillari*. Around the dons there swirl a miscellaneous company of clergymen, bursars, University officials and senior researchers: around the undergraduate flutter people writing theses for higher degrees, exchange students, *au pair* girls, and a few of those benevolent aesthetes, in silk scarves and sunglasses, who linger in all university towns in a condition of perpetual demi-youth.

Oxford's chief contribution to educational practice has been the intimacy that exists, at least in theory, between these two groups.

In this democracy the undergraduate plays no governmental part, except through committees of dons and students reluctantly set up under the pressures of the times. But he is traditionally encouraged not to be overawed by his seniors. In the past his disrespect was often bawdy—'Cut it short! Give him beer!' cried the undergraduates when Matthew Arnold delivered the Creweian Oration in the Sheldonian in 1864. Today it is less explicit. The Oxford teaching system is based upon the tutorial, a weekly hour-long meeting between the undergraduate and his tutor, in which an essay is read and criticized, conversation revolves around the subject of study, and some of the older man's wisdom and experience is supposed to alight like a mantle on his pupil. No undergraduate was compelled to go to any one of those Wednesday lectures, and some of them, I dare say, were totally unattended: it is said that when an undergraduate found himself waiting all alone for a lecture by one of the more formidable theological professors he was so demoralized by the aged footsteps of the scholar, shuffling along the corridor outside, that he climbed down a drain-pipe to evade the experience.

The University's rules of discipline are not onerous. Proctors must be obeyed, private aircraft must not be kept within 20 miles of Oxford, and a few things of that sort. Generally the University treats its junior members as adults, fining its recalcitrants without much rancour, and only occasionally condemning them to rustication—exile from Oxford for a week, a term or for ever. This equality is part of the legend of the place, and the romantic view of Oxford is dominated by dreams of dons and undergraduates linked in improving intimacy—talking about Life over sherry and Bath Olivers, talking about Literature on reading-parties in the Alps, striding together over Cumnor Hurst on white winter evenings.

Nowadays it does not often happen, and most tutors meet their pupils only once or twice a week, when they have to. The mystique is a relic of a period when the University was principally concerned with the formation of character, and its point was best illustrated by the fertile contact of don and undergraduate. This was a passing phase, encouraged by the religious revivals of the nineteenth century: for Oxford's notion of her own purpose has seldom been clear, and often fluctuates. Some see the University chiefly as a research institution, some as a nursery of Church and State, some as a liberation of the spirit, some as a microcosm of all society, some as a forcing-house for first-class intellects, some as a training-ground for the economic struggle, some as a channel of accepted wisdom, some as a probe towards new knowledge.

William of Wykeham, who founded New College in 1379, thought its task was to produce 'men of great learning, fruitful to the church of God and to the king and realm'. Benjamin Jowett, who was Master of Balliol from 1870 to 1893, said that he wanted to 'inoculate England with Balliol'. The Victorian divine Edward Pusey felt passionately that the main purpose of the University was 'not simply or mainly to cultivate the intellect', and Matthew Arnold thought mere patriotism a degrading emotion for so great an institution. Lewis Carroll, whose real name was C. L. Dodgson, and who was a mathematical tutor at Christ Church, strongly believed in the microcosmic function, and greeted one proposed reform with the sarcastic jingle:

> *Then, then shall Oxford be herself again,*
> *Neglect the heart and cultivate the brain—*
> *Then this shall be the burden of our song*
> *'All change is good—whatever is, is wrong'—*
> *Then Intellect's proud flag shall be unfurled,*
> *And Brain, and Brain alone shall rule the world.*

Thomas Gaisford, on the other hand, who was Dean of Christ Church from 1831 to 1855, once assured his undergraduates that the study of Greek would 'not only enable them to read the Scriptures in the original, but also qualify them for positions of considerable emolument': and Dr. Philip Shuttleworth, a nineteenth-century Warden of New College, is chiefly famous for the revealing couplet, part of a youthful apostrophe to the goddess of Learning:

> *Make me, O Sphere-descended Queen,*
> *A Bishop, or at least a Dean.*

Lord Curzon thought Oxford ought to be 'a focus of culture, a school of character, and a nursery of thought'. Bernard Shaw said the business of Oxford was 'to make a few scholars and a great many gentlemen'. Boswell approvingly defined the place as a Seat of Learning, Orthodoxy and Toryism.

The University Committee set up to consider the Robbins Report of 1963 said that the University 'has no consciously affirmed general policies, and lacks adequate machinery to evolve them'. People have certainly entered it for every sort of reason—to follow in their fathers' footsteps, to be sure of getting into Shell, to investigate the principles of Maori Land Tenure, to row, to prepare commentaries on Hesiod's theogony, to get some really practical, I mean *vibrant*, stage experience, to find a husband, to grow up, to slack off, to stay young—even to die, perhaps, though Swinburne thought that nobody in Oxford could be said to die, 'for they never begin to live'.

Every now and then a convulsion of reform overcomes Oxford, as one of these philosophies gains paramountcy, or the machinery lags too grotesquely behind the times. Sometimes the reforms are self-engendered, like the revolutionary new examination methods introduced in the first half of the nineteenth century. Sometimes they are imposed from outside. The first of the Royal Commissions investigated Oxford in 1850: the Duke of Wellington was Chancellor at the time, and he took the Commission's report to bed with him on the night he died—'with a pencil in it', so his housekeeper reported. There have been several more since then, and several fundamental changes in the University—the admission of women, for instance, and the acceptance for the first time of Government money. In 1964 the University, finding itself (not for the first time) the target of everybody's cockshy, foresaw yet another investigation, and set up its own Commission of Inquiry to forestall it: no don escaped its questionnaires, and no iconoclast was too vehement to be refused a public hearing.

Oxford is archaic in many ways, but only intermittently moribund. 'Beautiful city!' Matthew Arnold could sigh a century ago, 'so venerable, so lovely, so unravaged by the fierce intellectual life of our century, so serene!' It is no such Arcady now, and its University no longer whispers those last enchantments. It is a turmoil, always dissatisfied, always in disagreement. There is a brash element to its affairs, exemplified by opinionated dons in public controversies, and radical students picketing unwelcome visitors, and there is sometimes a touch of petulance. During its periodic moments of reform there is also a pervading air of uncertainty. 'Strange bits of Liberalism are joggled in amidst old prejudices and bigotries, and Past and Present are engaged in a never-ending conflict for dominion over the conscience of the University'—*The Times* was pronouncing judgement in the 1860s, but the phrase fits the

1960s just as well. The progress of this University is no disciplined march of intellectual legionaries, but more the groping, quarrelsome, skirmishing and sometimes comical advance of a posse of irregulars, blowing trumpets and jostling their way across a soggy sort of battlefield.

Whatever the reality, the forms die hard. The superficials of Oxford University have not changed much in the past fifty years, and add to the illusion that the fundamentals have not altered either.

Take the Oxford idiom. It is overlaid, of course, with general contemporary slang, but much of it survives from one century to the next. High Street is the High, Broad Street the Broad, Cornmarket the Corn. St. Edmund Hall is Teddy Hall, University College is Univ., Brasenose is BNC, Christ Church (*Aedes Christi*) is habitually The House, one never calls New College simply New, Magdalen is pronounced Maudlin (which is more or less how its founder spelt it). Cambridge is, at least in the drearier after-dinner speeches, 'the other place'. The Honour School of *Literae Humaniores* is Greats, the School of Philosophy, Politics and Economics is Modern Greats or P.P.E., you can win a Blue by being good at games, or a First, a Second, or a Third by sitting for a degree examination. The Oxford terms are called Michaelmas, Hilary and Trinity: you come up at the beginning of term and go down at the end of it, unless you are sent down by authority in the middle.

Oxford perfected that peculiar form of double-talk, born at Rugby School, in which a word is changed or abridged and given the suffix *-er*. This once seems to have been almost universal in undergraduate conversation, so that the Radcliffe Camera, for instance, became the Radder, and Jesus College was Jaggers. Today it has entered the language in examples like rugger, soccer and bedsitter, and remains fitfully alive in Oxford, where the Torpid boat races are still called Toggers, and you occasionally even overhear somebody's name distorted in an original coinage. A recent Principal of Brasenose, W. T. S. Stallybrass, was born Sonnenschein, and changed his name by deed poll during the first world war: he was affectionately known as 'Sonners' until the day of his death—which he met by falling out of the midnight train from Paddington in 1948.

All these usages, which mostly have Victorian upper-class origins,

are scorned by the rebels and reformers, but somehow they linger
on: many an undergraduate still blushes, to hear his mother inquire
how many undergrads they have at New, and the most resolute
scoffer at tradition soon falls into the habit of posting his letters
in the High. Nor do the undergraduates much change, however
startling they seem to each new generation of observer. The social
proportions have shifted, but the same classic figures stroll these
quadrangles. Here is the poor Welsh scholar, black-haired and dis-
approving, and here is the Duke's son on his way to dinner at the
Gridiron Club: the ambitious still stalk contemptuously among the
frivolities, the heedless still race up to London with lovely girls in
powerful sports cars. There is still a Civil Service in gestation here,
and a vast corps of potential schoolmasters, and a fringe of actors,
journalists and artists. Many undergraduates still look, as they
always have, unmistakably degenerate, and for all the economic
revolution many still manage to throw excellent champagne-parties
in college rooms on summer evenings. The long curled hair common
among men undergraduates in the 1960s was certainly nothing new.
In the seventeenth century Dr. Ralph Kettell, President of Trinity,
used to walk up and down his dining-hall with a pair of scissors
concealed in his muff, waiting to snip off effeminate coiffures—'I
remember he cut off Mr. Radford's hair', John Aubrey tells us with
respect, 'with the knife that chops the bread on the Buttery Hatch';
and when John Ruskin came up in 1836 he had to swear before
the Vice-Chancellor 'not to cut or comb my hair fantastically'.

The Oxford undergraduate still occasionally wears an odd little
truncated black gown, with loosely hanging tapes for creditors to
catch him by, and in their glass lodges beneath the gate-houses the
college porters still sit as crusty and gimlet-eyed as ever. Until a
few years ago the Proctors still patrolled the Oxford streets, three
nights a week, preceded by their Bulldogs: and accosting some bleary
undergraduate staggering down the Turl, they removed their
mortar-boards with a steely academic courtesy, put the age-old inquiries: 'Are you a member of this University? Name and college,
please?' and strode on, diffident but dignified, into the night. The
great occasions of Oxford are still marvellously rich in scarlet, black
and velvet, with grave tall Doctors and silver staffs and Latin oaths,
and bells pealing among the spires.

Above all, the *presence* of this institution remains inviolate, however its details change or its intentions vary. Ancient fretted cluttered buildings, plonking tennis balls and laughter off the river; the smells of wood, printer's ink and beeswax; the great dome of the Radcliffe Camera, like a huge old egg beside the Bodleian; green grass everywhere, and notice boards fluttering with a thousand announcements; a feeling of easy going irony, like a wink behind an admonition; a tacit assurance that here you may do, look and especially think how you like; a sense of generosity, tolerance and humour impregnating the very stones of the place, the very paragraphs of those incomprehensible Statutes: like it or not, all these really do survive, and raise this University and its patron city into the upper ranks of human artifacts, up there with the works of art, the codes of law and the philosophies. Sometimes as I walk through Oxford, cursing at her traffic, marvelling at her obscurity, and wondering when on earth they are going to bring her up to date, this old magic momentarily dazes me, and I lean against some gold-grey stone beneath the ragwort, and think how lucky I am to be grumbling there at all.

5. Ornery

With such a prodigy at the centre, it is not surprising that Oxford is nearly always up in arms. Everything in this city is sub-divided, cross-fertilized, and every smallest segment is pugnaciously determined to preserve its independence.

The most famous Oxford snook was cocked in 1687. King James II hoped to subvert the University to his own Catholic faith, and he tried to insinuate a Papist nominee into the Presidency of Magdalen, one of the proudest of the Oxford colleges. This was against the college statutes, and the Fellows of Magdalen angrily defied him, electing their own candidate instead. They were unmoved by the Court of Ecclesiastical Commission, headed by Judge Jeffreys in his most ferocious form. ('Who is this man?' the judge screamed at one point in the hearing, pointing to an elderly divine. 'What commission has he to be impudent here? Seize him! Put him into a dark room! What does he do without a keeper?') They even refused to obey the king himself when he came down to Oxford in person, and tried to force upon them, as second-best, the lick-spittle Bishop of Oxford. ('Go home!' cried the king. 'Get you gone! I am king! I will be obeyed! Go to your chapel this instant, and admit the Bishop of Oxford!') A special commission, escorted by cavalry, was sent to Magdalen to install the Bishop anyway: but when he was sworn in (by proxy) only two members of the college attended the ceremony, and almost all the Fellows preferred expulsion to submission.

Almost at the same time, up the road, the City Council flatly refused to accept a new team of officials nominated by the king, and in the end Oxford won. The undergraduates refused to doff their caps to the new President. The Council elected officials of its own. A public fund was opened for the expelled Fellows of Magdalen. Only two months before his own removal from the throne

King James gave in, and allowed the Fellows to return to the college
with their own elected President. Ever since Magdalen has celebrated October 25 as Restoration Day, with a peal of bells and the
toast *jus suum cuique*—'justice for all': and to this day Magdalen
Tower is remembered, at least in the guidebooks, as 'the tower
James II ran his head against'.

Oxford's relations with Authority have often been prickly—it is
said that one reason for the establishment of the University here was
the fact that the bishop of the diocese then had his see at Lincoln,
a safe 100 miles away. Wadham College proudly admitted Carew
Raleigh to its membership, almost immediately after James I had
executed his father, Sir Walter. Brasenose put up the royal coat of
arms, above its smaller doorway into Radcliffe Square, at a time
when the college was virtually governed by Cromwell's Parliamentary Visitors. When Parliament evicted the Dean of Christ Church,
Samuel Fell, in 1648, Mrs. Fell flatly refused to leave the Deanery,
and in the end she and her children had to be carried out on planks,
'going like so many Pyes to the Oven'. Jacobitism has always been
an Oxford cause: tradition says that the wrought-iron gates at the
east end of Trinity College garden will never be opened until a
Stuart returns to the throne (but it is a back-handed sort of myth,
for in fact they are not gates at all, only railings, and could not be
opened if the Blessed Martyr Charles himself commanded it).

In George I's day Jacobite feeling was so strong that a regiment
of dragoons was dispatched to keep order in the city, and a local
poet, noticing that Cambridge's loyalty to the Hanoverians had been
rewarded with a royal gift of books, remarked the contrast in a celebrated epigram.

> *The King, observing with judicious eyes,*
> *The state of both his universities,*
> *To Oxford sent a troop of horse, for why?*
> *That learned body wanted loyalty:*
> *To Cambridge books he sent, as well discerning*
> *How much that loyal body wanted learning.*

Back came an answer from the other university, astutely touching
the bloody-minded streak in the Oxford character:

> *The King to Oxford sent a troop of horse,*
> *For Tories own no argument but force.*

With equal skill to Cambridge books he sent
For Whigs admit no force but argument.

Oxford prides herself upon her pragmatism, her empiricism, her supreme ability to see the other point of view. There is, however, a profound stubbornness to the character of the place. At five minutes past nine each evening the great bell in Tom Tower, at Christ Church, is tolled 101 times—once for each member of the original foundation. Why *five past* nine? Because Oxford is 1° 15′ west of Greenwich, and when the clocks of the kingdom show five past it is really only nine at Carfax.

And if she is ornery in one cause at this end of town, at the other she may be entrenched in a diametrically opposite prejudice. At Magdalen James II is remembered only with distaste, but a few hundred yards up High Street, above the inner arch of University College gate tower, he is fulsomely honoured in a statue, standing in a posture of commanding rectitude, and wearing a toga. There is only one other statue of this unpopular king—in Trafalgar Square. A third once stood on Sand Hill, Newcastle upon Tyne, but a mob threw it into the river, and it was later salvaged to be turned into a peal of bells.

The oldest of Oxford battles is the battle between Town and Gown, which is as old as the University itself, and has often erupted into bloodshed. In 1355 there was a riot between students and citizens on the Feast of St. Scholastica (not, as you may suppose, a kind of abstract holy person, but the sister of St. Benedict). It began with a brawl at the Swyndlestock Tavern, whose site is marked still by a plaque on the wall at Barclay's Bank, Carfax, and developed into a glorious free-for-all. The townsmen rang the bell of Carfax tower; the students rang the bell of St. Mary's; thousands of wild country folk came screaming in, thonged and hooded, carrying a black flag and crying: 'Havac! Havoc! Smyt fast, give gode knocks!' If we are to credit the old chronicles, these unnerving yokels plundered the students' hostels, scalped a number of chaplains, attacked a procession of friars, buried several scholars in dung-hills and virtually depopulated the infant University.

More than 60 students were killed, we are told, and most of the others ran away, but the result was an overwhelming victory for the University. For 500 years after the event, each St. Scholastica's Day, the Mayor and 63 citizens—one for each dead student—were obliged to process in penitence to St. Mary's, to bow before the Vice-Chancellor and pay a fine of a penny each. They often found it difficult to muster 63 citizens, but it was only in 1825 that the ceremony was abolished—the City returning 'the warmest acknowledgements to the University for this act of grace' (though John de Beresford, 'ye mayor in ye time of ye conflicte', was a popular hero in Oxford several centuries after the last gode knock was smyten).

Though the City long pre-dated the University, for centuries the dons were dominant. The very first of the University's endowments was an annual fine imposed upon the townsmen in 1209, after an affray in which a clerk was hanged by the citizenry: the fine is paid to this day, by the Treasury, and forms part of the Vice-Chancellor's Fund for Needy Students—it used to be £1. 12s. a year, but has increased, in just three-quarters of a millennium, to £3·08. The mediaeval scholar was, as often as not, a turbulent swaggering fellow, quick to drink and to draw, and the presence in the little town of two or three thousand such young toughs must often have been a trial. As the book says, massacres were somewhat frequent. Sometimes the students were rioting among themselves, sometimes they were rioting against outsiders, and the violence was so frequent and so vicious that almost every inch of pavement between Carfax and St. Mary's, we are told with relish, at one time or another ran with blood. Once they locked the door of St. Mary's against the Archbishop of Canterbury, and defended it with bows and arrows. Once they bombarded Lord Norris with stones from the top of Magdalen Tower, when a student was arrested for poaching the king's deer: the earl's retinue protected themselves by carrying tables on the tops of their heads.

There were Town and Gown riots as late as the end of the nineteenth century—Charles James Fox once jumped out of his window at Hertford to take part in one, and in Brasenose Chapel there is a memorial to an undergraduate killed by a butcher's knife in 1857, with the lofty epitaph *Inter Tumultum Plebis Obdormivit*—'He Fell Asleep Among the Tumult of the People'. At many crises of Oxford's history, too, City and University have been on opposite sides. The City was Parliamentarian, the University Royalist. The

City wanted the railway works, the University resisted them. In the seventeenth century they even licensed rival coaches to London, the University unfairly forbidding its members to use the City service.

For centuries, however, the odds were unfair. The City was small, ordinary and provincial. The University was rich, clever and had powerful friends at court. Chancellor, Masters and Scholars acquired an ascendancy over Oxford so complete that their rights were almost capitulatory, like the privileges of foreigners in Khedivian Egypt. 'Privileged persons' of the University, who included everyone from Vice-Chancellor to college scullions, were exempt from all the normal obligations of citizenship, even from the jurisdiction of the law courts—precisely as the very dragoman at the Portuguese Consulate at Assiut, in the heyday of the Capitulations, could claim full diplomatic immunities.

In the seventeenth century the situation was officially described, in a charter from Charles I, as 'An Ocean or Great Sea of Privilege'. The University had a right to weigh the market produce, license stage performances, supervise lodging-houses, hear its own court cases, check drains, banish 'people of vicious life' and arrest citizens walking the streets after dark—noctivagating, as Oxford still likes to call it. The policing of Oxford at night was exclusively a University concern until 1868, and the poor women of the streets were hauled before a University court in all the grim majesty of the Convocation House, where they were probably bullied in Latin by withered clergymen. The students, on the other hand, could do almost what they pleased. In 1821, when the scholars of the anatomy school needed a body for dissection, they breezily snatched the corpse from a passing funeral.

The whole life of the City, impoverished by the decline of the wool industry, came to depend upon the grace of the University. Shopkeepers were cautiously subservient, and when the students dispersed for the long summer vacation half Oxford was out of work. Even within living memory the commerce of central Oxford was dominated by shops selling gowns, blazers, meerschaum pipes, college crests on wooden plaques, and other such old-school Varsity products. The aristocrat of Oxford working men was the college scout (as servants have been called in this place at least since 1718—'possibly an obsolete word for a cricket fieldsman', is the best deriva-

tion the dictionaries offer). It was symptomatic of the state of things
that though Magdalen Tower was left in all its tall glory, Carfax
Tower was cut down a few feet, in case the citizens started dropping
boulders too.

Now the pendulum has swung the other way. For the first time in
many centuries Town faces Gown on equal terms, and to many
Oxford people, once again, the students are there on sufferance.

The riots are over, but in many ways the two sides in this ancient
dispute, inextricably jumbled though they are, are not yet properly
fused. Even Lord Nuffield, who had a deep prejudice against universities, was apparently concerned by this. He really founded Nuffield College, I am assured, because he wanted to build something
impressive in a dingy corner of Oxford, but his declared purpose
was to bridge the gap that existed between industry and intellect—
between Cowley, that is, and Radcliffe Square. Most University
people never see the Cowley works from one year to the next.
Engineering of their kind is not a speciality of the University, and
though one or two academic scientists are now starting small industrial enterprises of their own in Oxford, there is no equivalent here
of the vast electronic plants and commercial laboratories that sprawl
along Route 101 at Cambridge, Massachusetts, with their affinity
of interests and even interchange of staffs with Harvard and the
Massachusetts Institute of Technology. Conversely, to most Cowley people Oxford is only a crowded shopping centre, or a place
to catch a train, or an evening at the cinema: you seldom see Oxford
citizens sight-seeing in the colleges, there are very few University
graduates among the Cowley executives, and nine people out of ten
in an Oxford street could not tell you the way to Jesus College or
even the Bodleian Library.

The University's political dominance has been whittled away, by
the abolition of its seats in Parliament, and reduced membership
of the City Council. Nevertheless its powers in Oxford are still formidable. Almost a quarter of the city area is owned by the University
and its colleges: successive plans for inner relief roads in Oxford
run into University opposition so persistent and so powerfully
backed that the scheme for a road across Christ Church meadows,
for example, was argued for at least 30 years, and subjected to a
whole succession of public inquiries, before it was finally scotched

by the doggedness of dons. The two greatest open spaces in the city centre are owned respectively by Christ Church and the University: both are private property—the Parks can be closed to the public at the academic will, but resident members of Convocation can have their own keys. The University even elects its own Clerks of the Market, impotent relics of old privileges: they are usually scholars of enormous distinction, who would scarcely know a bushel from a hogshead, and they are paid £5 a year for their dignity.

Even now, too, the University can claim several legal privileges, often buried away in the cobwebs of ancient legislation. 'Clerks of the University', which seems nowadays to mean undergraduates, may still demand to be heard before the Chancellor's Court if they are summoned by the police for misdemeanours, or sued in civil cases—in theory they could do so when picked up for bad driving or illegal parking. Once every few years somebody does, and the case is then heard by the Assessor to the Chancellor's Court in the fifteenth-century Convocation House. In 1978 four Oxford solicitors were entitled to practise as Proctors of this court, and there is an official called the Registrar of the Chancellor's Court, and a whole body of special procedure for its hearings.

At a pinch the Chancellor's Court may try criminal offences, too, and by a flick of its constitution it may transform itself into an ordinary magistrate's court, with jurisdiction in Oxfordshire and Berkshire (a metamorphosis it last undertook in 1926). What is more, far in the background there stands a darker and more ominous figure still, the High Steward of the University, who has his own and yet more dreadful jurisdiction. The special duty of the High Steward, who is elected for life, is defined by the Oxford Historical Register as being 'to hear and determine criminal causes of the gravest kind, like treason or felony, whenever the accused is a scholar or a privileged person resident within the precincts of the University'. In legal theory this meant that until capital punishment was abolished in England, *Universitas Oxoniensis* could not only rusticate you, fine you for keeping a private aeroplane in the city, or demand your name and college during noctivagations, but actually hang you, too.

They are obscure powers nowadays, like so much else in England, and are not likely to be arrogantly exercised. The Bulldogs are fatherly sort of men, and there is no counterpart here of the Harvard police force, flashing lights on big blue estate cars, still less of the university prison they show you in Heidelberg, where they used to chain refractory students to the wall. In Oxford, all the same, you can never be quite sure. I once told a Proctor that I proposed to follow him and his cortège through the streets that night, to see how the undergraduates responded (they were usually scared stiff, even in the last days of proctorial patrols, by the weird authority of the visitation). He advised me not to follow too closely, in case the Bulldogs took offence at my attentions, and summoned me to the proctorial presence. I bristled a bit at this. They'd better not, said I, I was a free citizen, I knew my rights, I could walk where I liked when I liked, nobody could pull antique usage over my eyes, he and his minions certainly had no authority over me. The Proctor smiled darkly. 'Are you quite sure?' he inquired: and by Heavens, remembering the bit about the High Steward and the felony, on second thoughts I wasn't.

6. College Spirit

Scarcely less prickly than the prides of Town and Gown are the 34 separate prides of the colleges—each a corporation in its own right, each fortified by its own endowments, some bold, some shy, some tucked away hole-in-corner, some in magnificent buildings like royal palaces, with parks for gardens and little cathedrals for chapels.

Before the invention of the colleges the Oxford students lived in halls of residence, presided over by a Master they themselves elected. There were at least 120 of these halls, at one time or another—at one period there were 27 in High Street alone, which must have given it rather the feeling of the main street at Lourdes today, lined with pilgrim hostels and souvenir shops. There was an Ape Hall, an Aristotle Hall, a Cat Hall and a Sparrow Hall: but though their names are still remembered here and there, in the Kemp Hall Bindery or the Drawda Hall stationery shop, St. Edmund Hall is the only one that has survived the centuries as a University institution.

They were replaced by the colleges, stronger bodies with money of their own and permanent foundations. Every undergraduate belongs to a college, which chooses him, feeds him, supervises his work and houses him for most of his university career: and it is the existence of these old and varied entities that still gives Oxford its meshed feeling—metaphysically, because each is a little society of its own, physically because they are all different, complete and secluded, like so many small townships side by side along the city streets. They are turned this way and that, with hidden entries and back gates and annexes and enclaves. Even habitués of Oxford do not often realize that a corridor of Trinity protrudes between St. John's and Balliol, in St. Giles, or that the east wall of All Souls' inner quadrangle actually belongs to New College; and only the man from the bakers would know that he could deliver the bread for Balliol Junior Common Room by pushing it through a window opposite the church of St. Mary Magdalen.

Sonorous are the corporate titles of these bodies—'The Provost and Scholars of the Blessed Mary the Virgin in Oxford, commonly called Oriel College, of the Foundation of Edward the Second of Blessed Memory, sometime King of England', or 'The College of All Souls of the Faithful Departed, of Oxford', or 'The President, Fellows and Scholars of the College of the Holy and Undivided Trinity in the University of Oxford of the Foundation of Sir Thomas Pope, Knight'. Each has a complex history of its own, ranging from Balliol, which was founded by John Balliol of Barnard Castle as a penance for having been rude to the Bishop of Durham when drunk in 1264, to St. Antony's, which was founded by M. Antonin Besse of Aden in 1948, and given its title because its donor wrongly thought that Antony was the English translation of his own Christian name. They are extraordinarily resilient old organisms. Very few have ever died (though London College only lasted five years in the fifteenth century). Even Hertford, which was reduced in 1814 to a complement of one, and in the end actually fell down with a cloud of dust—even Hertford bounced up again, and went on to educate Evelyn Waugh.

Each has a different constitution. The chapel of Christ Church is the Cathedral of Oxford, and the college head is the Dean, appointed by the Crown. All the others are entirely self-governing. New College is headed by a Warden, Exeter by a Rector, Trinity by a Président, University by a Master, Worcester by a Provost. Six colleges are for graduates only, five for women only, five have undergraduates of both sexes. New College demands a degree from the University instead of supplicating for it like all the others, Exeter, Pembroke and Jesus all have scholarships open only to boys from the Channel Islands, the scholars of Merton are called Postmasters, the scholars of Magdalen are called Demics, the Fellows of Christ Church are called Students, many of the Fellows of All Souls only come to Oxford at weekends.

They are strange structures indeed, expressing a mixture of militance and domestic satisfaction. They began as little fortresses in a generally hostile city, self-sufficient for minor sieges, with their own treasure-houses, vegetable gardens, water supplies and sewage systems—the cess-pit at New College was so large that during the first 300 years of the college's history it never had to be emptied. Even now the colleges do not encourage strangers, and the Oxford City Police sometimes have difficulty in getting their plain-clothes men inside, when some visiting bigwig needs protection. Their buildings are open to the public only with reluctance, and it is odd how often college porters forget to turn the little notices outside their lodges from Closed to Open.

They often look redoubtable still. Their outer walls are high and frowning, sometimes castellated, sometimes viciously studded with spikes or broken glass to prevent undergraduates climbing in after hours. Above the gate there rises a squat watch-tower, with a turret at one corner and sometimes arrow-slits: in the old days the Master himself used to live up there, keeping a paternal eye upon his students inside, and a wary one upon strangers approaching the portals. A porter sits watchfully in his lodge beneath, sometimes courteously curious, sometimes downright arrogant, and at night heavy wooden gates are closed upon the street, barred with iron, locked with elaborate padlocks, pierced only by a small postern and powerfully suggesting chain-mail and boiling oil.

Behind these defences, though, all is delightful intimacy. The college is probably divided into two or three quadrangles, lawns in their centres, gravel paths around the perimeter, creepers over the walls (unless the place has been scoured of all organic growth by recent restoration). On all sides, through little cottage doorways, you may see scrubbed wooden staircases winding upwards between blank wooden doors: Oxford colleges are traditionally built around staircases, rather than along corridors, a system which makes for quiet and privacy, and enables half a dozen men to live together in conditions of hugger-mugger fraternity. Some college rooms have double doors, and if an undergraduate really wants to be undisturbed he can close both of them—a porcupine gesture which used to be known as 'sporting the oak' ('the oak alone goes far', Shelley said once, 'towards making this place a paradise'). There is a dim chapel with stained-glass windows, and an old library like a room in some splendid country house, and a hall with family portraits on the walls and smells of soup and table polish: and tucked away inside, shaded by trees and protected by old stone walls, there is probably a delicious garden, half lawn, half herbaceous—and perhaps an orchard, too, with potting sheds in it.

No other buildings are quite like these. Some people think their structural origins are monastic, developed from cells and cloisters. Some think they were based upon mediaeval country houses, with their separate buildings around a compound. Others again see in them the mediaeval inn, with its central yard and surrounding lodges, like the fine old hostel called the Golden Cross which still thrives as a restaurant around its yard in the Cornmarket: certainly at New College individual rooms used to have names of their own— the Serpent's Head, the Christopher, the Rose or the Vine—just like an old-fashioned coaching inn. Lewis Mumford says the Oxford colleges are the historical prototypes of the 'super-block', as at Brasília, and of precinct planning. They serve very handily as conference centres during vacations, when squadrons of probation officers or strategic planners are sometimes to be glimpsed listlessly toying with baked beans in draughty dim-lit dining-halls; and I often think that if one of them fell upon really hard times it could conveniently be converted into a cut-rate motel.

But they can be exceedingly comfortable—especially for their senior members, whose common rooms, splendidly stocked with wines, constitute some of the best clubs to be found in Europe today. For a taste of their urbanity, I recommend the Betting Books which All Souls has privately published now and then, and which enable one almost to sniff the cigar smoke and savour the port of many a pleasurable, if intellectually demanding, evening. The stakes are seldom high, but the subjects are all-embracing. Here Hardinge bets Reichel 1s. that there exists such a tense as $\tau\varepsilon\tau\upsilon\varphi\theta\acute{\eta}\sigma o\mu\alpha\iota$, to which Reichel retorts that $\tau\varepsilon\tau\upsilon\varphi\theta\acute{\eta}\sigma o\mu\alpha\iota$ is the grammatical 'paulo-post' as against Hardinge's $\tau\varepsilon\tau\acute{\upsilon}\psi o\mu\alpha\iota$ ('I shall have been on the point of being about to be beaten'). Asquith bets Malcolm 1s. that twice around Malcolm's stomach is less than the combined perimeter of Malcolm's stomach and head, and Steel-Maitland bets Edgeworth that with three exceptions no monument exists within a radius of five miles from the centre of Rome, built between 100 B.C. and A.D. 300, possessing an arch with a lateral thrust. Hardinge once unaccountably bets Doyle 1s. that Admiral Benbow was a black man, Curzon bets Talbot 1s. that the man who stuck a pen-knife through a roll in the Old Testament was not called Jehudi. There was once a bet to the effect that *Home, Sweet Home* was written by a divorced German Jew, and between the wars Corbett succeeded in proving that he could in fact hang upside down by the grip of his toes for 10 seconds on the common-room door.

Inside the gates of such a community you can feel most comfortably insulated. All is on your side, and all is yours for ever. I don't know if it is actually possible nowadays to strike a name from any college records, but I imagine the procedure would be at least as awful as the Form Ordained for the Unfrocking of Primates. Once a member, you are never altogether dispossessed, and however undistinguished your college record, when you step inside those precincts again you will be welcomed as a right. The porter may be grumpy to outsiders, but he is all smiles to you. No hostile lout is going to storm through that postern, screaming Havac, Havoc. The librarian will find you your book as obligingly as ever the great lord's resident chaplain looked out a necessary Breviary. So pregnantly private indeed is the atmosphere of an Oxford college that when I once assured two American ladies that they really need not talk in whispers in Christ Church dining hall, they replied with nervous giggles that after a day in Oxford they didn't think they would ever learn to talk out loud again.

For a college is a kind of family, or so it likes to think. It is governed by its Fellows—dons who are mostly tutors, and who vary in number, college by college, from a dozen to nearly 60 (its undergraduates are not represented on the Governing Body, though they were in the earlier years of the women's colleges). In most ways it is perfectly autonomous. The head of the college is elected by the Fellows, and so for that matter are the Fellows themselves.

This has often led to in-breeding. Fellows have understandably chosen more of their own kind, and often the college statutes used to give preference to candidates connected by birth with the college. Between 1814 and 1857, for instance, 78 of the 113 Fellows elected to the graduate college of All Souls were kin to its founder, the fifteenth-century Archbishop Çichele. (Social graces counted, too. One unsuccessful candidate during this period, we are told, took off his shoes at dinner during the examinations: a beast of a rival kicked them out of his reach, and when they adjourned for the port he was found *altogether* unsuitable for a Fellowship.)

As for the undergraduates, University admission standards are the same for all, and academic performance is much the most important factor nowadays, but the colleges do have extra criteria of their own—character, school, keeping a proper balance, sustaining a family tradition, improving the academic reputation or trying to put together a decent boat crew. You cannot enter Oxford University as an undergraduate without first being accepted by a college: but you could be the young Einstein himself, and still have no claim to college patronage. The colleges often feel themselves to be outside the public domain, and if their attitude to the people at large is sometimes snooty, their regard for their own members is correspondingly possessive. 'Be assured,' wrote Dean Jackson of Christ Church to the young Robert Peel, when the future Prime Minister was new to Parliament, 'that I shall pursue you as long as I live with a jealous and watchful eye. Woe be to you if you fail me.' Even inanimate objects count. I once had a talk with the Treasurer of Christ Church about the great bell called Tom, in Tom Tower, and soon fell into my informant's affectionate habit of referring to the thing as 'he'.

Some colleges have close links with particular schools—Christ Church with Westminster, New College with Winchester, St. John's with Merchant Taylors. There are also some recherché regional links. Exeter has strong West Country connections. Queen's is traditionally North of England. Jesus is the Welsh college; at one time it could be said that most of the Welsh gentry had been educated there, and when in 1863 the set subject for the Newdigate Prize Poem was *Coal Mines*, who else *could* have won it but Thomas Llewellyn Thomas, Scholar of Jesus?

Long ago the colleges thus acquired their several reputations, and some of them are still relevant. Christ Church is traditionally both grand and liberal, proud enough to specialize in Etonians and noblemen, big enough to admit every kind of promising poor scholar—as recently as 1918 this tremendous college matriculated the composer William Walton at the age of 16. Magdalen is clever, rich and progressive, New College earnestly rational—its Fellows startled everybody in 1964 by proposing the admission of women undergraduates, after nearly 500 years of masculinity. Since Victorian days Balliol has stood for brain-power and worldly influence. Worcester, though small and poor, has a certain dash to its name, as of an irrepressible younger son. Trinity, though its reputation is changing, remains to most people monumentally public school and sporting. University always seems pleasantly tolerant and easy-going: and sure enough if you consult its history you will find that when, in the 1680s, its Master became a Roman Catholic, 'within the college there seems to have been no opposition, and Romans and Anglicans lived together in amity, the latter ignoring what they seem to have regarded as a foible of their Master, who otherwise had their loyalty and even affectionate regard'.

Keble, a High Anglican foundation once popularly supposed to be peopled only by weedy pietists, was so transformed by the arrival of a sporting Bursar that by 1964 six of the Oxford boat crew were Keble Etonians. When you think of Pembroke you think of Dr. Johnson. When you think of St. Peter's you think of the Chavasse family. It was founded in 1928 by Bishop Francis Chavasse, and in St. Peter le Bailey church, which serves as its chapel, you will find a large memorial to him; a stained-glass window dedicated to him; a pulpit in his memory; the grave of his son Christopher, the first Master; a cross removed from the grave near Ypres of his second son Noel, a double V.C.; a memorial to his third son Francis, who was killed in a car crash; a reredos in memory of his wife; and references in war memorials to Arden Chavasse of the King's Liverpool Regiment and F. Chavasse Squires of the Sikh Pioneers.

The more subtle of these characteristics only Oxford amateurs can appreciate. Most strangers, after a day or two in Oxford, can scarcely remember one college from another, and are left only with a hazed general impression of gargoyles and anecdotes. Some colleges are, however, distinctly different from others. They differ in size, for a start, and range from Linacre, which is a former small convent, to Christ Church, which sprawls majestically over several acres, and so easily absorbs the Cathedral of Oxford that at first sight the visitor hardly even notices it. They differ in self-esteem. 'Alexander the Great presents his compliments to Alexander the Coppersmith,' the Dean of Christ Church allegedly replied one day in the 1840s, when the Dean of Oriel asked him what time an examination began, 'and informs him that he knows nothing whatever about it.' When Francis Atterbury arrived from London in 1711 to take up his duties as Dean of Christ Church he was met on Shotover Hill by a welcoming party of 400 horsemen; and in the eighteenth century the Principal of Brasenose always hired extra horses for the last stage into Oxford, 'lest it be said that the first Tutor of the first College of the first University of the world entered it with a pair'.

They differ also in wealth. Some colleges are very rich, some are uncomfortably poor: and though the rich ones nowadays make contributions to the exchequers of the poor, the University acting as banker, still the gulf is very apparent. It is exceedingly difficult to discover the facts, especially about the rich ones, or those whose Bursars have a specialist knowledge of income-tax laws: but it seems safe to estimate that the endowed income of Christ Church, say, is at least 15 times that of Worcester, and that All Souls is probably 50 times richer than the richest of the women's colleges.

Precisely how all these moneys are raised and used, I cannot say— nor could the Royal Commission of 1850, which complained that only four colleges would produce statements of their revenues, or the Robbins Committee of 1963, which described Oxford's financial arrangements as being 'shrouded in general obscurity'. College accounts have not always been impeccably kept. When Cecil Rhodes left £100,000 to Oriel he stipulated that trustees must be consulted about its investment, 'as the College authorities live secluded from the world and so are like children in commercial matters'. For years certain debits in the accounts of Jesus College were merely entered as 'old and desperate debts', and when John Keble was looking after the books of Oriel his accounts showed an inexplicable deficiency of between £1,800 and £1,900, until it was discovered that he had added the date to the liabilities.

Things are less haphazard now, and the colleges are often slick business operations, run by astute professionals. Their sources of revenue are distinctly varied. At one end we have the story of poor Keble College, in its indigent Victorian beginnings, charging sixpence a head for a sight of Holman Hunt's picture *The Light of the World*, which hangs in the chapel: this so infuriated Hunt, it is said, that he promptly painted a replica of the picture, and gave it to St. Paul's Cathedral. At the other end of the scale we have Jesus College's possession of half London's South Bank, now one of the most valuable properties in Europe, until it was taken from them by compulsion during the war—and even then they were paid £100,000 for it. Most colleges have lately turned to stocks and shares, but traditionally their money has been in land, and estates up and down the country belong to the Oxford colleges. In Oxford itself most of the Banbury Road area belongs to St. John's, and the Mitre Hotel has been Lincoln College property since the fifteenth century. All over England you may stumble across signs of an Oxford landlord—a college crest beneath an eave, a Yorkshire pub called the University Arms, or a grandiose notice on a village green, regulating the public rights of access 'for air and exercise', and signed by the Steward of the Manor, The Queen's College, Oxford.

When Walter de Merton decided to found a college, in the thirteenth century, he wasn't sure whether to build it at Oxford or at Cambridge, so he bought land at both: and to this day Merton College, Oxford, owns a chunk of land at Grantchester, that most ineffably Cambridge corner of Cambridge, where Rupert Brooke went for honey with his tea. When Merton celebrated its seven hundredth anniversary, in 1964, tenant farmers came to the festivities from all quarters, and a sheep-farmer from Leicestershire gave a demonstration with his dogs on the college lawn. Sometimes, too, the Fellows of a college visit their farmlands, in a junket called a progress, pleasantly helped along with champagne, chicken sandwiches and college servants: these are by origin rent-collecting tours, and when the Warden of New College makes one he is accompanied by an official called the Outrider, chosen from among the Fellows, to guard the cashbox from highwaymen.

Another kind of rural stake is the patronage of church livings, which many colleges originally acquired in order to provide parishes for their Fellows. The Oxford colleges have hundreds of livings at their disposal. The names of many North Oxford streets are taken from the country livings of St. John's—Crick in Northamptonshire, Belbroughton in Worcestershire, Bardwell in Suffolk, Linton in Herefordshire, Leckford in Hampshire, Bainton in Yorkshire. Christ Church is the patron of church livings in 24 counties, and even Jesus, with its Welsh affinities, supports the benefices of Scartho in Lincolnshire and Nutfield in Surrey, not to speak of Pottersbury with Furtho and Yardley Gobion in deepest Northants.

All this variety makes some colleges proud, some selfish, and some covetous—maps of All Souls College sometimes lay claim to the adjacent garden of the Warden of New College, rather as Arabian sheikhs nudge their frontiers in the direction of neighbouring oilfields. The selfishness is very unattractive. When they first proposed to build a road across Christ Church meadows the division of opinion among the colleges was not difficult to analyse: those whose own calm would not be affected were for the road, those nearer the noise were against. It is largely because of college self-interest that so much of Oxford has been despoilt: even Cornmarket, now a tumult of chain stores, was once college property, and the great Cowley works themselves were built on college land thoughtlessly sold by heedless dons, who have been grumbling about them ever since.

The pride is often more endearing. Brasenose College was so proud of Walter Pater, a Fellow there for 30 years, that his memorial in the college ante-chapel shows him in the centre of a plaque surrounded by four peers—Leonardo da Vinci, Michelangelo, Dante and Plato. As for University College, if you look at the stained-glass window in the chapel that tells the story of Jonah, you will see that the ship from which he was thrown overboard flies the college flag (itself taken from King Alfred's putative coat of arms, invented in the true Aluredian tradition several centuries after the event).

I doubt if all this independence can survive, as the world shrinks and uniformity presses in. A century ago Oxford detested the idea of State aid, on the grounds that the paymaster normally called the tune: now people are more likely to think that if the public is footing half the bill, Oxford University has a duty to re-tune its old melodies to the mode of the times.

The autonomy of the colleges is sure to be weakened. For years Professors of the University have been *ex-officio* members of various colleges, whatever their personal style—the American Eastman Visiting Professor, for example, is always a Supernumerary Fellow of Balliol. The central authority of the University becomes stronger, as laboratories become more elaborate and more expensive, and things like computers and nuclear accelerators emphasize the smallness of the college unit. More and more undergraduates go for their tutorials in other colleges, or in University science departments, weakening the college sense of family completeness: and the college spirit itself, which figures so heartily in every Victorian novel of Oxford, with all its insignia of scarves, blazers, college ties and beer mugs—the very college spirit is half discredited, as undergraduates come to feel the need for wider loyalties, and deliberately discard the emotions of the past.

The old Oxford guidebooks list all kinds of Quaint College Customs. At New College a chorister used to call the members to dinner by standing at the garden gate and shouting '*Eat-manchet-toat-senivat*'—a corruption, we are assured, of '*A mangervous, seigneurs.*' At Magdalen, on the first Monday in Lent, two Bursars distributed among the members small screws of paper containing coins—two fourpenny pieces for each Fellow, twopence each for choristers. At University College on Easter Sunday each member chopped at a wooden block with a cleaver, while the college cook stood by with a plate for Easter offerings.

Most of these traditions are dead, and the survivals are mostly kept alive by dedicated traditionalists—like the eighteenth-century antiquarian Thomas Hearne, who declared when they gave up apple fritters for dinner at St. Edmund Hall that 'when laudable old customs dwindle, 'tis a sign learning dwindles'. At some colleges the custom of the sconce is still upheld. The undergraduate guilty of committing certain old-school solecisms at the dining table—notably talking about work, women or politics—is condemned to drink some vast quantity of beer, from some gargantuan container, at a single draught. (In 1961, it is claimed, an Oriel undergraduate swallowed $2\frac{1}{4}$ pints in six seconds.) A good deal of hilarity still attends such occasions; if the youth succeeds in drinking the beer he does not have to pay for it; but if you look around the hall you will see many young faces, unamused, which seem to be muttering something about the perfectly crippling legacy of the historical past, and wondering how we shall ever adjust the trade deficit, let alone make any decent films, if we will insist on preserving such archaic tomfooleries.

7. No Good Aire

O ne cannot imagine such a city, so snarled and contentious, in a climate of perpetual sunshine. The sun suits Oxford visually, and seems to fructify her golden stones—'I have seen no place', wrote the poet F. W. Faber,

> ... *by inland brook,*
> *Hill-top, or plain, or trim arcaded bowers,*
> *That carries age so nobly in its look*
> *As Oxford with the sun upon her towers.*

The temper of the place, however, depends upon the Oxford climate, which is ghastly. It always has been. The earliest weather records in Europe were kept at Merton in the fourteenth century, and they show that the climate was just as dismal then, though the winters were perhaps a little milder. Anthony Wood, the best known of Oxford antiquarians, wrote in January 1678 that the city was full of 'colds without coffing or running at the nose, onlie a languidness and faintness. Certainly Oxford is no good aire.' Generations of citizens have agreed with him since. Thomas Hardy called it 'an extinct air, accentuated by the rottenness of the stones', and almost every biography of an Oxford worthy records chronic catarrh, periodic fits of depression, or an ill-defined malaise that unhappily prevented the completion of his commentary on the Second Epistle to the Thessalonians. 'The air of Oxford does not suit me,' wrote Cardinal Newman. 'I feel it directly I return to it.'

So do I. It is only undergraduates, with their brief sojourn in the place, who think of Oxford afterwards as a city of unremitting vivacity; and a tragic handful even of them, nowadays, commit suicide in despair, or sink into the sordid misery of drug addiction. For half the year it is a heavy, dank, enervating environment, and the damp seems to rot your energy, and surround you in a fog of

permanent procrastination. Even your feet swell. If you fly over
Oxford early on a winter morning, you will see crisscross lines and
patches of vapour arising all around the city, from ponds and water-
meadows and country ditches, from the rivers and their multitudinous rivulets, from the queer marsh of Otmoor to the north: and
all this damp exhalation seems to be investing Oxford, so that her
towers and spires must reach over the miasma for fresh air, and
the mist creeps along her streets below, and sidles through her alleyways. On the windows of Boar's Hill, I am told, there is sometimes
a deposit of sea-salt, brought in by the winds from the west. The
valley air carries no such tang. The winds are often bluff, but seldom
exhilarating, and sometimes blow so cruelly through the buildings
that one gateway near the cathedral is called Killcanon in their
honour—and vicious indeed can they be there, when you turn the
corner out of Tom Quad on a raw January morning, and find them
howling through the tunnel in your face. Oxford can be horribly
cold. July and August are the only frost-free months, and a great
old cedar in Wadham gardens was once killed by a snowstorm in
the middle of the summer term.

Plagues and epidemics blotch the pages of the Oxford histories,
from the epidemic which sent the young Philip Sidney hurrying
away for good in 1571 to the great influenza epidemic of 1918, which
was so severe in Oxford that in the poor districts of Jericho and
St. Ebbe's families were sometimes unable even to bury their own
dead. In the Middle Ages most of the colleges had country retreats,
as refuges from the perennial plagues—Trinity had a house at Gars-
ington, Corpus Christi at Witney, Magdalen at Brackley, All Souls
at Stanton Harcourt. One plague lasted, virtually without relief,
from 1440 to 1540, and there was a time when Oxford's record of
disease seemed likely to drive the University out of town once and
for all.

Erasmus, writing at the end of the fifteenth century, was appalled
by the insanitary habits of the city: the floors of the Oxford buildings, he said, were lined with rushes that were often left undisturbed
for 20 years, 'harbouring expectorations, vomitings, the leakage of
dogs and men, ale-droppings, scraps of fish'. Three centuries later
Christ Church, believing that a cholera epidemic had emanated
from the underground waters of the Trill Mill stream, put up a high
wall to keep its unwholesome vapours out of the college precincts,

and the Regius Professor of Medicine suggested lowering the water level of the Thames below Oxford to reduce the incidence of phthisis among the city's poor. Even now there is something horribly suggestive to the tall iron columns, like old-fashioned lamp standards, that stride beside the river towards Iffley, ventilating the sewers beneath: and poor Erasmus would not be much encouraged by the ice-cream cartons, old newspapers, banana skins and cigarette ends that often blow like some vile tumbleweed around the shopping centres.

Today, though, the muck and climate of Oxford is more lowering than lethal, and the infant mortality rate is among the lowest of any English industrial city. Even in dirtier days, more robust philosophers soon accustomed themselves to local standards. Along Brasenose Lane, off Radcliffe Square, there still runs one of the last of the Oxford kennels—cobbled gutters in the middle of the streets down which the open sewers used to swill. In the eighteenth century one of these ran down the middle of High Street, and it is said that the heavy figure of Dr. Johnson himself used sometimes to be seen with his feet astride it, lost in unhygienic thought.

Sunk in her bowl of damp green, with floodlands all about, Oxford is scarcely designed for snap decisions. It took them 35 years to decide whether to build the Christ Church meadows road, 20 years to acquire a site for the Radcliffe Camera, and 50 to decide whether to install electric light in the Sheldonian Theatre—in the end their hand was forced, when it was needed for evening lectures during the first world war, but the Convocation House across the way is lightless still.

Newcomers to Oxford often begin as irrepressible go-getters, writing witty letters of protest to the Editor and preparing their lectures before breakfast, but it does not often last: slowly the languor creeps in, the carbon copy does not seem so necessary after all, and the letter-writer learns to cultivate the convenient habit of counting 10 before putting pen to paper. This is a city of uncompleted projects. In almost every house I know some small scheme of improvement hangs wanly in the air, indefinitely delayed because the builder never turned up, or the plumber left to do another job, or somehow it doesn't seem worth while after all. A craftsman I once invited to carve a wooden ship for my porch did not answer my letter for a year, took two years to make the thing, put it up in the wrong place and never sent the bill. Oxford's telephone system is perpetually on the brink of better things, but in the meantime talks dimly on through a maze of crossed lines, wrong numbers and crackling interventions, as though all the wires in its grand central exchange, off St. Aldate's, have been corroded by river water or nibbled away by shrews. Oxford's garages, which can't normally undertake to put a new bulb in your headlight until the Thursday after next, would all have been in fine new premises long ago, with room and time enough for a thousand cars, were it not that the planning permission has not come through, or they're waiting for the necessary joists, or the boss is thinking of changing his mind and turning the premises into a self-service betting-shop.

On a higher plane, too, Oxford is paved with noble aspirations. Never was a city more magnificently imagined than Oxford has been in her successive private and public development plans, drawn up at immense expense by famous architects, richly illustrated with maps, plans and models, and doomed from the start to non-fulfilment. There is scarcely an Oxford college that does not possess, tucked away in its archives, some high-flown plan for its own reconstruction. The colleges have always aimed at splendour: it is said that when the blind Bishop Fox, founder of Corpus Christi, visited his buildings for the first time, the considerate Fellows led him twice around the quadrangle, to make it seem grander than it was. These ambitions have often fizzled out for lack of money, leaving only the architectural plans—which were often by the most distinguished practitioners of the day, and thus form a curious sort of architectural treasury.

Hawksmoor, for example, drew up plans for Worcester and for Brasenose—plans which, if implemented, would have tilted the Oxford balance decisively from the Gothic to the Classical style. At about the same time there were plans to rebuild most of Magdalen in the Classical idiom: the block called the New Buildings, beside the deer park, is the only part they built, and you may still see on its southern façade the beginnings of its great quadrangle. A century later they had another try: the senior tutor of Magdalen returned from his holidays in 1822 to find a demolition crew happily at work upon the cloisters, but he testily interrupted them, and made them put it all together again. Then in the 1880s G. F. Bodley pro-

posed to build an elaborately buttressed bell-tower above the hall
staircase at Christ Church—higher than Tom Tower, and twice as
noticeable. Charles Barry, architect of the Houses of Parliament,
once did a plan for Worcester; Sir John Soane prepared a High
Street façade for Brasenose; it was once intended to drive a ceremonial way down the Turl to Trinity, striking from High Street
to Broad Street, and thus connecting in proper grandeur the two
principal streets of the University area.

They once intended to build the Examination Schools, which
now face east into Merton Street, northwards into the High. They
once intended to build a grand hotel on the banks of the Isis,
upstream from Folly Bridge. They once intended to build a college
within the castle walls, and if Lord Nuffield had not rejected the
original plans with contemptuous dislike, Nuffield College would
have been built in a style nearer Byzantium than the Cotswolds.
Three colleges—Magdalen, Queen's and Exeter—have all been
turned on their axes at one time or another, and now face in a different direction. The vaulted passage that runs between the hall and
the chapel at All Souls ends unexpectedly in a poky little doorway:
they once intended to rebuild the whole front quadrangle of the college and connect the passage with a central cloister. If you look
closely at the interior walls of the Divinity Schools, you will see
that several ornamented mouldings have been left unfinished: this
is because they had second thoughts half-way through its construction, and decided to finish it in a plainer style. There used to
be a cupola on the top of St. Michael's church, and railings around
the Radcliffe Camera, and an ornate water conduit in the middle
of Carfax—which still exists, reconstructed, in a field at Nuneham
Courtenay, eight miles out. The original version of the plan for a
road across Christ Church meadows envisaged it passing down
Broad Walk, an avenue of elms only 300 yards from the walls of
Merton College, and almost immediately outside the southern gates
of Christ Church: the architect's drawings, however, did not look
alarming, for only two or three very small cars and a respectful lorry
seemed to be passing at any one moment.

Sometimes afterthoughts have proved expensive. The members
of Merton College developed such a violent dislike for the Grove
Buildings erected for them by William Butterfield that in 1930, less
than 70 years later, they had them totally rebuilt (though Balliol

once rejected an offer of £20,000 to pull down Butterfield's chapel and reconstruct the one that had been there before). And when, in 1856, the Fellows of Exeter decided to replace their seventeenth-century chapel with a copy of the Sainte Chapelle by George Gilbert Scott, the old structure so resented their infidelity that they had to blow it up with gunpowder.

For much of this humming and hawing, I like to think, the climate was responsible, and the architect, financier, Master or engineer awoke one dreary Oxford morning, morosely drank his tea, and decided that life was just too short. It takes a double effort, to get things properly done in Oxford.

The palsied or leprous look that used to characterize the city was mainly due to the poor quality of the later Headington stone, still sold after the best seams had been exhausted—and sometimes before, when unscrupulous quarrymen preferred not to dig too deep. Several Oxford buildings, however, have actually fallen down, including at least three churches. The bridge over the Thames at Osney collapsed as recently as the 1880s, 'carrying with it unfortunately into the River', Mr. Henry Taunt recorded racily soon afterwards, 'a child or two'. When the wall of Worcester College hall was restored in 1964 the Fellows found they had been cheated by jerry-builders 200 years before—the wall was only two inches thick, instead of the four inches contracted for. The shoddy Victorian building of the Jericho quarter is popularly (though wrongly) supposed to be the origin of its name—if you blew a railway whistle loud enough, the walls would fall down. As for the contemporary buildings, half of them seem to be coming apart already. Doors don't shut properly, windows won't open, concrete is sadly streaked, pavement slabs are cracked or tilted, wrought iron is rusted, inscriptions are illegible, plaster is peeling. In the Bodleian Library they treasure the key which was used by the King of England in 1945 to open the huge extension in Broad Street: it broke when he turned it, and lies there snapped ignominiously still, with a note in the royal hand to explain what happened.

Does the Oxford blur or sidestep affect her scholarship, too? Jowett of Balliol apparently thought so. The depression that habitually overcame him in Oxford 'begins', he once wrote, 'with the stomach, extends itself to the head, where it dries up the fountains of the intellect, and is not wholly unconnected with the weather'. When the Bodleian bought, in 1698, its copy of the fourth book printed in France, its Curators seriously thought they were buying a manuscript. More humiliating still was the immortal *gaffe* achieved by the Oxford printer in the very first book ever printed in the city itself. This was a commentary on the Apostles' Creed supposedly by St. Jerome, and it was produced only a matter of months after Caxton's original experiments in London. It was the first of all the Oxford books on the first of all the Oxford presses: yet somehow the printer, befuddled no doubt by a heavy grey morning, contrived to make a misprint in the *date*.

8. Fauna and Flora

He put 1468 instead of 1478, but perhaps he was only in a hurry to take his children for a picnic lunch, or go bird-watching on Port Meadow. The damp effluvia of Oxford make for catarrh and lassitude, but also keep this city miraculously green. Sometimes the place seems to drip with flowering creepers: and sometimes the foliage seems so inexorable, the trees grow so fast and the gardens need weeding so often, that Oxford feels as though she survives only by the forbearance of nature—in the 1880s, indeed, a root of the ivy which then covered the masonry of Magdalen Tower penetrated the wine cellar beneath, groped its way through the cork of a bottle, and drank up all the port inside.

Enthusiasts of every degree pore over the botany of Oxford. In one kind are those innumerable elderly ladies to be seen stooping over rockeries on summer afternoons, earnestly identifying gentians and sometimes popping a cutting skilfully into their handbags: in quite another are the towering academic experts of the University, like the Curator of the Claridge Druce Herbarium, who once replied, when I offered him some more parsnip at the dinner table, that he 'seldom ate umbelliferae'. The Oxford Botanical Garden, behind high walls opposite Magdalen, is the oldest in Great Britain: and what with its crumbled stones and shaded benches, its urns and pots and greenhouses, the Cherwell flowing sweetly beside its lawns and the goldfish who twitch in its ornamental pond—with the great tower of Magdalen serene above its gate, and the spires peering always between its foliage, there can be few better places in England for the contemplation of flowers.

Thomas Millington discovered the secret of pollen in Oxford, and it was here that John Sibthorp, the eighteenth-century botanist, prepared his monumental *Flora Graeca*, still the most sumptuous of all flower books. During his 36 years as Professor of Botany Sibthorp

gave only one lecture, and that was a flop, but his mind was on
higher things—in particular, on compiling a catalogue of all the
plants mentioned in the great sixth-century Natural History of Dio-
scorides. This delectable project occupied the last 30 years of his
life, and entailed several adventurous visits to Greece. Once he was
held up by Barbary pirates. Once his companion fell out of the window in his sleep. Once his travels were delayed by a revolt of the
pashas. Alas, he died before all this passionate labour reached frui-
tion, and *Flora Graeca* appeared 10 years after his death. He left
his entire estate to pay for the production, and the work, in 10
volumes with 966 plates, cost £15,572. 6s. 10d. to prepare—the
most extravagant botanical work ever published. Only 31 copies of
the original edition were printed, at £240 a set.

The yellow ragwort, now common throughout southern England,
began its British career in Oxford. It was imported in the seventeenth century—either from Greece, or from Sicily, where it still
thrives on the lavas of Mount Etna; and it spread along the clinker
ash of the railway lines. By 1890 it had reached Swindon, by 1909
Gloucestershire, by 1916 Denbighshire, by 1922 Rugby, and by the
1940s it had stormed London with such spirit that in the bomb sites
of the capital only rosebay willow-herb and groundsel took root
more boisterously. The fritillary grows within sight of Magdalen
Bridge, as well as in the couplets of every other Oxford poet. A kind
of orchid which grows in a ditch at Godstow, near the Thames,
grows in only one other place in England. Wild tulips flourish in
Christ Church meadows. Cardinal Newman was so attached to the
snapdragon that grows on old Oxford walls that he thought it to
be 'an emblem of his own perpetual residence unto death in the
University': Newman, becoming a Roman Catholic, left Oxford in
a blaze of publicity in 1845, but he did not convert the snapdragon,
and it thrives here peacefully still.

No wonder this place has green fingers. There can scarcely be
another city where plants and flowers are so cherished, and many
susceptible visitors to Oxford remember the place more for its
gardens than its libraries. Through almost every college gateway
some fragrant garden beckons you: and though Oxford lawns are
not half so velvety as the old books imply, the college gardens of
Oxford are perhaps the finest concentration of domestic gardens in
the western world. Some are subtly half-wild, like Wadham's;

some are magnificently formal, like St. John's; some are best
glimpsed tantalizingly through locked gates, like the Fellows'
garden of Christ Church, or the garden that is secreted at the foot
of the old Radcliffe Observatory; some are all handsome gravity,
like Worcester's, and some are all escapism, like Merton's, which
has an enchanting summer-house and a lovers' walk along the city
wall. 'Capability' Brown, it is said, laid out St. John's garden, and
the path that undulates beside the Fellows' garden at Exeter is
believed to have been planned by the artist Hogarth—it follows the
same serpentine course as the line, drawn on a palette in his
self-portrait of 1745, which he used to define his principles of
beauty. Nearly all of them share a sense of easy, spacious, sweeping
style. Oxford is no place for itsy-bitsy flower beds. When they deposited a formal rose garden opposite Magdalen Tower, at the
expense of a well-meaning American, it looked so footling with its
dainty bowers and trellis-work that an ungrateful joker crept out
one night among its bushes and peopled it with terra-cotta gnomes.

Through them all march the great trees, which feed upon the
damp, and only look lusher when the drizzle falls about them. The
Oxford tree most sure of immortality is the stag-headed oak high
on a ridge above Hinksey, which an infatuated Matthew Arnold took
for an elm—'the signal-elm that looks on Ilsley Downs, the three
lone weirs, the youthful Thames': they call it the Poet's Tree now,
its upper branches are dead, and if you know where to look you
can still see its silhouette, away to the west, from most high Oxford
vantage points. The most significant Oxford tree is unquestionably
the lone sycamore in High Street, without whose presence the whole
flavour of that celebrated thoroughfare would be different, and which
Thomas Sharp the town planner called one of the most important
trees in Europe. The most successful Oxford tree was the gargantuan wych-elm which used to grow in Magdalen Grove, and whose
remains you may still see there, cautiously surrounded by an iron
wicket, in case it starts to grow again: this was blown down by a
storm in 1911, and was thought to be the largest timber tree in
Britain. It is said to have grown so large because buried beneath
its roots was a deposit of mammoth bones, giving it an unfair
nutritional advantage over its rivals—when Oliver Wendell Holmes
visited Oxford he measured its girth with a piece of string, found
it larger than the biggest he had measured at home, but 'stood before

it', we are told, 'admiring it without a single word of envy or disappointment'.

The most historic Oxford tree was perhaps the Magdalen Oak, which stood not far away, and was traditionally specified by the founder of the college, William of Waynflete, as the northern limit of its precincts: a seventeenth-century pedant reckoned that 256 horses might stand within its shade, or 3,456 men—but it dropped dead in 1789 without a breath of wind to fell it, and they made a chair out of it for the President's lodgings. The most procreative Oxford tree is the London plane, which began as a chance hybrid in this city, and has since so flourished, not least in polluted city streets, that London would scarcely seem the same without it, and more than one American interior decorator would be lost without its lacewood. The most forlorn Oxford tree is the large cedar which stands bleakly in the main quadrangle of St. Catherine's, which was broken at the top when they moved it to this futuristic site from a comfortable garden in North Oxford, and now looks as though progress is too much for it. The most interesting Oxford tree is perhaps the sycamore carved in stone upon the canopy of St. Frideswide's shrine in the cathedral, which is thought to be the oldest representation of a sycamore in Britain. The most prophetic is the horse chestnut which overhangs Brasenose Lane from Exeter Fellows' garden: it has long been said that when this tree, which is periodically pruned, grows long enough to touch the wall of Brasenose across the lane, Exeter will beat Brasenose on the river—and sure enough, at least twice in living memory, when it did, so did they.

Trees are very important to Oxford. The policy of the Curators of the University Parks, it is elegantly declared, has been to provide 'as many interesting trees as possible without detracting from the natural beauty of the indigenous by an excess of the exotic'; and the trees do greatly help to create Oxford's feeling of slightly spiced Englishness. Mulberry trees abound in Oxford, all among the elms and apples; many of them were planted by order of James I, who wished to foster the silk industry, but the one in the Warden's garden at New College was planted by Dr. Spooner's mother, and from its fruit they make mulberry ice-cream. The famous fig in one of the canons' gardens at Christ Church was brought from Syria by Edward Pococke, a seventeenth-century Professor of Arabic who had been chaplain to the Levant Company at Aleppo. The *Crataegus durobrivensis* in the University Parks is a specimen of a tree found for the first time in 1900, beside the Genesee River in New York State, and the Dawn Redwood nearby was rediscovered in Szechwan in 1945, after centuries in which it was known only as a fossil.

Trees also figure prominently in the lore of Oxford. Turn left at the top of Headington Hill, and beside the lane that leads to Barton you will find a plaque upon a wall, commemorating the site of Pullen's Elm. This tree was planted by a famous seventeenth-century character called Josiah Pullen, of Magdalen Hall, and it became such a favourite destination of donnish exercise that the footpath up Headington Hill was built by public subscription to lead to it. Richard Steele the essayist said that his regular walks to Pullen's Elm as an undergraduate enabled him to reach 'a florid old age'; and it was beneath this beloved tree that Robert Holmes, an eighteenth-century canon of Christ Church, walking out from college in full canonicals, used to be met by a servant with a hat, a gun and a dog—and throwing off his cassock and surplice, to reveal shooting clothes below, off he would stride to Stanton Woods for an afternoon's sport.

It is said that Sir Thomas White, the founder of St. John's, was guided to the site of his college by a dream in which he saw two elm trees growing from one trunk; and even the Norman abbey of Osney was founded because Editha d'Oilley, wife of Oxford's Norman governor, met some magpies in an elm who told her that they were really souls in purgatory, and needed a church to rest in. 'Now *De pardieux*,' the lady cried, 'if old Robert will give me leave, I will do what I can to bring these souls to rest'—and old Robert presently complied. The nonagenarian President of Magdalen, Dr. Routh, was once brought the news that the acacia tree outside his lodgings had been blown down by a storm. 'Put it up again,' was all he said: and up, of course, it went.

The fauna of Oxford, lively or extinct, has been studied to the last vein in a gnat's wing—it is said that Port Meadow is biologically the best-documented plot of land in England. Oxford is so full of coppices, alluvial meadows, gardens and streams that the ornithologist, entomologist, lepidopterist or ecologist need never go far for his pleasures. Scarcely a passing bird remains unrecorded, hardly a woodlouse's stone is left unturned. 'It may confidently be stated,' wrote Commander James J. Walker, R.N., in 1926, 'as regards nearly all Orders of Insects, that very few if any districts of the same extent have been so thoroughly and exhaustively worked, as that of which the ancient City of Oxford is the centre.' There! It was on the back of an Oxford slug that an observant clergyman found the first specimen of one the rarest of all coleopteras, *Ptinella britannica*, and at least 84 species of fungus-gnat have been noted, at one time or another, on the windows of the University Museum.

It is surprising what you can see in such an English city, if you keep your eyes open for a couple of centuries. Cormorants, alpine choughs, sturgeons, American hairy woodpeckers, mole crickets, even pelicans have all been spotted in these parts. The cockroach *Blattella germanica*, it was observed darkly in 1926, 'was at one time recorded as present in the Randolph Hotel kitchen'—but then the pseudo-scorpion *Chthonius rayi* was once reported from the cellars of the Mitre. There were once some black swans on the Thames, imported from Australia, but the emu that used to live at Magdalen died of eating too much currant cake, and the wallabies of Worcester are there no longer: one was drowned when he went sliding on the frozen lake, and the rest turned out to have such an insatiable appetite for roses that they were swapped for some ornamental birds from the zoo at Ilfracombe.

Deer are common enough in the Oxford countryside, and are often flushed out by foxhounds in the neighbouring woods—most of them refugees from great estates requisitioned or neglected during the second world war. The only herd inside the city lives in Magdalen Grove, and appears dappled and ethereal in nearly everybody's memories of Oxford. Its deer are looked after by the forester from the college woods at Tubney, outside Oxford, and when some have to be shot, to keep their numbers down, a marksman picks out his victims from a shadowy window of the New Buildings, so as not to scare the others. It used to be a favourite undergraduate prank to intoxicate these animals with port-soaked sugar. Lawrence of Arabia once planned to steal them all and drive them into the inner quadrangle of his own college, All Souls—Magdalen would be assured, when they asked for the animals back, that they were mistaken, and that this was the traditional All Souls herd, pastured in that quadrangle since remote antiquity. In the 1830s an elderly

Fellow of Magdalen fell out of his window in the New Buildings, breaking his neck: his corpse was found in the morning, and all around it the little deer stood in a silent circle.

Oxford does not feel a city of pets. Tadpoles possibly, for all those clever children in North Oxford to study genetic development with; rats perhaps, for experimental purposes at the Radcliffe Infirmary; beagles certainly, for the elegant young undergraduates of the hunting set; hamsters and guinea-pigs in the animal shop in the covered market, where the children stand on packing-cases to press their noses against the window; but if I were a sentimental spaniel, or a tabby in need of sympathy, I think I would avoid this ironical, analytical city, and go somewhere soppier—Paris, perhaps, or Manhattan Island. It is true that the Parson Jack breed of fox terriers was bred from a bitch once owned by a nineteenth-century vicar of Marston—she was called Trump, and still heads the genealogy of the breed. It is true that old Dr. Routh had a dog named Romulus which had been brought up by a cat, and washed its face with its paws. Most of Oxford's animal traditions, though, are of the caustic kind, and are told without much affection.

In David Loggan's print of Corpus Christi, drawn in 1675, a small animal is to be seen on a chain in a courtyard, gazing statuesque towards a blank wall: this unhappy creature is a fox, kept there in memory of Bishop Fox the founder, and he has a small kennel at his back, and a container for his water. At a garden party in the Botanical Gardens in 1847 a bear called Tiglath Pileser, dressed as a Student of Christ Church in cap and gown, was mesmerized in public by Richard Monckton Milnes. An eighteenth-century Principal of Jesus, Joseph Hoare, died in his ninety-fifth year after being bitten by a cat: 'he inadvertently placed the leg of his chair on the cat's leg,' says one Victorian chronicler, 'not noticing it, or hearing the peculiar sound emitted from the tortured animal; and thus the Head of a House died the death of a mouse.' In the 1820s an Oriel don called Richard Whately, later to be Archbishop of Dublin, used often to be seen surrounded by admiring crowds in Christ Church meadows, as he showed off his dog Sailor's trick of climbing trees and diving into the Cherwell. Later in the century a number of young swells at Christ Church rounded up all the cats they could find in North Oxford, released them in a field, mounted their horses and had a cat-hunt.

They are not, on the whole, very kindly stories. Oxford is not
an animal-city, and even in her art creatures are not conspicuous—
off-hand I can think of a whiskered cat beneath a stone mitre at
St. John's, a lion without a head outside a house at Folly Bridge,
monsters and freaks among the gargoyles and misericords, a svelte
stone retriever outside the University Surveyor's office, near the
castle. One creature there is, though, and that the most famous of
Oxford's fauna, which is eminently in this city's style. In an old
glass case in the University Museum, surrounded by a wild
assembly of dinosaur bones, geological specimens and busts of eminent thinkers, like Aristotle and the Prince Consort, there is preserved a curious collection of small bones—one spiky claw, one
long-beaked skull. It is all that is left of Oxford's dodo. Nowhere
else possesses much more, for Oxford is a metropolis of *Didus ineptus*—a clumsy obtuse bird, fat and flightless, which lived only on
the island of Mauritius, and was never seen alive after 1681. There
are dodo relics in several countries, but it is to Oxford that the really
dedicated dodoist first makes his excited way. 'Ever since the Scientific Renaissance in the 17th century,' says an announcement in the
Museum of the History of Science, 'Oxford has been renowned for
its Dodos.'

The museum exhibit is only a sad remnant of the best known
of all dodo skeletons, which came to Oxford in 1683 with the rest
of the Tradescant Collection of Rarities. It was listed in the original
catalogue as 'Dodar, from the Island Mauritious; it is not able to
flie being so big'. By 1795 it was getting rather decrepit, and the
curator ordered it to be burnt, only its head and its right foot being
preserved to conform with the terms of the Tradescant bequest.
Around these a putative skeleton was once again constructed, with
the help of odd extra bones—sceptics said it was made of a vulture's
head and the legs of some great gallinaceous fowl: but the purist
savants of the 1890s would have none of such shams, pulled it
all to pieces again, and mounted that beaky head and that skinny
foot as we see them today. As Hilaire Belloc said of this very
bird:

> The voice that used to squawk and squeak
> Is now for ever dumb:
> But you may see his bones and beak
> All in the Museum.

Of the 12 living dodos known to have been brought to Europe, one came to Oxford ('Dodar, a blacke Indian Bird', seen here in 1634), and another is the subject of an engraving preserved only at the Bodleian Library. What really makes Oxford the last capital of the dodo kingdom, though, is the fact that here, in this city of mists and fantasies, the bird achieved immortality after all. The dodo's oily flesh, we are told, 'cannot chuse but quickly cloy and nauseate the stomach'. It was eaten up all the same, by hogs, sailors and monkeys: and it was Lewis Carroll, here in Oxford, who trium-phantly resuscitated it for the bewilderment of Alice in Wonder-land. Carroll identified himself with the dodo, and when, under his own name of Dodgson, he found his way into the *Encyclopædia Britannica*, the two of them were happily placed side by side.

Today no sensitive lover of *Didus ineptus* can enter Oxford with-out imagining its presence, waddling gravely through the drizzle with its walking stick, sheltering from the wind around the corner from Killcanon, dimly glimpsed in the far wet reaches of Port Meadow, or simply standing silently at your side with one finger on its forehead—the position in which you usually see Shakespeare, in the pictures of him.

9. Sorts and Conditions

Around the turn of the century there used to be a well-known Oxford character, a graduate of Oriel, who wore a beard and short white trousers, and was known to everyone as The British Workman—or sometimes, in the jargon of those days, The Britter. He died just after the first world war, and was buried in the cemetery of St. Sepulchre—the gloomiest and most enthralling of the Oxford burial-places, lying in the hulking shadow of Lucy's works, between Walton Street and the canal. On the left-hand side of the cemetery stands his modest tomb, and upon it the following regal inscription still shows:

OPERARIUS BRITANNICUS: HERBERTIUS JACKSON B.A.
1851–1921

Oxford is a microcosm of England, and in no way more revealingly than in her social structure. Here the English social classes are displayed for all to see, as in geological layers, and an epitaph like Mr. Jackson's, with its suggestions of gentle social irony, perfectly fits the temperament of the city. Oxford knows all sorts. There has scarcely been a time, for seven centuries, when some monumental social lion, a king, a prince or at least a maharajah has not been resident in the place—'Campion Hall Man To Wed' was the insouciant headline in the undergraduate newspaper *Cherwell*, when Prince Carlos Hugo of Bourbon-Parma, by getting engaged to Princess Irene of the Netherlands, almost turned Holland into a republic. Conversely casual labour of the more mobile sort is often attracted to the city by the easy money of the car industry; and between the extremes every kind of individualist crosses the lines at random, sometimes inspiring a wayward phrase on a tombstone, and happily compounding the complexity of the place.

Not so long ago an Oxford college itself must have been a regular showcase of the classes—a lesson, as Gladstone thought, in the structure of society. The dons stood above the college servants. The servants stood above the tradesmen. Undergraduates of noble birth took precedence over gentlemen commoners, who took precedence over servitors—men like Dr. Johnson who worked their way through college, and who not infrequently, like the great Doctor, felt ashamed to go through the gateway of Christ Church because of the state of their shoes. Each college was a closed hierarchy of its own, paternal and assured. In Wadham chapel you may still see the cramped back pews for the college servants, behind the screen, and in the cloisters at Christ Church a characteristic period memorial commemorates 'William Pound, Many years one of the porters of this College, Who by an exemplary life and behaviour, and an Honest attention to the duties of his station, Deserved and obtained the approbation and esteem of the whole society'. In Worcester College chapel, a gloomily flamboyant structure redecorated in the 1860s, the words of the *Te Deum* are strung out in painted panels around the stalls, generally so arranged that the words must be divided into groups of three or four letters, and adjacent Fellows' stalls are inscribed with apparently cabalistic devices like E. WOR   SHI   P.TH   EE. . The designer, however, knew his place, and he so ordered the letters that when he reached the Provost's seat, beside the door, he had one complete word to put upon it. It was the best, indeed the only word for such a position: GOD .

In those days the student body was dominated by the governing classes of England, whose sons moved almost instinctively from Eton or Winchester to Oxford or Cambridge, before going on to run the world. Grand names and ancient pedigrees resounded through the college registers, and it took half a dozen menials to support each undergraduate in the style to which an aristocratic society had long accustomed him. There have always been poor students at Oxford, but in the Victorian century especially, when servitors were no longer admitted, this University was synonymous with privilege. Even the dons, generally clergymen of more modest origins, sometimes found their social instincts sharpened by acquaintance with *la haute*. A window in Oriel College hall is embellished with the armorial bearings of Regius Professors of Modern History, and outside Queen's College chapel there is a memorial to Joseph Smith, an eighteenth-century Provost of the college, which brilliantly manages to convey the information, in half a dozen lines of epitaph, not only that his wife's grandfather was Governor of Pontefract Castle but also that his daughter married a grandson of the Archbishop of York.

It was not just snobbery. Many Oxford educators believed that the wholesome influence of their University could best be exerted through the ranks of the ruling classes. Jowett of Balliol thought so, liberal though his social ideas were, and Dr. Plumptre, a nineteenth-century Master of University, used to allow the young Lord Egmont to skip lectures twice a week to go hunting—it was, he said, 'so suitable'. The very word 'tuft-hunter' was coined in Oxford—titled undergraduates used to wear a gold tassel, called a tuft, upon their mortar-boards. In the Museum of the History of Science there is a magnet presented to the University by the Countess of Westmorland: it is a very large magnet indeed, it supports a slab of iron weighing 160 lb., and around its middle gratefully reclines a coronet.

Socially the patrician undergraduate stood at the head of the University pedigree, and often treated the dons exactly as he felt inclined to—as a rich man to his employees. In 1869 Lord Rosebery was ordered by the Dean of Christ Church to give up his racing stud—he had already entered a colt for the Derby: he refused, was sent down without a degree, but became Prime Minister anyway. Winston Churchill tells of his father, Lord Randolph, that he was summoned once to receive a rebuke from the Warden of Merton, but so swiftly intimidated the don that by the end of the interview Lord Randolph was standing spaciously with his back to the fire, and the Warden was reduced to chilly embarrassment. The very fashionable young man has often sneered at Oxford's donnish ways—it is no coincidence that both Beau Nash and Beau Brummell left this University without taking degrees—and the very powerful young man does not much care anyway. Even now, a petty sheikh or obscure central European princeling generally gets fairly fulsome treatment from authority, and the more practised Oxford mendicants generally know where to go, to which corner of Christ Church or Balliol staircase, to find a likely touch of the old school. 'I'm not going around the colleges again,' remarked Mr. James Burns, when charged in 1964 with stealing a threepenny bun from the rooms of the Earl of Ancram, 'if they are going to start taking liberties like this.'

The social brilliance of Oxford reached a peak in the years before the first world war, when this was the most glittering university in Europe. The lists of the dead in the war memorials at Christ Church include two viscounts, three earls, seven lords by courtesy, four baronets, 11 honourables, an Italian marquis and a French count. The war moderated this grandeur, together with the national shift in social conscience and the compression of English society. By 1928 rather more than half the undergraduates came to Oxford on scholarships or on public grants. By the 1960s the proportion was more than two-thirds, and most Oxford undergraduates now come from the State-maintained schools.

There are still rich young men at Oxford, and life at this University still offers most of the appurtenances of an opulent past—hunting, polo, smart clubs, lavish summer balls, scouts to make your bed or experienced landladies with a nose for Debrett. Only a minority, however, makes use of it all, and nobody nowadays could seriously call this University, as critics have for generations, a playground of gilded youth. In manners it seems to me much less polished than Harvard or Princeton, and in personnel it ranges from the exquisite to the downright boorish, by way of a thousand dullards. When St. Catherine's was being built in 1963, among the casual labourers working on the site was the Master's son, on vacation; and the Bulldogs tell me that whereas before the second world war all the town boys tried to look like undergraduates, nowadays Gown does its best to be mistaken for Town (whose faces frequently are, as a matter of fact, much more interesting to look at). This is no longer a ruling class in the moulding. You may still be able to tell an Oxford graduate by his command of the absolute position of equilibria, or his unexpected ability to quote the younger Seneca in the context of an income-tax demand: but you could not tell him, as once they say you could, just by the way he walked into a room.

Only a fool would resent these changes, which make the University less magnificent than it was, but much more representative of the nation. The dons, too, now come from every background, grand or humble (though they are officially graded by the Registrar-General in Social Class 2, below bank managers or doctors). Perhaps the only whole-hog reactionaries left in the University are college scouts in the old tradition, who maintain the Victorian values of Oxford more staunchly than anyone else, and are often to be heard in pubs talking in the University slang of half a century ago—language in which the Varsity seems engaged in a perpetual old billy-oh of Toggers and Rugger, and the homely Oxfordshire dialect is overlaid with echoes of Edwardian clericalism. Today it is hard to find college servants—the design of the new St. Anne's dining-hall revolved around the supposition that if the kitchen looked out on the road, it would be easier to get cooks—and even in the 1920s T. E. Lawrence successfully organized a strike of scouts at All Souls. The traditionalists among them, though, are still haughty men, pugnaciously conscious of college superiorities, and sometimes tremendous snobs.

An elderly servant of one of the grander colleges himself told me the story of a squelch he once administered to Lord Nuffield. To such an old retainer, long since accustomed to crowned heads and Nobel prize-winners, Nuffield was no more than a jumped-up Oxford tradesman—and a suspiciously sharp one at that. When the millionaire emerged one evening after dining at the college, full of good food and old port, the servant handed him his hat in the hall outside, as was the custom of the place. 'How d'you know it's mine?' inquired Lord Nuffield as he took it. 'I don't, my lord,' the scout replied, 'but it's the one you gave me.'

Outside the college gates a wider hierarchy exists, and you may see paraded for your analysis all the social grades of an old and prosperous city of the English Midlands. One way to start is to look at the houses, for here almost the whole gamut of English domestic design may be inspected in a morning, providing a key to the kind of people who have inhabited the place.

There are the mediaeval houses first, gabled and higgledy-piggledy, like the row that survives in St. Aldate's, and makes you think instantly of thanes, plagues, tonsures and scurvy. Then there are the modest manor houses, embedded now within the city, which remind us of the days when this was the capital of the Oxford wool country. One such house is Kettell Hall, now part of Trinity

College, which seen through half-closed and imaginative eyes might still be settled comfortably on the edge of pasture-land, with a dingle in front and cow stalls at the back. Another stands next door to Holywell church, in a street still called Manor Road, and a third forms part of the offices of British Leyland, long since acclimatized to the Cowley turmoil.

There are some grander country houses next, splendidly encouched in trees and lawns, breathing the spirit of eighteenth-century ease, and now inhabited either by schools or hospitals, or by scholars of such eminence that one imagines them permanently thronged with visiting philosophers and members of the Royal Swedish Academy. The Judge's House in St. Giles is a pleasant country mansion of the smaller kind, and ought to have a lake in front of it, and a ha-ha—when it was built in 1702 it stood all by itself among green fields. Not far away two small areas of planned Georgian and Regency town houses form elegant oases in the city centre—Beaumont Street and its ancillary roads, including the delightful gas-lit livery lane called Beaumont Buildings, and the handsome crescent called Parktown, a breath of Bath beyond the Engineering Department.

But then the Victorians fall upon us. At their best they made north Oxford, a large rich suburb built in the 1880s, when dons were first allowed to marry. This is a great success. The size of the houses, now mostly divided into flats, the width of the streets, the abundance of trees, the parish church of St. Philip and St. James that stands so comfortably in the middle of it all, the exuberance of towers, turrets, balconies, conservatories, sculpted figures and gabled porches—all testify to the confidence of the Victorian governing classes, only 30-odd years after Peterloo, at a time when an English revolution was still a distinct possibility.

At their worst, on the other hand, the Victorians gave us the slums of Oxford, which must have made the revolution a more distinct possibility still. These were the other side of the sovereign, and until the 1960s straggled half-derelict and bedraggled along the western side of Oxford, between the railway and the city centre. They were condemned for years and years, but disappeared with surprising suddenness, leaving car parks and shopping centres behind them, and street names that vary from the sadly anomalous (Paradise Square) to the brutally factual (Gas Street).

Next let us wander bemused through the acres of houses built, mostly by private enterprise, between the two world wars. These lie like a swathe around Oxford, filling in the gaps between her ancient villages, and they are mostly built in that peculiar style of bloodless semi-Tudor—a beam or two of timber, gables above the bedroom windows—which will always be the hall-mark of the English twenties and thirties. They express nothing but vacuous Philistinism: houses built in a hurry, at a profit, by uneducated men, for the new middle classes that were emerging out of the first world war. They look gimcrack, but in a maddening sort of way perfectly fulfil most people's domestic aspirations—with their gardens, their bay windows and their air of semi-detached satisfaction, to this day they still fetch good prices on the market, and form an object of ambition for many a poor homeless young bride, queuing for a council house and trying to share a kitchen with Mum.

Much more attractive are the estates, mostly built by the City Council, which appeared in every corner of the city after the Second World War. The best of these have a properly permanent air, and in them you may recognize many lessons learnt from the English New Towns—lessons especially of scale and humanity. They are generally gentle in style, though there are a couple of high-rise blocks at Cowley, and are carefully designed to satisfy English predilections for privacy. Even the blocks of flats, like those beside the river at St. Ebbe's, contrive to give the feeling that each apartment is a proper homestead, complete to itself: and the best of them all, built up of terraced houses, happily continue the English cottage tradition, and have garden gates to hang over, fences to snub neighbours across and lawns to accuse that slut Mrs. Wirraby of allowing her children to throw sweet-papers on.

So, if you have a keen enough interest and a car, you can see the way the English have lived, from cottage to council house, gazebo to Elsan, in a few short hours of Oxford contrast—with a detour, if you have a moment, to some of the caravan sites and houseboats which, distributed in odd patches of the city limits, in creeks off the river or fields beside the ring roads, provide some flimsy shelter for those many of the English who still cannot get a home at all. Nothing is far from anything else. This is not a socially segregated city. There is hardly such a thing as a bad address. Retired diplomats and celebrated novelists live in semi-detached villas in boring suburban roads, and it is only a step from the railway brick of Jericho to Beaumont Street's urbanity of dentists.

There used to be a notorious exception to this principle. In the early 1930s the owners of a modest company housing estate off the Banbury Road erected two brick walls across its roads to cut off their property from an adjacent municipal estate. They were hideous structures, seven feet tall and topped with revolving spikes, for all the world like prison barriers, and they became notorious as the Cuttleslowe Walls. On one side lived the middle-class tenants of private enterprise, on the other the working-class tenants of the city, and they were divided as scrupulously as ever blacks were split from whites in Alabama.

The connecting streets were cut into two and renamed, the housing company rejecting a sly municipal suggestion that one half might be called Cardinal and the other Wolsey, and for more than 25 years the Cuttleslowe Walls stood horribly firm. Nobody could get them moved. The Communist Party tried, led by a popular demagogue nicknamed Bill Firestone because of his success as a strike leader at the Firestone Rubber Company. The City Council tried, even at one time considering building walls at the other end of the company's estate, to bottle all its tenants inside. When the City plucked up its courage to knock the walls down, in 1938, the High Court ordered them put up again. When a sympathetic tank ran into one of them during wartime manœuvres the War Office had to pay for the damage. In vain did air-raid wardens complain that they could not get their fire hoses over the walls, in vain did City Councillors ask what would happen if their bricks became impregnated with poison gas. Editorials were written, petitions were organized, left-wing dons addressed protest meetings, Sir Stafford Cripps charged £537. 10s. for legal advice, and all the time the people on one side of the wall were virtually invisible to the prople on the other.

It took a complete change of social climate to knock down the Cuttleslowe Walls, as the issue slowly lost its point, the council tenants became indistinguishable from their neighbours, and a new generation saw the walls only as a ludicrous eyesore. They were formally demolished at last in 1959, by which time the housing company had been wound up and most of its tenants had bought their own houses. In a garden at the point where Wentworth Road becomes Aldrich Road, however, you may still see a last segment of their brickwork, with the spikes on top. A man living on the private side of the barrier told me that the first morning after the demolition of the walls his walking stick slipped on a gobbet of phlegm on the pavement—something, he swore, that had never happened before: and even in the 1960s the No. 2 bus, like a horse encountering a spectre, used to stop short at the place where the walls were, turn round with a whinny, and make a laborious detour to the other side.

Oxford is a rich city. The heads of colleges live in almost unrivalled comfort, in lovely old houses with attentive servants, with antique silver on the tables and tapestries upon the walls. The industrial grandees live in decorously lavish villas on the surrounding hills, with garden paths sometimes illuminated by superannuated gas standards, and boats beside the garage. Through curtain chinks in almost any corner of Oxford you may catch glimpses of cultivated comfort, pictures and books and decanters and carpets. The average income for Oxford as a whole is the highest for any English city, and when they built Woolworth's in Cornmarket it was the largest in Europe.

Poverty, however, is not far behind, and is not forgotten. North Parade Avenue, off the Banbury Road, is now a pleasant and rather rustic little shopping street, popular among dons' wives for its village flavour: but 50 years ago it was the misery of this street that first turned the schoolboy mind of Hugh Gaitskell towards Socialism. I have myself met an Oxford man whose wages, when he started work as a boy of 14, were a penny a week, with nothing to eat but bread and lard. There was still a hiring fair for domestic staff at St. Clement's in the 1930s, at a time when a new house for the Secretary of the Rhodes Trust was being built with 30 rooms, seven bathrooms and quarters for eight servants. Before the first world war unemployment seemed an inescapable economic fact in Oxford— 'a permanent part of the social life of the city', as one contemporary sociologist put it. The lovely little high-arched bridge across the Cherwell in the University Parks was built in 1923 as one of the first public works designed to relieve unemployment: it was paid for jointly by the City, the University, the colleges and individual subscribers, and is ironically the most blithe and graceful structure erected in Oxford between the wars.

Trade unionism did not really catch on in Oxford until the second war. Morris did not encourage it at Cowley, which he ran as a paternal autocracy, and until they were taught militancy by workers from elsewhere, Oxford people did not much want it anyway—to this day you do not often hear a native Oxfordshire voice in the picket lines. Lawrence's strike at All Souls was only a flash in the pan, and most of the college servants remain unorganized to this day. Even the Co-operative movement took time to take root (and the University's own Co-op, founded in a flush of social aspiration in 1914, foundered seven years later—unlike the Harvard 'Co-op', much the best shop in Cambridge, Massachusetts). It was as though the Oxford townspeople, subdued for so long by the authority of the University, had almost lost the will to better themselves.

Perhaps it was this background of fatalistic poverty, set as it was against a dazzle of privilege, that made Oxford a city of petty crime. Even now violence is rare, but thefts are more common than in most English cities—especially of pay packets from Cowley houses on Friday nights, wallets and transistors from undergraduate rooms, or church collection boxes. When the Assize Judge used to stay in the Judge's House during sessions a policeman always stood guard outside: this was because not so long ago, when the Judge was handing out sentences in court one day, somebody slipped into his bedroom and rifled his belongings.

Vandalism is an Oxford scourge, perhaps encouraged by the old and wretched traditions of undergraduate hooliganism. Today the students do not often set fire to things, squirt hosepipes at policemen or paint the city scarlet on Guy Fawkes Night, but there seems to be scarcely an Oxford churchyard without its upturned gravestones and mutilated angels. The Oxford propensity for false pretences also has academic origins: an old tradesmen's trap for unwary freshmen was to offer them unlimited credit on sight, effectively ensnaring them for their whole university careers: dud cheques and false identities thus became common Oxford currency, and every now and then you still read of a bogus Doctor of Philosophy unsuccessfully trying to diddle a jeweller, or some unhappy undergraduate forging his uncle the Bishop's signature.

Sometimes it breaks out into something worse. The earlier chronicles of Oxford record some really whole-hog local crimes. All the Danes in the city, for instance, were once burnt alive in St. Frideswide's priory, and in Oxford Edmund Ironside is alleged to have been murdered by Canute's agents, just after the two kings had signed a treaty sharing England between them—he was killed, according to one chronicler, by a mechanical figure of an archer which shot an arrow when you touched it. Fair Rosamond, mistress of Henry II, is supposed to have been murdered at Godstow by the jealous Queen Eleanor, who presumably inspired the famous epitaph inscribed on her tomb at Godstow Nunnery, beside the river—'In this tomb lies Rosamond, the Rose of the World, the fair, but not the pure.' Some say Eleanor poisoned the girl, some say she was stabbed, and my own favourite version is the one that has her bled to death in a hot bath.

In the University Church, curiously back-to-front before the altar, a memorial tablet tells us that somewhere in the church is buried Amy Robsart, wife of Queen Elizabeth's favourite Robert Dudley, who died in highly suspicious circumstances at Cumnor, just outside the city. She was first buried at Cumnor, but was exhumed at Dudley's orders and deposited here in an unmarked grave: if anyone had any doubts that he had murdered her it was certainly not the Rector of Lincoln of the day, who preached the funeral sermon and tripped up once or twice, we are told, 'by recommending to their memories that vertuous ladie so pittefully murdered, instead of so pitifully slain'.

Murder does not often happen now—the last man hanged in Oxford prison died in 1951. Between the wars there was a famous case in which the corpse of a college servant, murdered by a mad theological student, lay for four days on a rooftop overlooking the Banbury Road. In 1940 a schizophrenic conscientious objector at University College lay in wait for a group of heartier undergraduates, and let fly at them with a rifle from his rooms in the front quadrangle, killing one and wounding two more. In 1963 a girl was strangled in the allotments behind Magdalen College—a few hundred yards from the site at Holywell where, as late as the eighteenth century, undergraduate highwaymen were put to death on Gownmen's Gallows. But most of the best-loved Oxford crimes have been more bizarre than horrific. There was the case in 1946

of the woman who set fire to the church of St. Michael, allegedly
because the vicar was trying to rid the belfry of pigeons. There was
the attempt in 1938 to kidnap Lord Nuffield. In this project it was
proposed to bundle Nuffield upon a yacht, equipped with instruments of torture and lying ready off the Essex coast: he would then
have his thumbs twisted or his spine elongated until he signed a
draft for £100,000. The plan was thwarted by a disloyal accomplice,
and its originator, sentenced to seven years' imprisonment, died in-
sane. Most curiously of all, there was the case of the gold chain in
the Ashmolean Museum. This was a relic of Elias Ashmole, the
founder of the museum, and one day in 1776 it was found to have
been shortened by three or four links—as you can still see for yourself, if you compare the chain in its glass case with the portrait of
its owner, in full regalia, inside a frame by Grinling Gibbons directly
above. The man who stole this bauble was Jean Paul Marat of the
French Revolution, who gave it to his landlord in Liverpool in
payment for board and lodging, and was presently assassinated in
his bath.

Squalid episodes, every one: and there is squalor still in Oxford,
Heaven knows. There used to be a place called Penniless Bench,
where the indigent assembled for comfort or charity in the shadow
of Carfax Tower: and often enough the indigent are to be found
there still, hangdog in frayed trousers in the winter dusk, among
the leather-jacket louts and tarts of the English evening. When an
Oxford man was charged recently with ill-treating a pony his address
was given as c/o The Piggery, Stratford Street, and when he was
turned out of that sty he went to live instead in the grandstand of
the University rugby football ground.

Physically Oxford has been enormously improved in recent
decades, its grubbiest streets restored or eliminated, even its traffic
congestion perceptibly relieved, but it still has its blighted corners,
and its poor. A Russian tourist who visited Oxford in 1963 noticed
a wooden effigy of an emaciated boy which stands in the Cornmarket
to raise funds for famine relief abroad: he was amazed, he reported
in the Ministry of Culture magazine when he returned to Moscow,
to find such a city advertising its own miseries so flagrantly—'victims of famine in wealthy England!' This was pitching it high, and
anyway some of the shabbier parts of the city shelter its cosiest and
closest-knit communities. But you can still feel pathos in Oxford

poignantly enough if you wander through the poorer quarters some dismal Sunday afternoon, when the frail Pakistanis and their wives wander cold and forlorn towards the railway, and through the street windows families of Jamaicans may be seen hugger-mugger at oil-clothed tables eating a stew in damp parlours (cat-food stew, so the supermarket girls say). Taxi drivers will tell you where the harlots are to be found, satin-swathed in private houses or haunting the bars of well-known pubs; and somehow or other in this homely city the poor young drug addicts manage to maintain their terrible connection, graduating only, all too often, from grass to heroin.

Oxford has lately been feminized—partly by the gradual equalizing of the sexes that is occurring everywhere in England, more specifically by the reluctant recognition of women's rights by a mordantly masculine University. Until the 1880s Oxford dons, except Heads of Houses and professors, were not allowed to marry. The earlier All Souls betting books are full of ironic wagers about matrimony. In 1883, for instance, Curzon made a bet that Maguire would be married before he was himself: Maguire won the bet, it is said, by postponing his own wedding a couple of days. Even when the celibacy rule was relaxed, some colleges fought dogged rear-guard actions. At Brasenose Fellows were only allowed to marry by the vote of two-thirds of their colleagues—by secret ballot, mercifully—and at All Souls even now certain categories of Fellowship are usually forfeited upon marriage.

This meant that old Oxford neither understood nor much admired women. 'A woman is a creature,' declared Dr. Whately once, 'that cannot reason and pokes the fire from the top.' When a women's college was first suggested, in the 1870s, Dr. Liddon of Christ Church said that all its students would be atheists, and declared it to be 'an educational development which runs counter to the wisdom and experience of all the centuries of Christendom'. 'Inferior to us God made you,' Dean Burgon assured the female sex in a sermon at New College in 1884, 'and inferior to the end of time you will remain.' 'What was your lady-love like, dear Master?' asked Margot Asquith of Jowett, when told that he had once been in love with Florence Nightingale. 'Violent,' the sage replied. 'Very violent.'

But women had always been more influential in the place than old bachelors might care to admit. Both Wadham and Balliol were founded by women—it was Dorothy Wadham who had the good sense to suggest that the library might be built above the kitchen, to keep the books dry. Several talented Jewesses were prominent in the business life of mediaeval Oxford, and several wives of college heads cut formidable figures in later centuries. 'Mrs. Jenkyns and Master Balliol,' is how a footman once announced the stumpy little Dr. Jenkyns, a nineteenth-century Master, and his stately wife, and we are told that when, at two o'clock in the morning one night in the 1830s, the idea flashed upon Dr. Buckland, Professor of Geology, that the Cheirotherium footsteps might be testudinal, his wife instantly got up and made some paste on the kitchen table, to test a tortoise's footprints in. Bishop Robinson of Oriel, when he built a new building at the college in the eighteenth century, had the grace to put an inscription above the door attributing the idea to his wife (though he ended the lines enigmatically, as you can still see, with the maxim *Man is the Increase of Mould*—in Runic).

> *I am the Dean, this Mrs. Liddell*
> *She plays the first, I, second fiddle.*
> *She is the Broad,*
> *I am the High—*
> *We are the University.*

So sang the misogynist dons of Victorian Oxford, but they were perhaps more hypocritical about women than they knew themselves. Women might not be able to poke a fire properly, and sometimes made fools of themselves lording it over their husbands in public, but there had been a woman professor at Bologna University as long before as the fourteenth century, and most of the great European universities had given degrees to women in the past. Until the Reformation women were often guests at Oxford college tables, and the sharp-tongued ladies of Charles I's court were, I am sure, well able to hold their own with the most acidulous donnish conversationalist. 'Inferior to us God made you': but the precepts of fundamentalist religion were doubtless buttressed by the fear that if ever women got into Oxford things would never be quite so comfortable again.

So they *sidled* in. Treated by and large as beings somewhere between butterflies and gorgons, they were not ashamed, like the lady with the bustle in the *Punch* cartoon, to try sideways. In the 1830s a girl named Rachel Burton, daughter of a Canon of Christ Church, competed under a pseudonym for the Newdigate Poetry Prize, and won it. In 1873 somebody called A. M. A. H. Rogers came first in the Oxford Senior Local examination for schools: Worcester College at once offered the candidate an exhibition, hastily withdrawn when the initials were found to stand for Annie Mary Anne Henley. Ruse by ruse, concession by concession, the women eased their way into *Universitas Oxoniensis*: in unofficial associations, in societies without college status, in colleges of their own, and finally in a few of the men's colleges. Many dons were sympathetic, but for years the University as a whole treated women students rather as old President Routh treated railways—by refusing to recognize their existence. Twenty years after women began sitting for University examinations the Statutes still declared flatly that only members of the University—that is, men—could be admitted to them at all. 'Since there is only one person present,' said an old-school don when he found that his audience consisted of one man and one woman, 'this lecture will be postponed until tomorrow.' *a /*

When girls did become members of the University they were severely circumscribed and segregated. The unhappy chaperon, an elderly bored lady knitting her way through endless hours of Mediaeval French or Early Saxon Land Tenure, was one of the classic figures of late Victorian Oxford: so was the chair-man, who propelled young ladies in Bath chair from one call to the next in the early days of married Fellowships, while their proud husbands walked starched and stiff beside them. As late as 1914 the Professor of Human Anatomy, uncomfortably surveying the femaleness of females, refused to teach women students unless they worked in separate dissecting rooms. Only in the 1970s did the first of the men's colleges agree to admit women undergraduates, and they are still debating whether it was a good idea or not.

It took guts to break down all these taboos and restrictions, and some powerful women emerged from the struggle for academic emancipation. Of all the faces that greet you from the portraits in the Oxford colleges, perhaps the most daunting is that of Charlotte Moberly, first Principal of St. Hugh's—an arrogant, tight, almost fanatic face, such a face as I would not care to cross repartee with:

and this is not surprising, for she was the daughter of Bishop Moberly of Salisbury, who believed himself to be a great-grandson of Peter the Great, and whose wife only once, so legend says, called him by his Christian name.

The arrival of the women has fertilized and mellowed the University, especially now that success has set them free. It has made Oxford less aloof to the standards of the world outside. In the old days a man's memories of his Oxford years had a sensual lilt to them: the emotional impact of the city was itself warm and vivid, and often the friendships formed within his college were highly charged—if not overtly homosexual, certainly shot through with rapturous undertones, in an age torn between puritanism and the libidinous liberties of classical Greece. College loyalties and personal friendships were all diffused in a cloud of golden recollection, illuminated at its edges by poetry.

Today the Oxford man's regard for his college is generally more detached and more precise, and as likely as not this is because half his heart was always up the road, behind the stern lady porters of Somerville and St. Anne's. We do not hear much nowadays of homosexual misadventure at Oxford, but a perennial of controversy is the problem of the undergraduate caught with a girl in his cupboard before breakfast. The interminable adolescence of the boarding-school boy is not quite so protracted as it used to be, now that the women come up to Oxford: the affinity between Town and Gown is closer, now that each has a girl on his arm.

Yet in a way perhaps those old die-hards were right. The presence of women has fructified Oxford University, and made it more sensible; but it has also, I suspect, blunted its edge. The Oxford temperament was moulded by the caustic but tolerant give-and-take of men's conversations, helped along by an abundant flow of liquor. Now that most dons dine domestically with their wives I fear some of the sting has gone, the *bons mots* come harder and feelings are more easily hurt. The women's colleges pride themselves on their high proportion of first-class degrees: but their emphasis on brains, on work and on examination results is out of Oxford's character. Gibbon, De Quincey, Swinburne and Ruskin all, for one reason or another, failed to sit for degrees at all; Shelley, John Locke and Sir Richard Burton were all expelled from the University; neither Matthew Arnold nor Cardinal Newman got firsts; but the

new Oxford standards, so ably supported by the women, sanction
no such magnificent failures, and prize a first-class mediocrity above
an idle genius.

The women's colleges are like presentiments of things to come—
dedicated, efficient, highly competitive. Times have changed since
John Ruskin could write in a birthday book, without fear of offence:
'So glad to be old enough to be let come and have tea at Somerville,
and to watch the girlies play at ball.'

Nobody tried harder than old Ruskin, all the same, to integrate the
sorts and conditions of Oxford. Though he opposed the idea of
women's colleges at the start, he became their influential advocate,
and unlike too many dons he was always conscious of the dismal
Victorian gulf between rich and poor. 'No demons could contrive,
under the earth,' he once told an undergraduate audience of a visit
he had made to the slum districts near the railway, 'a more un-
comfortable and abominable place for the condemned souls of dirty
people'—sound art, policy or religion could not exist in England
until such places were restored to decency. Ruskin was Slade Professor of Fine Arts at Oxford, and here he vigorously pursued his
campaign for the revival of Gothic craftsmanship—for the recognition of the labourer as a creative member of society, and of manual
labour as an honourable pursuit for any man. No trace is left of
the village road which he laboriously paved at North Hinksey,
helped by a gang of young idealists that included Alfred Milner,
Arnold Toynbee and Oscar Wilde: any level parts of it, Ruskin himself admitted, were due to his gardener—grandly summoned, rather
against the spirit of the thing, from the Professor's country home.

The University Museum, however, is the supreme structural
illustration of his 'gospel of labour'—pathetic sometimes, comical
occasionally, but also noble. He was interested in the whole concept
of the building, but it was the decoration especially that was to con-
firm his belief in the powers of the natural, untrained artist. The
workers on the site were mostly Irish, and were encouraged to evolve
their own ornamental designs. They were helped along by daily
prayers in the messroom (in which, Ruskin innocently tells us, there
were 'various volumes placed for their use'), and they formed among
themselves one of the first of the Oxford co-operatives. A talented
family of Irish sculptor-masons, the O'Sheas, were to do the chief

sculptural decoration—all, according to Ruskin's tenets, 'informative, conveying truthful statements about natural facts', and all executed by the men who designed it. In its decoration the Museum was intended to be 'somewhat the same as a great chorus in music, in which, while perhaps there may be only one or two voices perfectly trained, and of perfect sweetness ... the body of sound is sublime'. Ruskin himself, with disciples, erected one of the brick pillars inside the building, and the O'Sheas went to work with a Dublin vengeance, carving monkeys, cats, fruits and vegetables all over the place.

As a memorial to these lofty aspirations, the Museum is something less than sublime. 'The building will shortly sink into insignificance,' Sir Henry Acland wrote in 1860, 'when compared with the contents it will display, and the minds it will mould.' This prophecy has scarcely come true, for the building remains among the most fervently cherished and implacably detested in Oxford: but its decoration, that hymn to the gospel of labour, has weathered the generations badly. They worked at it intermittently until 1907— I have met a man who remembers seeing a mason actually carving a pillar, freehand, from a specimen of a carnivorous plant in a bottle at his side. It was never finished, though, partly because the money ran out, partly because the volatile O'Sheas, angered by interference from dons, went off in a huff: some of the windows on its façade are elaborately embellished, some are altogether unadorned, and some peter out into austerity half-way through. At one moment the most talented of the O'Sheas was found to be carving, just inside the porch, alternate images of parrots, owls and Members of Convocation: he was ordered to knock their heads off, to obliterate such disrespect, and their half-formed images are there still—birds and dons alike in perpetual embryo. Ruskin's own pillar was so ineptly erected that it had to be taken down and put up again by professionals, and it is only in our own times that the Museum, splendidly restored and supplemented by an underground library, has really achieved fulfilment.

Ruskin himself is properly honoured in Oxford. The Ruskin School of Art draws its students from Town and Gown alike. Ruskin College, though not part of the University, gives working men and women two years of study in the Oxford pattern. Bernard Shaw once refused to lecture there, on the grounds that 'a workman ought

to have a vulgar prejudice against Oxford': but so far it has unexpectedly survived the English social revolution, and gets its recruits from astonishingly varied sources—in recent years it welcomed students awarded scholarships by the National Coal Board,
the Distressed Gentlewomen's Aid Society, the Great-Britain-
U.S.S.R. Association and the Kuala Lumpur Municipal Services
Union. Ruskin was one of the few great social idealists Oxford has
produced—Tolstoy acknowledged him as his master—and one of
the few famous Oxford dons to have a heart matching his head
(though how clear his head was academically we may have leave
to doubt, for because of illness he never sat for his degree, and was
awarded the ultimate in consolation prizes, an honorary double-
fourth).

At least he tried to bridge the gaps, and now that those old social
gulfs are narrowing, the sons of the O'Sheas are often undergraduates themselves and even the Cuttleslowe Walls are down, it is
pleasant to see some of his aspirations cheerfully, if unconsciously,
guyed. When they were renovating the Sheldonian Theatre a few
years ago they built a mess hall for the workers there, too. Work
did not begin with morning prayers, and various volumes were not
placed there for their use, but outside the door those craftsmen
erected a fanciful embellishment which undoubtedly conveyed
truthful statements about natural facts. It was a coat of arms—quar-
terly, with a cup in the first and fourth and three spoons palewise
in fess in the second and third, and a chief charged with a teapot.

10. Pleasures

Oxford has a gift for pleasure. Discontented schoolgirls do not always think so, and sometimes write letters to the editor complaining about the lack of discos, but if you circle over the city in an aircraft on a fine day at the end of June the scene below you looks a regular carnival. All along the river the boats are idly swinging, punts and skiffs and motor launches, with the oblique white wings of the yachts at Binsey, and here and there the tiny plop of somebody diving in. There are the cricketers, poised in mystic circle, and there are the white hats and blue blazers of the ladies on the bowling greens, and motionless along the sedgy reaches of the canal you may see the hermit anglers, plunged in morbid hope.

Perhaps there is a garden party down there, and the lawns beneath the elms are sprinkled with scarlet hoods, silk frocks and such frou-frou hats as only the wives of Oxford professors can wear with just the right mixture of absurdity and command. You can see the sight-seers clumped on the balcony of St. Mary's tower, or processing behind their guide through Tom Quad at Christ Church. You can see the big bright coaches streaming in from London or out to Strat-ford-on-Avon. Other little aeroplanes are buzzing about the airport, west of the city, and two or three girls are galloping their ponies up and down Port Meadow like Mongols on the rampage. On half a dozen green patches among the colleges stand the striped awnings, marquees, band-stands and tables of the commemoration balls, shameless social anachronisms which have survived with such panache that the smartest of them think nothing of hiring four separate bands for an evening, with a couple of cabarets thrown in and an all-night ladies' hairdresser, and some years ago one of the prizes offered was breakfast in Paris next morning—an aircraft stood by at the airport to whisk the winner off at dawn.

On such a day the city down there, clustered about its pinnacles, seems to be waving flags, playing fiddles, trailing its fingers among water lilies and positively wallowing in pleasures.

Pleasures of green fields first, for *mens sana in corpore sano* used to be an Oxford motto, and nothing expresses the old Oxford ethos better than the vision of young Mr. Gladstone walking his statutory 10 miles each weekday afternoon. Every sensible Victorian undergraduate went for rambles in the countryside, or roamed the hills on his bicycle. The correct dress for a student of the 1830s, we are told, was 'black frock coat, and tall hat, with the neatest of gloves and boots, and in this costume he went out for his country walk, the admired of all beholders'. The best of Oxford's celebrants, Matthew Arnold, perfectly captured these old pleasures of the fresh air in *Thyrsis* and *The Scholar Gypsy*—poems that seem to rustle still with the meadow grass of the high Hinkseys, veiled in white fog, yellow with cowslips, or echoing with the voices of 'a troop of Oxford hunters going home, as in old days, jovial and talking'. The ideal of the Renaissance man was still alive in those days, and in Oxford it was interpreted as the cult of the jolly good all-rounder.

You may still meet him now and then, and especially in the famous old club called Vincent's, in upstairs premises off the High. This is pre-eminently a sporting club, but its members were to be elected, so the original statutes said in 1863, for their 'all-round qualities—social, physical and intellectual qualities being duly considered'. Today most prominent undergraduate sportsmen are elected, but past members have included two Prime Ministers, a Viceroy of India, several archbishops and any number of judges. At Vincent's, whose walls are lined with photographs of eminent members, and whose undergraduate membership is limited to 150 at a time, you may still feel the allure of that old philosophy. There is nothing ham-handed to the character of the club, roisterous though its smoking room may become after a victorious rugger match. It is mellow and unexpectedly subtle. It is named after the printer whose shop happened to be on the floor below the original premises. Its committee invented the kind of tie that has a pattern of crests all over it. Rule IV of its original rule-book decreed that tea, chocolate, coffee and beer were to be free to all members for ever. In an England of shifting convictions, Vincent's feels supremely sure of itself: and if ever you feel like scoffing at its values,

take care of the young men you meet on its stairs, who always look
to me suggestively light-footed.

It has certainly been derided in its time, for Oxford's pleasure
in manly exercise was long ago tainted by the association of
organized sport with things hearty and crudely Philistine. It was
Oscar Wilde, a double-first, who mocked the progress of the
oarsmen as 'travelling backwards to Iffley Lock', and whipped the
huntsmen as 'the unspeakable in pursuit of the inedible'. Before
the second world war the undergraduate body was unhealthily split
between Hearties and Aesthetes—the former descending often to
cruel horseplay and even violence, the latter sometimes carrying
delicacy so far that Oswald Mosley the Fascist called them 'the
shimmying half-men of Oxford'. There was a time when Brasenose
College came perilously close to the American system of awarding
scholarships to very able sportsmen, and there have been periods
in the University's history when the *élite* of the undergraduate body
was formed entirely of its notable athletes. Even now in some
English circles a blue is more admired than a first, while in others
it only raises a supercilious eyebrow and a second-hand aphorism.

But the antipathies have weakened, and in Oxford herself nowadays nobody much cares whether you spend your afternoons torpid
in the sunshine of the cricket field or violently exerting yourself at
the library table. The carefree amateurism of Oxford sport has faded
a little—you may often find an Olympic runner or two in the
bar at Vincent's, and it was at a match between the University and
the Athletics Association that Bannister first ran a mile in four
minutes: but at least the sportsmen only play because they really
want to, not because shame has driven them to it, or the example
of Mr. Gladstone.

The team spirit is at a discount, but the sporting pleasures flourish still. You may still win a blue at cricket, rugby, hockey, athletics,
soccer, tennis, rowing, golf, boxing, squash, swimming, yachting
or cross-country running, or a half-blue at Real Tennis, Eton Fives,
Rifle and Revolver Shooting, or Archery. Visiting cricket Test
teams always come to Oxford for a game; the annual Oxford and
Cambridge match at Lord's is one of the happiest events in the
cricket calendar; the university Rugby match is so great an occasion
for hundreds and thousands of enthusiasts that the very name of
Twickenham, the London suburb where it is played, has become

synonymous with the game—rugger men ask 'Going to Twickenham this year?' as a cardinal might inquire of a colleague if he will
be dropping in at the Vatican.

Even the field sports survive, the most picturesque relics of this
University's posher past. It is said that Oxford bags, those floppy
grey trousers of the 1930s, were invented so that smart undergraduates could wear them over riding breeches, enabling them to slip
out to the hunting fields immediately after tutorials: conversely the
open-fronted and unbuttonable surplices worn by Christ Church
men in chapel were designed, tradition says, so that hunting pinks
could not be concealed beneath them. The annals of Oxford are
full of hunts, shoots, drives and meets. They used to hunt boar in
the royal forest of Shotover, on the eastern heights, and it was in
Bagley Wood that an early student thwarted an angry hog by stuffing a copy of Aristotle down its throat—'*Graecum Est!*' cried the
resourceful youth, and the beast fell dead. The world's most lethal
rabbit shoot was held outside Oxford in 1898, when five guns killed
6,943 rabbits in a day. There have always been hunting men among
the Oxford undergraduates, and today the Bullingdon Club boisterously sustains the tradition. There is a drag hunt still, point-to-
points prosper, and often you will see a swagger of pinks on a crisp
autumn morning, disappearing through Tom Gate for a day with
the Heythrop.

Christ Church and New College have a joint pack of beagles.
Every Boxing Day the pack meets at some neighbouring country
house, and revives for a few brisk and jolly hours the spirit of an
earlier Oxford—a more dashing but crueller Oxford, the Oxford
of the English aristocrats. All is still there, at such a meet of Oxford
sportsmen. The wine is mulled, there are adorable children on the
lawn, fine women in suede jackets stride about the rosebeds. The
faces around you are long firm English faces, and there is an emana-
tion of leather, mud, lavender scent and universal acquaintance. A
few dons stand on the fringes, eccentrically dressed in high old-
fashioned boots, or Polish topcoats. A few exceedingly modern girls
chat about each other's cousins. The hounds look sleek, fit and
hungry: the huntsman looks like a Stubbs jockey; and presently,
with a high shrill toot of a hunting horn, the Master and his whip-
pers-in lead you away down the drive—undergraduates of such a
burnished elegance, such an easy swinging pace, such an air of

certainty, that you can see them striding with the same commanding pleasure through all the centuries of English history, cracking
their whips and laughing.

Pleasures of the river: the long lines of punts idling foreshortened
up the Cherwell, with their Carpaccio boatmen at the stern, and
the slanting forest of their punt poles against the trees; bathing in
the nude at Parson's Pleasure; fishing in the dusk off the gravel
bottom at Binsey, when the evening bream are biting, and the
midges are whirring in the shrubbery behind; drifting through the
mists on the morning after the ball, crumped pink nylon and champagne bottles in the well of the boat; above all the long easy stroke
of a racing eight, with the panting of its crew and the creaking of
its sliding seats and sometimes a sharp blasphemous exhortation
from the cox in his gay peaked cap.

Much the most famous of the Oxford pleasures is rowing. No
proper Victorian novel of Oxford life was complete without its hero
in the college crew—'all rowed fast,' as Ouida is maliciously alleged
to have put it, 'but none so fast as stroke.' It is the Oxford and Cambridge Boat Race which has so oddly captured the public imagination. This began at Henley in 1829, but is now rowed at London, on
a course between Mortlake and Putney. It is one of the great sporting events of the English year, and the most supremely successful
publicity stunt ever mounted by academic institutions. All over the
world, if you mention the name of Oxford, people will instantly light
up with some eager phrase of recognition, such as 'Ah, the regatta
of the boats!' or 'Ha, ha, where Cambridge always wins, isn't it?'—
it being an almost universal belief that Oxford invariably loses,
though the statistics show that she has won 53 times out of 122
(and once, legend says, the umpire tumbled out of a bankside pub
just in time to announce 'a dead heat for Oxford, by quarter of a
length').

It is one of the social curiosities of modern Britain that when this
race enters the news columns, in the same tone of voice as the Cup
Final, say, or the Olympic Games, the schools and colleges of the
oarsmen are still carefully recorded; and you may see how complete was the ascendancy of these universities in their social heyday
in the fact that until recently scarcely a soul in Britain was not a
fervent supporter of one crew or the other—Light Blue for Cam-

bridge, Dark for Oxford. *'I sticks ter Orxfud Collidge, I dew,'* sang an archetypal Cockney in a 1906 skit—

> *I'm nuts on sport, whatever it is, I'm keen on the*
> *boat-rice dye,*
> *When I tikes my third ter Putney Bridge*
> *and it's fust-class all the wye.*
> *There's some as changes and chops about, but*
> *mine's no turncoat gime—*
> *I've allus bin Orxfud Collidge myself,*
> *and my mother were just the sime.*

Until the second world war girls all over England used to make Boat Race favours out of twists of wool, and small boys spat at each other defiant jingles like *Cambridge upstairs putting on their braces, Oxford downstairs winning all the races.* Today the partisanship is not so violent, or so universal; the image of Oxford is less shimmering and unapproachable than it used to be; but the Boat Race still dominates the television for the afternoon, and the most unexpected of your neighbours, in the days preceding it, may accost you with theories about weights, breath control or the advantages of spoon oars.

The Boat Race is a straight contest, start to finish, but because the Thames at Oxford is both narrow and sinuous, a special kind of rowing race was long ago devised for the University. It began, we are told, when oarsmen who had pottered down to Sandford for an evening drink started for home at different times, and made a custom of trying to catch each other up: and it has developed into an elaborate system of competitive rowing, in which college crews start at equal intervals and try to bump the one in front—thus taking its place in the next race. A kind of ladder is formed, and the crew that bumps its way to the top of it, in a week of daily racing, becomes Head of the River, celebrates with a college binge, and chalks its insignia proudly on the quadrangle wall. There are two such annual regatta weeks, for different standards of crews, but the big one is Eights Week at the end of May. Rowing is not so important as it was at Oxford, and college enthusiasm for the races is not so fervent. Even so, in Eights Week the pleasures of Oxford are in their fullest bloom—possibly, like the evening of some splendid rose, getting a little blowzy.

The traditional vantage-point used to be the deck of one of the college barges, which were moored in a colourful line all along the river bank of Christ Church meadows, downstream from Folly Bridge. Until the 1960s these queer old craft, now replaced by balconied boathouses, were among the archetypal sights of Oxford. They were descended from the ceremonial barges once used by the Livery Companies of London on State occasions and Lord Mayors' Shows, and were gloriously embellished with whirligigs, rosettes and figures of classical mythology (though some of the last to be built were made of concrete). The first of them actually were old Company barges. Thus the Skinners' Company barge, built in 1738, was used by Queen's College until 1900, and the Merchant Taylors' barge was the first headquarters of the University Boat Club—it was built in 1800, of 'good sound seasoned English oak, free from Red Rot, sap and prejudicial knots', and the great crest from its stern, removed before the sale, still hangs in the Company's hall in the City of London. Later the colleges built their own barges, in Oxford boatyards, and today superannuated survivors are scattered over the city, sometimes as raffish dwelling-places, sometimes high and dry on water-meadows, frequented only by rats and ducks.

Today only St. Catherine's maintains a college barge, all alone and fairly forlorn, and for Eights Week you would do better to get yourself a seat on one of the boathouse roofs. There the Oxford of popular legend seems miraculously alive again. This is not Hotspur's Oxford, like the afternoon of the beagles: this is golden vicarage stuff, a dreamy Edwardian Oxford, all on a summer afternoon. All around you are summer frocks, proud mothers, experienced fathers and public-school accents—rowing being a sport cultivated especially at the independent schools, it has been more impervious than most Oxford pleasures to social change. The river flutters with pennants and bright colours. A noisy crowd of undergraduates seethes up and down the towpath, threaded by earnest rowing coaches carrying megaphones on bicycles. Wherever you look there are colours, blazers and white flannels, straw hats with ribbons, lemonade bottles and crested caps. A ferryman conveys a crew from one bank to the other, its oars standing upright in the punt like lances in a Spanish painting. A hired motor launch chugs self-consciously past, like a shopper who, looking for Inexpensive

Hats, finds she has to run the gauntlet of Model Dresses. On the other side of the river you may see a cow in a field, and some cricketers statuesque against the green. The splendid trees of Christ Church meadows look vast and motherly. The traffic crossing Folly Bridge seems altogether remote and silent; and presently, almost as an afterthought, the boats come by.

There go the two officials of the Water Authority, grandly in yachting caps and an old varnished motor boat, and soon there advances upstream a wave of sound, as the college enthusiasts on the bank run beside their boat shouting encouragement—You're going up, Balliol!'—'Come on, The House!'—'Teddy Hall! Teddy Hall!' A flash of oars you see first, with the drip of the water off their painted blades, and then the first of the racing shells comes sweeping to the finishing line—eight very English young men, with the wiry little coxswain bawling at them from the stern, and a raggle-taggle party of supporters still staggering breathless along the bank; and the girl beside you turns to her brother and asks vacuously which boat it is, and the father says testily that it's all on the race card anyway, and the mother tidies her back hair and murmurs well, Susan only asked, after all it *is* only a sort of game, and presently the whole affair bursts into strawberries, cool drinks, the splashing of coxswains thrown into the water, and happy little groups of people, white and blue and polka-dotted, strolling through the meadows back to college.

The pleasures of performance next. Play-acting has old traditions in Oxford, and actors have always been welcomed here—one of my favourite Oxford scenes is the currently fashionable restaurant after a first night that has gone with a swing at the New Theatre, when the actors celebrate with the gayest of dinners and drink to the almost interminable run they foresee for the show when it gets to London. Shakespeare himself, so Oxford likes to think, used to put up at the Crown Inn at Cornmarket, on his way to the Globe. The landlord's son was the poet Will Davenant, to whom Shakespeare stood godfather—possibly in the old church of St. Martin's at Carfax, just along the road from the Crown—and on these somewhat flimsy grounds of tradition, every year on Shakespeare's birthday they drink malmsey in a surviving room of the old inn, now called the Painted Room at No. 3, Cornmarket. I once went to one of these festivities, chiefly to see what malmsey tasted like, but inspecting the label on the bottle afterwards, I found it described as an 'old world luxury wine of Regency days, from sunkissed island vineyards whose quality you can depend on'.

Oxford has long specialized in satirical licence. Until 1783 a character called the Terrae Filius, a kind of University jester, used to stand up at degree ceremonies and deliver a monologue of stunning scurrility—in 1733, for instance, he denounced the Bishop of Oxford as 'a mitred Hog and father of 18'. Nowadays some young men come up to Oxford chiefly because of her theatrical tastes— the prestige of her University Dramatic Society, the O.U.D.S., her endless opportunities for acting and directing in a score of college companies, her fortunate station as one of those places on the professional stage circuit where plays are often tried out before they go to London (though once it was the other way round—'plays which had been enthusiastically applauded in London', Macaulay wrote of seventeenth-century Oxford, 'were not thought out of danger until they had undergone the more severe judgement of audiences familiar with Sophocles and Terence').

There is nothing in Oxford like the great American university theatres. The New Theatre, nevertheless, is one of the largest in England, and the University has its own pleasant Playhouse. This has had its ups and downs. It began in 1923 in a house in the Woodstock Road that previously housed a collection of big-game trophies, and it collapsed in 1929 when the building was turned into a midget golf course. Now it is handsomely housed in Beaumont Street, and most of the famous English players have acted there at one time or another, generally in plays of fairly stringent appeal by Ibsen, Brecht or Strindberg—for 'if Oxford is not highbrow,' as Bernard Shaw remarked apropos of the Playhouse itself, 'what on earth is Oxford?'

More than one undergraduate production has gone straight from the Playhouse to the West End, such is the polish of Oxford University productions at their best (at their worst they can make you squirm). To most people, though, the theatre in Oxford means the theatre outdoors, beside the lake at Worcester, on the great shabby lawn at Trinity, or beneath the noble purple beech in the gardens of Wadham. I am not myself irresistibly attracted by the prospect of an evening with Beaumont, Fletcher and the midges, but I admit

the magic of those occasions if the evening is fine and you can watch
from an independent distance. I was once loitering around Magdalen on a classic May evening when I saw a company of players
making their way through the Grove for a performance of *A Mid-
summer Night's Dream*. They were moving swiftly in their cowls,
ruffs and velvets, all among the elms, and a few shy deer watched
them pass between the tree trunks. Their footfalls were silent on
the turf, their voices reached me faintly on the warm air, and they
disappeared into the shadows merrily, with Puck occasionally prac-
tising his jumps, and Titania lifting her crimson skirts, and a few
lumpish fairies skirmishing in the flanks. I never caught the spell
of the theatre more hauntingly, as I watched them across the fence,
and felt rather like Hamlet when the players came to Elsinore—' *You
are welcome, masters, welcome all.*'

If I had waited, I do not doubt, the charm would have been broken
by a tinny twanging of lute strings, intermittently amplified, for
Oxford's love of music is almost inescapable. It starts with bells.
'Oxford is a city', Elmer Davis once wrote, 'where too many bells
are always ringing in the rain.' I once listened hard in Radcliffe
Square, and counted 13 midnight chimes, with distant laggards still
opening up a full minute after Great Tom had reverberated into
silence.

This is campanologists' country. Change ringing, a peculiarly
English practice, has been flourishing in Oxford for at least 300
years, and at the neighbouring village of Appleton lives the most
famous family of English bell-ringers, the Whites—whenever some
specialist bell-work is required in the city the Whites are called in
to advise. Forty or 50 times a year the Oxford Society of Change
Ringers swings into action—at Christ Church, New College, Magdalen, Merton, St. Mary's or St. Giles's, celebrating events as dis-
parate as Holy Innocents' Day, the election of the new Lord Mayor
or the Duke of Edinburgh's birthday. The parish church at Old
Marston is a well-known centre of bell-ringing: in 1958 its ringers
rang a world record peal of doubles, 12,600 changes in 6 hours 20
minutes, beating a record established in 1775, and if you look at
the board in the belfry you will find that the methods they have
initiated there include the Magdalen Bob, the Wadham Bob, the
Nuffield Bob, and even one named for St. Frideswide.

'Too many bells'—and their king is Great Tom, the loudest thing in Oxford. This originally hung in Osney Abbey, and was removed to Christ Church at the dissolution of the monasteries, together with its companions Dounce, Clement, Austin, Hautclere, Gabriel and John. It was recast once in the garden of the Archdeacon's house in Christ Church, but the workmen got their quantities wrong, and molten lead poured out of the Archdeacon's door along the paths of Tom Quad. In the first world war, I am told in all seriousness, Great Tom was muffled, in case its sound guided the zeppelins to Oxford; in 1965 it was muffled again to mourn the passing of Churchill, as the train carrying the great man's body steamed past the city towards his burial place at Bladon.

Most Oxford churches have a chime—the composer John Stainer wrote one for Carfax Tower—and the best Oxford music is church music. Christ Church, Magdalen and New College all have choir schools, giving their chapels choirs of high professional standard. The organist at Magdalen used to be called the Informator of the Choristers, and in Elizabethan times one incumbent took his job so seriously that he kidnapped a promising treble at Malmesbury, and brought him to Oxford in chains. William Walton was a chorister at Christ Church, and Ivor Novello at Magdalen. At Christmas time all these choirs sing carols—carols at Magdalen on Christmas Eve, with the President himself dressed up as Father Christmas, carols in the splendour of Christ Church hall, best of all carols in the Town Hall for the citizens, when the Lord Mayor and one of the cathedral choristers sing *Good King Wenceslas* in antiphony, like an antelope and a rough old bear in a fable. And on May Day, in the chilly dawn, the choir of Magdalen sings an ancient Latin anthem on the top of Magdalen Tower: the traffic is halted, the river is crowded with punts, the city is hushed, and the distant harmony rides away from that tower upon the morning wind, as though it is capsuled, and is being projected into orbit.

There is a harpsichord factory at Headington—you may see an exquisite example of its work in the chapel of Nuffield College—and an organ works in St. Clement's. Oxford indeed is full of organs. Every college chapel has one, excepting only All Souls, whose instrument was torn out at the Reformation, and has never been replaced. Magdalen's was once stolen by Oliver Cromwell, who was knowledgeable about organs: after dining in the college one evening

he had it whisked away to Hampton Court, where Milton is said
to have played it, and parts of it ended up at Tewkesbury Abbey
in Gloucestershire, where they may still be seen. Christ Church,
whose old organ was said to be one of the two or three finest in
Europe, has recently been given a new one all the same. There is
an excellent organ in the Sheldonian, and a remarkable new one
at University College, and a very grand one in the Town Hall,
and a dear little one made by William Crotch himself near the
high altar of the cathedral, and a harmonium of delightfully innocent appeal in the village church at Binsey. Jowett himself gave
the one that stands in Balliol dining-hall. The one in St. Mary's
Church was the first to be built in England when the organ-makers
left their aircraft frames and returned to their pipes after the second
world war. There has been an organ at St. Peter's in the East so
long that in the accounts for 1488 there appears a sixpenny charge
for Holy and Ive agayne Christmas and Mendyng Organs. An
Oxford organ-builder was father to Lambert Simnel, pretender to
Henry VII's throne, and one of the happiest of Oxford's epitaphs
commemorates an organist of New College: *Here Lies one blown out
of breath, Who lived a merry life and dy'd a merry death.*

In the early nineteenth century to be fond of music was considered bad form in Oxford—even unnatural among men. A Doctorate of Music was not considered a proper doctorate at all, and
holders of the degree were not even allowed to sit with their peers
of other faculties in the Sheldonian. Long before, though, the city
had become an important concert centre—the delightful little Holywell Music Rooms are claimed to be the oldest in Europe—and most
of the great performers of their day have visited the place. Handel
wrote an oratorio especially for Oxford (though the embittered antiquarian Thomas Hearne dismissed him with a sneer as 'Handel and
his lousy crew of foreign fiddlers'). Haydn was given an honorary
degree—the Bodleian still has the round he wrote as his nominal
exercise, a curiosity which makes musical sense back-to-front or
even upside-down; his 'Oxford' symphony got its nickname because
it was played in the Sheldonian to celebrate the occasion. Elizabeth
Linley refused ever to sing in public again after her elopement with
Sheridan, but she made an exception for Oxford, and sang for Lord
North when, having lost America, he became Chancellor of the University. Jenny Lind bowled Oxford over in 1848, the Beatles dined

with the Principal of Brasenose in 1964. Among the list of subscriptions to the cost of the Bodleian Library extension in the 1930s is an entry for £780. 8s. 10d., 'Proceeds of a Concert given by A. Toscanini': it was in the New Theatre, and was the only concert he ever conducted in the English provinces.

You cannot get away from music in Oxford. Even the tone-deaf sing—as a contemporary observer wrote of Dr. George Horne, an eighteenth-century President of Magdalen, 'he did not, indeed, profess to have any knowledge of Music, but in those smaller Anthems which frequent repetition had rendered familiar to his ear, he was accustomed to join with remarkable fervency'. Organs rumble through every college quadrangle, pianos echo down Holywell, transistor radios swing along the towpaths, juke-boxes thump in pubs: and when, in the middle of a recital in some exquisite college library, the quartet rests upon its bows for a minute, and you look forward to a moment's silent reverie, contemplating the old books around you, or admiring the plaster-work on the ceiling—the instant the Mozart stops, *boom*, off goes old Tom, in the first deafening stroke of 101.

One strain of Oxford music, nevertheless, I would much like to have heard. In the Ashmolean Museum there is a superb Stradivarius, in mint condition. It is called *Le Messie*, The Messiah, supposedly because the world waited for so long for such perfection to arrive, and it is kept in a glass case purely to preserve its technical details. Nobody is allowed to play it, the whole point of it being its absolutely brand-new state, at a time when most of the Stradivarius violins are fast deteriorating with use. A few years ago, however, an American violinist travelled all the way from Virginia, bringing his own bow with him, simply for the pleasure of playing a few notes upon this legendary instrument. When he was told it was held there incommunicado he burst into tears. The Keeper relented, ushered him surreptitiously into the instrument room, and locked the door: and presently listeners in the corridor outside heard a soft and marvellously melodious sound emerging, such a sound, they said, as only a Stradivarius could produce, when played by an exceptionally happy man.

So to the pleasures of the table. Oxford has always done herself well. It is an old joke that when Cardinal Wolsey founded Christ Church

the very first building he commissioned was the monumental
kitchen, and when Archbishop Laud completed the new part of St.
John's in the seventeenth century he celebrated the occasion with
a couple of banquets that cost just half as much as the buildings
themselves. 'A feast it was,' exclaimed Erasmus in 1499, trying to
express the pleasure of a dinner at Magdalen—'a feast, and not a
symposium!'

In the past most of the college kitchens had their own specialities—fondues at Brasenose, wild fowl at Christ Church, venison at
Magdalen, dressed crabs and hare soups, so the gastronome George
Saintsbury tells us, at Merton. The Oxford restaurants have seldom
been much to brag about, though there are generally two or three
in the Good Food Guide, but food at college high tables can be
excellent, and the big feasts which most colleges throw now and
then, to celebrate an anniversary or honour some antique benefactor,
are very good dinners indeed—grand dinners in the old style, with
six or seven courses, and wines for every dish, and huge platters
of meat, and delectably indigestible puddings, and no speeches.

Even more has Oxford enjoyed her drink. This is a notoriously
bibulous city. Taverns, wine-shops and drinking parties figure
prominently in its records, and on festival occasions or election days
the public conduit at Carfax used to spout free claret for the people.
At Oxford hundreds of thousands of undergraduates have been introduced to alcohol, though pubs were only officially placed in
bounds in the 1950s (nearly two centuries after the Cambridge
taverns were opened to Harvard students). The wine party was a
characteristic of nineteenth-century Oxford, and was a favourite
subject of Victorian engravings, with elegant young men lounging
about in mortar-boards smoking cheroots, and aged scouts pottering
in and out with trays of steaming mulled claret. When the German
traveller C. P. Moritz arrived in Oxford in 1782 he sat up all night
in the Mitre drinking beer with a convivial group of parsons, all
in their gowns and bands—until at dawn one of the most convivial
got up with an oath and said he must be off now, because he had
to read morning prayers at All Souls. Dr. Johnson used to claim,
remembering the chimes at midnight, that he had sometimes drunk
three bottles of port at a go when being entertained at University
College.

Often it has been carried to sottish excess, and we read of dons falling dead on the floor with brandy bottles in their hands, a Vice-Chancellor dying of too much drink while at dinner with the Keeper of the Ashmolean, a line of doctors following each other in a drunken haze round and round the Radcliffe Camera in the small hours. The Dutch admiral Cornelius van Tromp, himself a tremendous drinker, was so generously entertained by the dons when he visited Oxford in 1675 that he had to be taken home to his lodgings in a wheelbarrow. Marshal Blücher, staying at Christ Church in 1814, found himself altogether at home: he drank a bottle of brandy before breakfast, and walked it off with a walk around the meadows. The Bodleian possesses a portrait of Isaac Fuller, the eighteenth-century Oxford painter, which shows him dressed as some kind of Oriental, and is said to have been painted by himself when quite sozzled—for his talents were, as the *Dictionary of National Biography* says, 'dissipated in ignoble indulgences'. When Richard Meinerzhagen dined at New College in 1897 he was invited to drain a whole bottle of port out of a fox's head. He did so, and never drank too much again all the rest of his long life.

No fluctuations of taste or fortune have weaned Oxford from the old addiction, sometimes gay, sometimes beastly. Through Papacy and Reformation, under Cavaliers and Cromwellians, through the evangelical years of the Victorians and the libertine years between the world wars, this remained a city that took great pleasure in its cups. It is no less true today. There is probably nowhere in the world where wine goes down more copiously, more enjoyably, more knowledgeably and more beneficially than in the senior common room of one of the urbaner Oxford colleges. Some of their cellars are magnificent. The port, in particular, is likely to be excellent, and I am told that in one or two purist common rooms, even now, palates are preserved by the custom of serving only sherry before a meal.

Most of the colleges used to have their own breweries. Queen's kept theirs until 1939, and when the parishioners of St. Michael's beat their bounds on Ascension Day they are still entertained at Lincoln with a peculiar college brew called ground-ivy beer—in which ivy gathered by the college butler has been steeped for a fortnight in a muslin bag jammed in the bung-hole of the barrel. (The ceremony ends when pennies are scattered in the quadrangle for the choirboys, half of them coins which have been heated in a shovel over the fire, and which are contributed by undergraduates, so

Canon R. R. Martin says in a delightful explanatory pamphlet, in order 'to observe the conflict of avarice and apprehension among the young recipients of their bounty'.)

Much good comes from Oxford's careful use of wines—wines meticulously chosen, lovingly cherished, and drunk with a happy gusto. William Blackstone, the great lawyer, who is said to have introduced the corkscrew to this city, wrote his commentaries with a bottle of port always at his side; and for all the impact of the new brutalism, I know of no more civilized pleasure of the table than the half-hour after dinner in an Oxford common room. At All Souls you reach for the nuts with an antique wooden claw. At New College the port is circulated, because of an awkward gap beside the fireplace, on a wooden iron-wheeled trolley, designed by Warden Shuttleworth after the model of the coal tubs in the Durham mines. The claret, the port and the madeira come round in bottles hung with elegant eighteenth-century labels. The candles are not too bright, the room is panelled with old oak, your hosts are all kind attention, and as the evening wears on, and one or two of the younger dons get slightly and engagingly tight, so you begin to see how Dr. Johnson managed it.

Drinking in a college is unquestionably best, but if you cannot arrange it, you may still drink pleasurably enough outside. The inns of Oxford have not always been admired. Before the railways came, when this was one of the prime coaching centres of England, they were said to be the largest and finest in the land, but by 1860 John Murray's guide could only say of them that they were all 'bad, dirty, comfortless and very high in charges'. Today there is no really *de luxe* hotel (by international standards) in Oxford, for all the superb gas lamps outside the doors of the Randolph. There are, however, innumerable pleasant taverns. The University used to be responsible for their licensing—in 1835 licensees included Henry Bugburd of the Plasterer's Arms and Barrington Buggins of the Crown—and many of the Oxford pubs still feel like academic appendages.

The Turf, for instance, settles most comfortably beneath the walls of New College, in a little maze of mediaeval alleyways, and is famous for steak sandwiches in the garden. The White Horse is jammed between Blackwell's bookshop and Trinity College, and is excellent for the conversations of elderly college servants and undergraduates of sporting tastes. The Bear, beneath the mighty shadow

of Christ Church, was once a great coaching inn; the ostlers' rooms
are all that survive, and the pub is now chiefly known for an extraordinary collection of neckties, all presented by customers, all
mounted in glass cases, and including such rarities as the official
ties of the First National Bank of the City of New York, the Royal
Commercial Travellers' Association, and the Thames Ditton Skiff
and Punting Club.

The King's Arms, which belongs to Wadham, goes in for wine
and sandwiches, and in summer spills cheerfully into the street outside. The Victoria Arms at Marston Ferry, with a nice peeling inn-
sign of the young queen, is a popular place to punt to for breakfast
on May Morning. The Welsh Pony, near the bus station, is a haunt
of aspirant actors. The Head of the River, by Folly Bridge, occupies
an old boat-yard. Doctors go to the Royal Oak, in the Woodstock
Road. Old Oxford men, when they revisit the *alma mater*, make sentimental journeys to the Trout at Godstow, which they fondly remember as a sweet tavern lost among its gardens at the river's edge,
but which is now within sight of a huge ring road and serves steaks
on platters with wines by the glass.

And outside the influence of the University there are many old
pubs of an earthier or homelier allure—pubs that serve beef sandwiches, like the Grapes in George Street, pubs that Irishmen love,
like the New Inn or the Old Tom in St. Aldate's, pubs for assembly
line workers, like the Original Swan below Gate 12 at the Morris
works, Jamaicans' pubs, like the Angel in New Road, old bargees'
pubs, like the Jolly Waterman at Osney, trim little local pubs, like
the Rose and Crown in North Parade, proper old country pubs,
like the delightful Jolly Farmers behind the castle, rough pubs near
the canal, tough pubs at Cowley, pubs with inn-signs showing the
harbour at Port Mahon (captured by the British in 1708) or General
Eliott (defender of Gibraltar in 1779) or a bearded Duke of
Edinburgh (died 1900) or Charles II in the royal oak, or an undergraduate falling off a punt, or the bells of Osney Abbey, or a raindrop
falling on an elf, or a Proctor's Bulldog chasing an undergraduate
across Christ Church meadows, or a Cavalier in a lace collar, or
Magdalen Bridge, or a baby on an eagle's back, or horses on one
side and a plough on the other, or guns, or mitres, or crossed keys—
the arms of the Archbishop of York, which dignify the inn at South
Hinksey because in a cottage opposite a sixteenth-century Arch-

bishop was born. The sign of the White Horse in Broad Street commemorates a mounted policeman who single-handed controlled an
unruly crowd at Wembley Stadium in 1923. At the Duke of Mon-
mouth in the Abingdon Road the Duke is portrayed facing the axe-
man at the scaffold; until a few years ago he was pictured on the
other side of the sign as a death's-head in his bed—he was tucked
up thus after his execution, it is said, to deceive the populace into
supposing he had died in his sleep.

There are pubs near the railway that look as though a smile has
never once illuminated their lugubrious interiors. There are pubs
built on housing estates in the modern manner, sprayed with
hygiene, and pubs with powerful shove-halfpenny teams, whose
fortunes you may follow in the weekly shove-halfpenny column of
the *Oxford Mail*. There are pubs that burst on Friday and Saturday
evenings into a deafening exuberance of electric guitars, drums and
rock groups. It is no coincidence that a Warden of Merton first suggested the process of fermenting sugar cane that gave birth to Jamaican rum. Oxford has an instinct for liquor. As blithe old Dean
Aldrich of Christ Church wrote 250 years ago:

> *If all be true that I do think*
> *There are five reasons we should drink:*
> *Good wine—a friend—or being dry,*
> *Or lest we should be, by and by,*
> *Or any other reason why.*

Love is not a traditional Oxford pleasure, if only because the
traditions of Oxford are based upon bachelor communities. It
happens, all the same. Some of the happiest and most ineffably boring of marriages have been contracted at Oxford, when two intelli-
gent young persons of similar tastes and intellectual values have met
at a session of the Film Society, and spent the rest of their lives
together discussing the opinions of the weekly reviews. Nothing
more piquantly enlivens the lives of dons than some properly
paradoxical scandal—a swop of wives between faculties, say, or a
suggestion that the Master is paying unmistakable attentions to
a red-headed waitress at the Mitre.

Such University love stories as survive have a touching pungency
of their own. There was the romance of R. S. Hawker, for instance,

a nineteenth-century undergraduate at Pembroke, who was told one day that his father could no longer afford the fees. Hawker instantly rode to Cornwall and successfully proposed to his opulent godmother, a lady 21 years his senior called Charlotte Eliza Rawleigh I'Ans. She returned to Oxford with him, riding pillion, kept him for the rest of his University terms, and lived happily with him until her death at the age of 81 (at her funeral R. S. Hawker, by then the Vicar of Morwenstow, wore a pink brimless hat for which, he said, the ceremonies of the Eastern Church offered sanction; in the following year he married Pauline Anne Kuczynski). Or there was the splendid gesture of the Reverend Edward Drax Free, a Fellow of St. John's, who was deprived of his country living in 1830 on grounds of profanity, intoxication, impropriety, gross immorality and selling the lead off the church roof: undaunted by it all, he barricaded himself inside his rectory with his paramour, and in an ecstasy of defiant romance fought off the Bishop's bailiffs for several days, his love at his side. Or there was the noble loyalty of Maud Royden, the preacher, who fell in love with the Reverend Hudson Shaw in Oxford in 1901. Shaw was married already, but Miss Royden never looked at another man: she became Mr. Shaw's unofficial curate, and was at last able to marry him when his wife died 34 years later. But by then he was 85, and eight weeks later he died, too—dividing Miss Royden's life poignantly into 67 years as a spinster, two months as a bride and 12 years as a widow.

But except in the transient ecstasies of students, this is not really a city of sex. Its romance, so rich and seductive, is of an impotent, solitary sort. The most obsessive of Oxford's love affairs are those sad embroilments that generations of victims have contracted with the city itself, which have often dampened a fine career, or shackled a lively spirit to this beautiful but restricting place. It is as though the genius of the city dries up the sap in you, and leaves you only in an intellectual thrall, moved only by the great stone shapes of its buildings, the shift of spire against spire, wall against wall, the invitations of those gardens through the gates, the juxtaposition of the shabby with the splendid or the secret.

People are often disappointed when they set eyes on Oxford for the first time: but the pleasure of this place is like an addiction, and often summons me back to the city at the end of a day's work—

not to do anything in particular, not to see anybody or examine an inscription on a wall, but only to wander about the streets by myself, absorbing the grey velvety feel of Oxford in the evening, and eyeing her silhouettes.

THREE

Oxford is a city of many kinds, and the look of the place varies: sometimes noble, sometimes ugly, sometimes edible, sometimes hole-in-corner, sometimes full of surprises and sometimes only suggestive of things that have happened here, or great men who have passed this way.

11. The Look of It

The allure of Oxford crystallizes slowly, to the stranger in these streets. High Street, described in every other guidebook as the finest thoroughfare in Europe, looks ordinary enough at first, with its bus queues and its traffic lights. The company of towers, spires and cupolas does not feel a company at all, until you have time to stand back, drive out to the hills, and see it in context. The University seems to have no form; the city seems to have no interest; and to the colleges that greet you on every corner there is at first a cold military sameness, box-like and aloof, which makes you feel you should not stare.

The shagginess of Oxford, so intoxicating to infatuated lovers of the place, looks only unkempt to the uninitiated visitor—corners of gardens that appear to need mowing, chunks of buildings that do not seem to fit, wastelands, allotments and railway tracks around the periphery. Oxford is very far from perfect. She is essentially frayed, or perhaps rusted, and the recent restoration of many University buildings, which makes the detail look more trim than it has for generations, only makes the general seem untidier. 'From no point', says Ward Lock's guide warily of the approaches to Oxford, 'is the visitor cheated of the pleasures of anticipation, now and again artistically heightened by a certain feeling of dissatisfaction.' I have welcomed many foreigners to Oxford, and that certain feeling generally seems to be uppermost, as we emerge from the dingy faubourgs of the railway station and trail away across the canal. Oxford, wrote Moritz in 1782, 'did not ... appear to me nearly so beautiful and magnificent as Mr. Maud had described it to me during our last night's walk'. Oxford's admirers generally do overplay their hand: but take my word for it, the city grows on you with time, and demands that you survey it, not in a single candid sweep of assessment, but in several frames or modes of mind.

Take the noble first—for Oxford has an air to her, and sometimes looks properly royal. This always feels a considerable city, with wide streets like a little capital, and few places in the world can look more splendid, when you catch Oxford in the right light. There is nobility to your first glimpse of the University Church, a single admonitory spire as you drive down the Cowley Road from the factories. There is nobility to the sudden glimpses you have, everywhere on the fringes of the city, of that celebrated skyline—suddenly as you cross the ridge from Newbury, and see it golden there beyond the railway lines and the pylons, or gradually as you come down the gentle hill from Littlemore, or dramatically on a winter's day wreathed in mist beyond Port Meadow, or best of all from an aircraft on a crystal day of summer, when the university city below you looks like one great gorgeous palace, sprinkled with gardens and vineries, with dower houses and orangeries and ducks on ornamental ponds.

Christ Church is terrifically noble: big, stern, rich, certain. In 1976 its establishment comprised, ordinary undergraduates apart, 1 Visitor, 1 Dean, 6 Canons, 48 Students, 22 Honorary Students, 15 Emeritus Students, 1 College Chaplain, 13 Lecturers, 17 Research Lecturers, 6 Senior Scholars, 80 Scholars, 53 College Exhibitioners, 6 Westminster Exhibitioners, 5 Academical Clerks, 1 Precentor, 1 Organist, 1 Schoolmaster, 6 Singing Men and 8 Choristers. Tom Quad is not only the biggest quadrangle in Oxford, but also much the grandest: with Wren's fine tower on the west side, and the cathedral spire, perhaps the oldest in England, on the east—on the south the superb hall, on the north the little archway that leads beneath Killcanon Tower to the great library and Peckwater quadrangle. Christ Church was founded by Cardinal Wolsey, and refounded by Henry VIII, and it remains a structure fit for prelates and noblemen. I once walked into its precincts on a Saturday afternoon and found a wedding reception rumbustiously in progress in the hall—with a haze of cigar smoke screening the portraits, a hubbub of shrill chatter and laughter, and eight little bridesmaids, all in white, tumbling about the great quad outside. It was as though I had walked into some dukely household, to the nuptials of a Spanish heiress.

Noble in a different kind is Magdalen, which is not so much regal as matriarchal—a setting for some voluptuous chatelaine, all pearls, roses from the east garden and instructions for the cook. Magdalen has a deer park. Magdalen has a river walk along the Cherwell, and 100 acres of meadow and garden. Magdalen has a gracious New Building, classical beside the Grove, and the quaint old remains of its grammar school, all crumbled and picturesque. Above all, Magdalen has one of the best towers in Europe, high above its bridge—not quite square, gently tapering to its eight pinnacles, out of true with its college and its chapel, but still so benignly autocratic that James I called it 'the most absolute building in Oxford'. The best way to see this beautiful structure is to walk down Rose Place, the little alley opposite, after dark any fine night. The lane is a cul-de-sac, and behind the locked gates at its end lie Christ Church meadows, dark, green and secret. Beside you there rise the gloomy cypresses and monkey-puzzle trees of the Botanical Gardens. A few yards away the ceaseless traffic is thundering down the High, but where you stand there is an isolated hush: and when you turn around and look back through the trees, there stands the great tower against the sky, gently lit by the street lights and the headlamps, looking wonderfully serene above the restless city, and apparently phosphorescent.

Oxford is not a soldier's city—she is much too slapdash and irregular. From Christ Church meadows, however, she can be seen in a fine military posture, on guard. You must juggle a bit with this view, and so position yourself that through the elms of the Broad Walk the tower of Merton chapel is roughly centred. Then you will see Oxford as a walled city, stony and defiant. To the left stands the gaunt cathedral, its rose window like a huge observing eye; to the right is Magdalen Tower, which really was a watch-post in the Civil War; in the middle is the grey cluster of Merton, looking squat and strong; and all along the foreground runs the city wall itself, with its bastions and its high walk for sentries. From this spot alone you may imagine Oxford as she was before the suburbs sprouted all around her—a fortified city of towers, rising as abruptly and dramatically from this English valley as an Ávila or a Segovia in Castile.

At the other end of the city is Keble College, which the Victorian architect William Butterfield built in a regular splurge of nobility, striping his walls with bricks of different colours, and sinking his quadrangle below the level of the streets to discourage riotous assembly. Only in our own times has Keble come into its own. Ruskin loathed it, even giving up his daily walks in the Parks because of it, and for years it was one of the jokes of Oxford, which clever undergraduates habitually took their parents to laugh at. Today its colours still offend most people, but its splendours of proportion are recognized at last, and are even said to have influenced the design of the new Churchill College at Cambridge. Keble was in fact shoddily built, for all the practical genius of its architect, but it looks like a piece of capable engineering, as though Brunel knocked it off between a railway and a suspension bridge; and with its huge humped chapel towering above its quadrangles, it seems to stand in loyal homage to God and Queen Victoria, side by side.

Noble lastly is the glittering modern building of St. Catherine's, designed by the Dane Arne Jacobsen with a lordly disdain for the environment, and built in a series of enormous rectangles. It is a severe, uncompromising thing, with its shivery expanses of concrete and its bare portentous hall, like an assembly shed in a munitions plant, or a trolls' gymnasium. Its vast windows are necessarily covered with net curtains. Its rosebeds are dotted with odd isolated walls, like baffles to obscure the noise of the jets, and its brick is a bilious yellow. It has clearly not grown up in these parts. But seen through the willows across the damp water-meadow called Mesopotamia, this hulking, crouching, alien structure has a truly exciting grandeur—not so calm or sublime as its predecessors, but possibly a little evil, like a younger son returned unannounced from foreign places, and waiting to poison the heir.

A few disfigurements next, for there is salt to every Oxford strawberry. 'Whatever else is said of them,' Ruskin is supposed to have observed of the Meadows Buildings at Christ Church, which several generations after his almost unanimously detested, 'nobody will venture to deny that they are beautiful.' It was one of his sillier *dicta*, for Oxford is a showcase of changing tastes, and there is no new building that does not seem hideous to somebody. 'Be you mad, Sir?' expostulates a don in a skit by Lewis Carroll attacking a proposed extension to Christ Church. 'Why, this is the very climacteric and coronal of all our architectural aspirations!' But when, a century later, St. John's College made a minor addition to their premises, the undergraduates of the University Design Society described it in print as 'a lumpish development, unimpeachable congealed traditionalism, unalleviated by some quirkish variations'.

Which buildings you think ugliest depends upon your age. If you are very old indeed, you are probably still fuming about the façade built in the High Street by Oriel College in 1909, which most of us scarcely notice nowadays, but used to be thought an absolute outrage. If you are in your sixties, nothing will reconcile you to the Bodleian extension at the end of Broad Street, which looks like a well-equipped municipal swimming baths, and replaced a nice corner of jostling old houses in the late 1930s. Middle age may be marked, in the Oxford amateur, by an almost irresistible desire to blow up the Waynflete Building erected by Magdalen College at the eastern end of Magdalen Bridge, and you may be fairly sure that your youth is over if you wake up one morning and find that James Stirling's mechanist Florey Building, almost next door to it, is *not* after all the best building in Oxford since the Sheldonian.

Whatever your age, you are likely to find the commercial middle of Oxford—Cornmarket, George Street, Queen Street, the Westgate shopping complex—ugly in a way peculiar to twentieth-century England. It owes its character to the special status of these islands, half-way between Europe and America. Part of it is old still, part of it very new, and in a half-hearted way it has been turned into a pedestrian precinct—buses and taxis may knock you down, but not the private motorist. It is as though some Illinois Main Street has been superimposed upon a mediaeval European thoroughfare, and it reflects a hybrid culture that exists nowhere else. Here, cheek-by-jowl with the old-school tailors and the leather shops, all the paraphernalia of mass Anglo-American commercialism thrives—always crowded, always noisy, with that special smell of Woolworth's seeping out into the street, and trading stamps all over. It could be a tart, or an entertaining mixture, but it comes out harsh, and gives a garish abrasive taint to the centre of the city.

There are less specific disfigurements almost everywhere: the hangdog ugliness of suburbia, rank upon rank towards the countryside; the ugliness of the traffic signs, plastered in their hundreds so insensitively across the city; the dingy remains of the slums; the ugliness of the traffic, clogged and sweaty at Carfax; the nightmare

ugliness of car parks, so blank and lifeless, like dry scabs on the
urban surface; the ugliness of the dreary bus station at Gloucester
Green, with the lonely vigilants sitting with their carrier bags in
the waiting room, and pale tired faces glimpsed through the steamy
windows of the Cheltenham coach.

But through it all the spark of Oxford shows, in small surprises,
hidden buildings, or views that seem, to judge by the tight clutter
of buildings all around, altogether unattainable.

One such little miracle occurs behind the former City Church,
now the library of Lincoln College. If you walk among the gravestones through the old churchyard you will find a secluded glade,
as still and separate as something in a forest, with a distinct atmosphere of private collusion, as though you are in honour bound not
to tell anyone else about it. Pleasant buildings in the Georgian style
surround this clearing, stone steps lead you from one level to
another, the church shuts it off behind, and if you are lucky you
may chance to see the Rector of Lincoln emerge from his house,
deep in the proceedings of the Hebdomadal Council, to take a turn
around his lawn—for all the world like Prospero beside his cell, with
you a Caliban among the tombstones.

Or if you walk down Queen's Lane, off the High, you will see
a small and unpretentious doorway in an old and not very interesting
façade. Turn into it, pass the neat little lodge that stands inside its
corridor, and in a step or two you will find yourself in the old part
of St. Edmund Hall, the most exquisite of the small Oxford quadrangles—a college in miniature, with creepers over its walls, a well,
and the complete appendages of a college, chapel, hall, rooms and
all, grouped intimately around a breakfast-table square. Perhaps
somebody is playing the piano, and the air is thick with pop or
Chopin. Perhaps a group of undergraduates is laughing boisterously around the well. Perhaps a pair of dons emerges from one
doorway, hands in pockets, to disappear talking hard into another.
All seems reduced to a lesser proportion, and if you felt like Caliban
behind the old City Church, here you are more like Gulliver.

Happiest of all is the surprise that awaits you in the Fellows'
garden at Exeter College (closed to the public, so a notice says, at
four o'clock each day). This is best seen in winter, and preferably—
for Oxford prohibitions are meant to be ignored—somewhere around

five, when the dusk is closing in and the lights are coming on. You must walk the length of the garden first, and climb the steps at the bottom, and presently you will find yourself sitting on a seat on the top of a wall, to survey the most satisfying of Oxford compositions. Below you there lies Radcliffe Square, the focus of the University, like the stage of a theatre. It is dramatically alive. The street lights glint on the shiny cobblestones, and the handle-bars of the bicycles in their racks. Everywhere there is movement: undergraduates hastening towards the Bodleian, porters looking out of Brasenose gate, the vicar of St. Mary's, cassocked and belted, talking to a parishioner in his porch. The great dome of the Radcliffe Camera almost fills this stage; the balcony of St. Mary's looks down like a royal box; and even as you watch from your position in the wings the lights go up in the Bodleian and the Codrington Library across the way, and the gilded crests spring into brilliance on the ceiling of Duke Humfrey's, and the whole scene is diffused in a glow of theatrically sumptuous learning.

Do not stay too long. Oxford rules are flexible, but there may be something chilling to the manner of the porter, when he courteously approaches you through the garden, and asks with innocent interest if you are a Fellow of this College.

Sometimes the look of Oxford seems to demand more than sight. It is the green that does it, and the age, and you feel you would like to stroke the scene before you, or swim in it.

The garden of New College has such an effect on me. This is the most perfect of the Oxford gardens, and easily goes to one's head. It is bounded by a slab of the old city wall, with a couple of bastions for effect. There are herbaceous borders around the edge, big rolling lawns and some glorious chestnuts, and in the very heart of it all, covered with trees and thick grass, stands a carefully untended eighteenth-century mound. Splendid wrought-iron gates separate this garden from the main college buildings, the sinewy tower of St. Peter's in the East peers perpetually over its wall, and if you look through the archway at the end you will see a large abstract sculpture by Barbara Hepworth, neatly framed in the yard beyond.

A more tactile allure is that of the old Radcliffe Observatory, now a medical laboratory (the Observatory itself has moved to South

Africa). This is one of those compact buildings, like models, that you feel you would like to pick up and place upon a table. It is a greatly enlarged copy of the Tower of the Winds at Athens, upon which Andronicus of Cyrrhus erected the first of all weathercocks, and the Regency complex around Beaumont Street was originally intended to form a horizontal frame for its vertical grandeur. It has lovely tall windows, and open terraces like patios at Cliveden, and is decorated with zephyrs and signs of the zodiac. At its side stands the Astronomer's House, in its lee is a hidden garden, and high on its roof, beside a bronze Atlas and his globe, the little black weather-balls busily whirl—paying tribute, 2,000 years late, to old Andronicus and his original revolving Triton.

Many people find Worcester College garden sensually satisfying. It is the only garden in the city with a lake, and is sensitively designed in the English patrician manner, park-like and private. It adjoins, however, the dismal old canal and the railway lines, and looks across the college playing fields to the drear tower of St. Barnabas, the parish church of Jericho. Its delights are therefore punctuated by the melancholy clanging and knockings of shunting yards, and it looks blighted at the edges. To strangers this effect is depressing, and makes the garden feel besieged by squalor, but to the true Oxford *aficionado* the mixture has just the proper indigenous tang. Worcester garden does not much work up any of my own appetites: but some of the waterfowl upon the lake, especially the pintail duck and some of the plumper ornamental geese, do look as though they might roast to perfection.

For sometimes they are gastronomic instincts that the look of Oxford excites in you. There is a little place called the Nuns' Garden, which belongs to Queen's College and is reached by following your nose through the classical formalities of the two college quadrangles: this quiet retreat, hidden beside the High, suggests all kinds of herbs, rosemary, thyme and marjoram, and is like a speckle of sweet spice upon a curry. The magnificent garden of St. John's, surveyed by the most splendid Renaissance block in Oxford, is like some diplomatic banquet, napkinned and white-tied. The new quadrangle of Pembroke, which has been formed by blocking the ancient thoroughfare called Beef Lane, and prettying up its various houses until they look like some felicitously contrived exhibition set, has a rather sickly, caramel sort of appeal. The bright new boathouses are like so many meringues along the river. The superb trees of Oxford, everywhere green, calm and friendly, are the freshest of garnishings.

And the leper hospital of St. Bartlemas is a gourmet's delicacy that hardly anyone tastes. It stands in a cul-de-sac off the Cowley Road, beside the playing fields of Oriel College. Once it was a haven for lepers passing through Oxford, with a holy well for cures, and a Warden for charity, and today you may still see its buildings in their fourteenth-century pattern. Here are the lodgings for poor lepers, now a row of dons' houses. Here is the Warden's house, rose-embowered. Here is the little whitewashed chapel, with a high-pitched roof in a garden. All is fragrant and meditative, and seems peopled by gentle ghosts. It is an ivory enclave, fastidiously preserved. It leaves a lingering after-taste, the very antidote to everything cloying or creamy: like oysters, in fact.

'And that sweet city with her dreaming spires,' wrote Matthew Arnold. 'She needs not June for beauty's heightening.' Nor does she. The particular magic of Oxford rides out the seasons. New York is brightest in the spring, Venice is nastiest in the winter, London looks best on a morning of high summer: but all four seasons suit Oxford, and each enhances the look of her in a different way.

No!

I once went for a walk around Christ Church meadows on the morning of Boxing Day. It was a proper Oxford winter morning, with a thin crust of soggy snow along the skyline, and a damp mist hanging everywhere. The meadows felt downright primaeval, so subdued and muffled were the trees, so empty was everything, so silent: I almost expected to see the thin smoke of a neolithic fire rising above the elms. Down on the river four very cold river men, huddled in waterproofs, were hammering piles into the river bed from a barge, their breath in clouds around them. Propped against a tree beside the Cherwell two elderly Irish lovers, looking as though they had been out all night, interrupted their embrace to wish me the top of the mornin'. I met nobody else, not even a swan on the river, and when I emerged into the Broad Walk, to see the city there in front of me, Oxford looked like some marvellous dead metropolis, long since abandoned in its valley, and left to rot in the fog.

In the spring the precision of Oxford best shows, when the trees are still half bare, and the outlines of buildings show clearly through the branches. These are the clearest days, between the dank winter and the languid summer, and old Oxford seems a kind of filigree— all chiselled pinnacles, corners, the laced meshwork of trees, the elaborate tracery of windows, spires and domes etched brilliantly against the sky, as though they have been engraved with acid. This is when the work gets done. In the spring you really feel you have the hang of things in Oxford: suddenly the shape of that thesis on Papuan Folk-Myths becomes apparent, a First in Greats is clearly well within your grasp, and you even ring up the carpenter to see if he can't make a start on the garage door.

Hurry! As soon as summer comes, and those clear-cut edges are lost in foliage, procrastination steals in. Then Oxford looks all hedonism, her green so green, her gold so gleaming, the tourists strolling happily through her gardens, her awnings, tents, hammocks, punts, inflatable mattresses and little yachts on trailers. The Cowley works close for their annual holidays, sun-blinds shade the shop windows of the High, and even the trains seem to pant and complain past Hinksey, as they make the effort to break away. In recollection every Oxford summer day is warm, bright and sunlit, like the pictures of Oxford on the old postcards. Summer is more summery here than anywhere else I know; not hotter, certainly not sunnier, but more like summers used to be, in everyone's childhood memories.

But the year does not die with the autumn. Some cities go nostalgic as the leaves begin to fall. In Oxford the opposite happens, for October is the beginning of the University year, and as the first cold snaps come in, so do the undergraduates. There are trunks everywhere, and shouts of recognition, and bespectacled freshmen buying fountain pens. Porters' lodges are busy as railway stations. Noisy sports cars race down echoing lanes. Sunburnt dons talk about Greece on street corners, and there is a smell of dubbin on new football boots. Autumn is the most powerful of the Oxford seasons. It feels as though the city is being recharged—as though, while the evenings shorten and the first winter fogs assemble over the river, the whole place is stocking up with energy.

This is a city of very strong character—too rooted to be much affected by a fall of leaves, a change of temperature or a cold in the nose. If you loathe it in January, you will detest it in July. If you are a devotee anyway, you will agree with another poet, F. W. Faber, who expressed his own unchanging admiration for this 'city of all seasons' in the breathless apostrophe:

> *Coy city, that doth swathe thy summer self*
> *In willow lines and elmy avenue,*
> *Each winter comes, and brings some hidden pelf,*
> *Buttress or Cross or gable out to view!*

I had to look up pelf in the dictionary, and found it to mean, at least in Faber's sense, treasure, wealth or riches. Oxford *is* a little coy about her possessions, and often keeps them cannily hidden away. She is not generally spectacular. There is nothing here so instantly breathtaking as the Backs at Cambridge, or the sweep of Princes Street in Edinburgh, let alone Park Avenue or the Golden Horn. This is a stippled city—'towery city and branchy between towers,' as Gerard Manley Hopkins thought, 'cuckoo-echoing, bell-swarmèd, lark-charmèd, rook-racked, river-rounded'. It is a city built up of dabs and details, like a pointillist painting.

The style of Oxford is reserved, and the scale is domestic. The famous curve of High Street is, as Lewis Mumford has pointed out, only the natural curve that any pedestrian follows, as he leaves his footprints in the dew of an open field. The covered market is essentially a family affair, with neat parallel arcades offering you a convenient short cut to Marks and Spencer's, a jolly red pillar-box in the central intersection, and a quaint Victorian hand-trolley, municipal property, propped in a corner like a beloved ancestral toy. The sight-seers looking down upon Radcliffe Square from the balcony of St. Mary's do not look dwarfed or overawed up there: on the contrary, they look only like guests in the gallery of some lavish drawing-room, or minstrels tuning up. Sometimes this smallness opens briefly into a Tom Quad or a great garden, but soon it closes in again, the lanes narrow and the walls grow higher, and you are back in the closet of Oxford, her strangely cramped and reluctant fascination.

A Gothic irregularity is one of the keys to it. If you stand with your back to Balliol's main gate, and examine the rows of buildings on the other side of Broad Street, you will see how romantically varied is the façade of Oxford. To the left is the Palladian block of the Clarendon Building, then Wren's peculiar Sheldonian, then the florid classicism of the Old Ashmolean; a slab of baronial follows, and the unyielding concrete of Exeter's modern building, and then a Georgian block with two oriel windows and a little tower; two sort of generally mediaeval structures next, a Victorian house with gables, more mediaeval, more Georgian, a kind of mock-Tudor chalet, a pseudo-Georgian shop, and finally a big building of the 1930s, at the junction with Cornmarket, for which I am at a loss to suggest any style at all. All these variegated structures stand there side by side, running into one another, and long since moulded into a patchwork unity.

Sometimes the allure is suggestively aged, as in the alley called Magpie Lane, off the High, along whose cobbled pavement, after dark, people's footfalls echo as in Venice; or in New College cloisters, as silent as the grave, with an ilex in the middle and an antique fire engine in a dark corner; or down the canyon of New College Lane, which Max Beerbohm called 'a grim ravine', and which creeps surreptitiously from Catte Street towards the High. The passages that lead off the south side of High Street feel infinitely musty and antique, with snatches of half-timber here and there, wooden staircases and rickety outhouses, skylights, fire escapes, the brass name plates of solicitors' offices and typists' coats hanging on wire coat-hangers through dusty Dickensian windows. From the south side of Holywell an alley unexpectedly strikes off into a little warren of mediaeval cottages that lies beneath the bulk of New College. It looks more like Cornwall than Oxfordshire. There are bright-painted cottage gates, and cobbled yards, and a crooked little fairy-tale lane, meandering through this manikin's Oxford, which leads between back gardens to the more boisterous pleasures of the Turf (itself, secreted away beneath those frowning walls, a proper pub for djinns or wizards).

Sometimes a modern architect conjures up just the same feeling of intricate reticence. Powell and Moya achieved such a wrinkled *tour de force* with the celebrated set of rooms they inserted into the structure of Brasenose in 1961, apparently lowering the building by helicopter among the quadrangles. It is faced with Portland stone, with lead slabs and a small shuttered lawn, and it looks at once monastic and faintly Japanese. Its staircases are scrubbed, its external lights are concealed under the pavement, and the whole building is squeezed into a tight corner behind the main fabric of

the college, where a junk yard used to be. You reach it down a corridor from Brasenose's inner quadrangle. A bare blank wall is the
first thing you see, and when you leave you will be hard put to place
a shape upon the memory: but the impact of this building, angular,
awkward and cramped, is a properly Oxford experience, true to a
diffident but urbane tradition.

And this taste for diminutive, domestic complexity infuses some
of the central buildings of Oxford, keeping even its grandest institutions down to a family size. The cathedral, for instance, is the
shortest in England (155 feet long, compared with Winchester at
530), and the prison is the smallest (120 cells, compared with Worm-
wood Scrubs' 1,258). For a time the passage at the north end of the
Bodleian was used as a pig market: and there is to the space behind
the Sheldonian, even now, almost a farmyard air. Straw on the
ground would suit it. The buildings are grouped about it in a
homely, practical way—the Clarendon Building like an estate office,
the Sheldonian like a barn, the Divinity School for deep litters and
the Old Ashmolean for the farmer's draughty house. It all fits
together neatly and compactly—like a toy farm, perhaps, where
tractors drop no oil on the path, and fences never need mending.

Yet it is a place full of meaning, where English Parliaments have
assembled, heroes and geniuses have collected honorary degrees,
and the whole history of the University has been enacted. For the
drama of Oxford you must look beyond her appearances, and remember, as you pass through her aloof and modest pageantry, all
that this city has meant to the world. These are the streets, so
Flecker said, where the great men go. The most famous sight in
Oxford is the grand sweep of the High, as you walk slowly westward
from Magdalen Bridge: but as its gentle curve unfolds itself, so
calm, so generous, as pinnacle succeeds pinnacle, Queen's gives way
to All Souls, St. Mary's to All Saints—as the stern façades inspect
your passage and the noble spire of the University Church austerely
welcomes you—as you glimpse the big dome of the Radcliffe down
Catte Street, and the grim façade of the Bodleian behind—as you
feel yourself swept onwards towards the noisy vortex of Carfax,
where the old tower stands guard above Penniless Bench, so you
will realize that in such a city the look of it is only ancillary to the
genius, and that all these grey and golden stones are merely Oxford's
index.

FOUR

The genius of this learned city has Christian origins, and propagates itself in individualism, fantasy and endless invention. Oxford overflows with queer and wonderful possessions: and though there is something cloying to her atmosphere, something which discourages poets and deadens inspiration, still there is scarcely a human activity that she has not enriched—from the art of nonsense to the ruling of the world.

12. Learning

My favourite Oxford street sign appears on a road near the Donnington Bridge. 'Chatham Road,' it says, 'Formerly Pitt Road.' They really changed the name because they found the Pitts had been honoured once too often in the city, but the sign's suggestion of historical awareness is very appropriate to Oxford. This is a city of learning, and scholarship seeps into most of its activities—chiefly excepting, I fear, the making of cars at Cowley, where the feeblest smatter of classical education would have named the Mini-Minor the Minimus. Newton, Herschel, Franklin, Aristotle and Luther all have their streets in Oxford: there is even an alley called Logic Lane.

In Oxford there is almost nothing you cannot learn. You can learn to fly a helicopter at Oxford Airport, or to be an airline pilot. You can learn pottery at the College of Technology, or foremanship at the Pressed Steel Training Centre, or skiing at the dry-ski school in St. Clement's, or shorthand and *savoir-faire* at the smart secretarial schools, or you can enrol in one of the several institutions, commonly named for lesser saints, which are housed in Victorian villas in north Oxford, advertise themselves in Olde English letteryng, offer tuition in anything from Anglo-Saxon to trigonometry, and often confuse poor strangers who assume them to have been founded by Alfred the Great. (I once met a Persian in the street who had come all the way from Teheran to enter such an Oxford establishment, and who was disconcerted to find that its entire academic plant apparently fitted into a single semi-detached house. 'Where, then, should I inquire to enter that college today as a student?' he asked me, pointing hopefully to Lady Margaret Hall.)

There are so many schools in Oxford that the Banbury Road, at half past four any term-time afternoon, is almost a parody of the happiest days of one's life—a cavalcade of gym tunics, cellular shirts, blazers, black stockings, house ribbons, satchels and mothers distractedly disengaging babies from gear levers. Rose Macaulay was at Oxford High School. Kenneth Grahame was at St. Edward's, an independent boys' school housed grandiosely in north Oxford, with a tunnel beneath the Woodstock Road to its playing fields, and a taste for aviation—at school celebrations they often have a fly-past of light aircraft, all flown by boys of the sixth form. T. E. Lawrence was at the City of Oxford School, where a plaque was unveiled by Churchill himself to commemorate 'the generous majesty of his nature': the family home was 2 Polstead Road, in north Oxford, and in its garden still stands Lawrence's own little bungalow, at the bottom of the lawn.

The Dragon School, where they play football with several balls, to keep all the players warm and happy, is a preparatory school with a daunting reputation for brain-power, and a personality so pervasive that when its old boys grow up to be Hugh Gaitskells or John Betjemans, you can still see its stamp upon them. Summerfields, along the road, is a famous breeding-ground for Eton, going in for admirals, judges and Mr. Harold Macmillan. Wherever you look in Oxford, at the right time of day, there seems to be a school bus, a crocodile, or a small harassed boy on a bicycle, three minutes late already, and desperately conjugating under his breath the future perfect of *rego*.

On the edge of the University, too, all sorts of independent research flourishes—inquiries into stuttering, or metal fatigue, or the orchids of the Chiltern country, or telepathy, or the mediaeval topography of the city itself. Culture rubs off almost everywhere. The *Oxford Mail* is one of the more civilized of the provincial evening newspapers, Radio Oxford is among the less abrasive, I am told, of the local radio stations, the Oxford County Council actually subsidizes the admirable Museum of Modern Art, in Pembroke Street. Even the Post Office paints the St. Giles telephone boxes grey instead of red, not to clash with the antiquity. The inscription on the fire engine in New College cloisters is written in Latin, and so are some of the *graffiti* you find chalked on the walls of Oxford lavatories.

Some Oxford businesses acquire an almost collegiate flavour, after busying themselves in this city long enough. Blackwell's the booksellers are popularly supposed to have their own domestic

1. Oxford: the ancient centre

2. High Street: clockwise from the front, the Examination Schools, the spire of the University Church, the dome of the Radcliffe Camera, the pinnacles of All Souls and, in the foreground, cupola'd Queen's College

3. The look of it: north-eastwards from Boar's Hill

4. In the covered market

5. The Arts End, Bodleian Library: seventeenth century

6. Port Meadow

7. The first M.G., 1925

8. The 'Brasen Nose' of Brasenose College; a twelfth- or early thirteenth-century
bronze knocker, now hanging in the College hall

bursar, and when they decided in 1960 to analyse one day's business in the shop, they found they had been asked for the Bible in Georgian, a catalogue of the finger rings in the South Kensington Museum, Tertullian's *Treatise against Praxeas*, the music of *Oh Dear, What Can the Matter Be?*, 'a good Argentine literary periodical', a list of books on the Quechua language and the Dutch National Anthem. Gills the ironmongers, who live in one of those alleys off the High, substantiate their claim to be the oldest ironmongers in Great Britain (established 1530) with a thoughtful little historical pamphlet, containing a family genealogy and a list of important events that have occurred in the lifetime of the firm—like the Gunpowder Plot, Votes for Women and the Invention of Green's First Chain Drive Mower.

The Morrell family, who have been synonymous with Oxford beer for 150 years, and were vintners here in Elizabethan times, also gave their name to Lady Ottoline Morrell, that celebrated literary chatelaine of the 1930s, whose house outside Oxford was a rendezvous for the liveliest artists and writers of the day. Pergamon the publishing house, whose offices are in a mansion at the top of Headington Hill, with peacocks in the garden—Pergamon was described to me by its founder, a former Socialist M.P., as 'one of the world's largest centres of dissemination of the latest results of research in the fields of science, technology and engineering'—research from 100 nations, he added, warming to his theme, representing a total cost of £2,000,000,000, with their own man in Moscow and a mass of matter from the United States. In the upstairs premises of Rosenthal's the antiquarian bookseller, above a toy shop in the Broad, there sat until his death in 1974 the scholar who bought the fourth-century Codex Sinaiticus from the Russians in 1933: they wanted £1,000,000 for it, but he beat them down in several years of inexorable negotiation, and the manuscript is now thought to have been the best of all book bargains—the Russians so badly needed foreign currency in the thirties that they let it go for £100,000.

All these activities revolve around the presence of the University in Oxford, which makes hard thought a local stock-in-trade. 'Brain Basil' is Oxford schoolboy slang for a clever boy, and in this city he comes two a penny. Nobody here is surprised to find that you earn your living with your mind. The bones of the Cetiosaurus in the Museum were discovered and identified by a local watchmaker, and in 1964 the chairman of the Freemen of the City was Lewis Carroll's successor as Mathematical Tutor at Christ Church. I know of no pleasanter place to write a book about. Almost nobody resents questions, and nobody at all is surprised to be asked. One drear and foggy winter morning, so thick that you could scarcely see across Carfax, I happened to be in the Fellows' garden at Merton when I heard footsteps along the path outside, in Christ Church meadows. I pushed my head through the railings, to see who could be out for exercise on such a day, and poised there like a gargoyle, with my nose through the iron bars, I was just in time to see the Warden of New College striding out of the haze. I must have been a disconcerting grotesque, suspended so eerily above him, but he was not - taken aback, for he knew I was writing a book. 'Ah,' he simply said, 'pursuing your investigations, I see'—and with a measured tap of his walking stick he melted into the mist.

For Oxford is built upon books—books being read, books being written, books being published, books in the dozen bookshops of the city, books littered through a labyrinth of libraries. The Clarendon Building, now the headquarters of the University, was actually built with the royalties from the Earl of Clarendon's *History of the Rebellion*—the author is portrayed in a statue on the west wall, contemplating with satisfaction what I have always enviously assumed to be his sales report.

Every Oxford college has its own library, chiefly for the needs of its own members, and between them all they add up to an assembly of books such as only the very greatest of universities can possess. They represent every stage in library technique, from Merton's, which is one of the best surviving examples of a mediaeval library, to the microfilm efficiency of St. Catherine's—whose books, one feels, ought really to be chosen to suit the architecture, like the dining-room chairs. Some college libraries are magnificently housed, like Christ Church's in its huge classical pavilion, or Queen's in the most gorgeous room in Oxford, or the Codrington Library at All Souls, from whose stacks busts of old college worthies brood in white marble down the generations. Almost all contain valuable rarities, and Oxford is full of specialist book collections— collections so scattered, in so many separate libraries, that they are covered by no general catalogue, and it is almost impossible for the stranger to discover where they all are. There are Shakespeare First Folios all over the place. Queen's College has Garrick's copy, and another, one of the last to be privately owned, is to be found in a secluded Victorian house chiefly decorated, as it happens, with old travel posters.

My own favourite college collection is the Allestree library at Christ Church. This was bequeathed by a seventeenth-century canon to be used in perpetuity by the Regius Professors of Divinity, and it remains unaltered to this day—the complete theological collection of a Restoration scholar. It is kept in a cold bare chamber above the cloisters, into which there has been inserted a washbasin for the use of the man in the rooms next door—his shaving brush stands beside the mirror, and on the window-sill he keeps, apparently to read while he washes, a file of the University *Gazette*. Everything else is just as Dr. Allestree left it. The books are fragrant with age, beatitudes and old leather, there is a little rickety table for writing sermons at, and through the windows you may look down into the cloisters beneath, watch the chaplains hastening into the south door of the cathedral, or project seventeenth-century injunctions upon passing heretics. For years the Regius Professor was the only man allowed to enter this magically evocative little room: now, I suspect, nobody uses Dr. Allestree's books from one ecumenical council to the next, unless the man with the washbasin, tiring of his lecture lists, reaches out a spare hand to thumb through an ordinal, or remind himself about the codicils to the Decrees of Trent.

Greater by far, though, than any college collection is the Bodleian, the central library of the University, which is named for a sixteenth-century benefactor, Sir Thomas Bodley. This is one of the three English copyright libraries—with the British Museum and the Cambridge University Library, it is entitled to a free copy of any book published in Britain (it does not want them all, and its selections are passed to a copyright agent in London, who sends the books down to Oxford once a fortnight by truck). Though perennially hard up, it is thus in a condition of ceaseless growth. It began modestly in the room now called Duke Humfrey's library, after Henry V's brother, Duke of Gloucester—a noble oblong chamber decorated with hundreds and hundreds of University crests, and still containing its original bookstacks. Then it extended itself into wings, and then into the lecture rooms of the old Examination Schools, downstairs. In the nineteenth century it acquired the great dome of the Radcliffe Camera, in the square outside. In the twentieth they tunnelled vaults underneath, housing thousands more books in sliding iron bookstacks: the reason you may not walk upon the grass in Radcliffe Square is the fact that there is only nine inches of soil between your feet and the roof of the library beneath.

It was still too small, and in the 1930s they extended it the other way, driving a tunnel beneath Broad Street and building the huge New Bodleian on the other side. A mechanical conveyor, modelled on the machines at the General Post Office in London, takes books from one side to the other, and queer clanking devices spew them out at unloading points in different parts of the building, rather as though some huge mechanical man is lying supine there beneath, occasionally pushing a dictionary up a shaft with a long tinny finger. Even so, some of the Bodleian's collections—on science, on law, on Eastern art, on imperial and American history—are kept elsewhere in Oxford, requiring a short walk to get there: and mechanical distributors or no, the library still provides its readers with knives, to cut the pages with.

It is a vast and baffling organism—some of it very modern, some desperately archaic. It is said to contain more than 3,000,000 books, including 50,000 manuscripts and 15,500 charters, and is partly built up, like a huge mosaic, out of dozens of separate collections, long since absorbed into the whole—Douce's Collection, Gough's Collection, Laud's Collection, the collection formed by Matheo Canonici, an eighteenth-century Venetian Jesuit, or the Oppenheimer Collection of Hebrew manuscripts, assembled by an eighteenth-century Chief Rabbi of Prague, and now forming part of one of the great Jewish collections in the world. Wandering through the Bodleian's corridors, vaults and tunnels is rather like inspecting the war chambers of Gibraltar, or Franco's subterranean cathedral outside Madrid. There are so many books, stored in so many different ways, in so many different parts of so many buildings, some facing this way, some that, some in manuscript, some carved in Tibetan characters on wood-blocks, some engraved in Pali characters on metal, some wrapped around with gorgeous stuffs, some so heavy it takes two people to remove them from a shelf, some priceless, some worthless, from the only known copy of the first edition of Shakespeare's *Venus and Adonis* to the Irish cross-channel time-tables on the open shelves of the Camera—there is such a staggering arsenal of books that the whole place seems to hum with knowledge, and vibrate to the movement of its conveyor belts. They have been producing a new catalogue for the Bodleian on and off since 1939: by 1978 they had, so the Keeper of the Catalogue assured me, 'definitively finished the letter T'.

In the early days of Oxford University books were so coveted that they had to be chained to their shelves. To see how the currency has declined you have only to glance at one of the requisition trays at the Bodleian. I once looked idly through the contents of such a tray to see what books readers were wanting that afternoon, and the first four volumes I found were *The Toys' Picnic Painting Book*; *Das Stumme Spiel im Deutschen Drama*; James Hesler's *America and the Weimar Republic*; and *An Analytical Index to the Series of Records Known as the Remembrencia, Preserved among the Archives of the City of London, 1579 to 1664*.

So complex is the structure of this library that only initiates can make head or tail of its catalogue references, and its messenger boys take months just to learn where to look for an item. Topographical books, for instance, are usually listed under the key-word Gough: this is because a topographical library bequeathed by the anti-quarian Richard Gough at the beginning of the nineteenth century forms the core of the Bodleian's topographical collection now. If you have a mind to consult the Harvard edition of the works of James I, you will find it listed as 24817 d. 122=S. Sir William M'Intosh's study of marine anelids, published in Cape Town in 1904, is 189469 dc 18b, and Claudia L. Woods's comedy *The Rummage Sale* is M.adds. 110e 1485 (1). There are, by my bemused count, more than 5,000 Oxford entries in the catalogues of printed books; they are closely preceded by Miss Sibyl Ouseley's *A Madcap Brownie* and *That Tiresome Lower Fifth*, and closely followed by *The Oyster*, by A Peer. The catalogue entry G.8.8.Th will lead you to a seventeenth-century book called *The best Religion, Wherein is largely explaned the Summe and principal heads of the Gospell*. You will not, however, be able to take it to your reading desk, for of all the 3,000,000 books in the Bodleian Library, G.8.8.Th is the only one that is still chained to its bookcase.

The treasures of this astonishing library have to be winkled out, so varied are they, and so withdrawn is the spirit of the place. The Bodleian never lets books leave its premises—you have to read them on the spot. Charles I was refused permission to take books away, and so was Oliver Cromwell. When Sir Richard Burton was forbidden to remove a manuscript of the *Thousand and One Nights* he retaliated by dedicating one volume of his great translation to the Curators of the Library: if they had let him take it, he said, he would have suppressed any tales that might have embarrassed the Bodleian, but as it was the volume owed its 'rarest and raciest passages' to their refusal. The very physical shape of the library is an impenetrable mystery to the stranger, and the Bodleian is full of surprises, stacked away behind those grey walls like bric-à-brac in the richest of all junk shops.

Not many libraries possess more of the standard bibliographical rarities, though for a time the Bodleian did not have a First Folio: a copy had been delivered in sheets at the time of its publication in 1623, but was discarded when the Third Folio came out—only to turn up again in 1905, when it was sent to Oxford for advice about its repair, was recognized by its binding, and bought by subscription. The lesser marvels are, however, often more interesting. There is a collection of scribbled notes, for example, exchanged by Charles II and his chief adviser, Clarendon, during sessions of the State Council: these often concern small personal matters, like a visit the king proposed to pay to his sister at Tunbridge, and they bring that dead council chamber marvellously to life. 'I intend to take nothing but my night-bag,' scribbles the king. 'Yet', says Clarendon, 'you will not go without 40 or 50 horses.' 'I counte that part of my night-bag,' retorts Charles—and when we see his scrawl there on the paper, so we can glimpse his gay and crooked smile, too, as he shoves the note across the table of State, and the councillors drone on around him. The manuscript of *The Wind in the Willows* is in the Bodleian, and so is the very manuscript of the *Rubá'iyát* from which Fitzgerald took his translation. The Bodleian's manuscript of Firdausi's *Shāhnāma* is the one illuminated for Tamburlaine's grandson. Its seventh-century Sardinian manuscript of the Acts of the Apostles is probably the copy the Venerable Bede used when he was writing his commentaries.

It is more like a living thing than a collection of objects. There

are many libraries more efficient, at least for the ordinary reader—
it sometimes takes an unconscionable time to get a book out of these
vaulted forests: but the Bodleian is given warmth not only by its
precious possessions but also by all its memories and meanings, all
the generations who have worked in it so lovingly for 450 years,
all the hands that have thumbed its catalogues and turned its millions of printed pages—till ten o'clock every night of term, until
the big bell at the end of Duke Humfrey's rings among the books
for closing time.

Half a mile away are the offices of the Oxford University Press,
above the printing works in Walton Street. This immense organization is controlled directly by the University—its Delegates are University officials who do the job free, and its Secretary is always a
distinguished scholar himself (the present one is an economist). Part
of its output is scrupulously academic—books which are published
under the imprint of the Clarendon Press, approved by the Delegates themselves and printed on the Walton Street machines.
Another part is efficiently, sometimes racily, commercial—books
they call General Books, which are produced by the General
Division of the Press, and may be anything from fairy tales to fish-
ermen's memoirs. No other university has such a publishing house
as this, with its music and map departments, its offices across the
world, its own American corporation, and its grave Delegates meeting up there above the presses, to decide whether or not the moment
has come for another commentary on Seneca's *Apocolocyntosis*.
    Some of the grandest works of scholarship, in any language, have
been sponsored by this house, and at any moment several enormous
projects are almost certainly under way. The *New English Dictionary*
was described by *The Times* in 1897 as 'the greatest effort which
any University has taken in hand since the invention of printing'.
(Its originator, warned at the age of 30 that he had only 18 months
to live, replied that if that were so he must begin to learn Sanskrit
tomorrow.) The *N.E.D.* was originally set up by hand, all 15,000
pages of it, and is now available in a miniaturized version, photo-
graphically reduced into two volumes, and supplied with magnify-
ing glass. It has also been compressed, like a Russian toy, into a
Shorter Oxford Dictionary, a *Concise Oxford Dictionary*, a *Pocket
Oxford Dictionary* and a *Little Oxford Dictionary*, and there is still

a permanent staff working on its addenda. Liddell and Scott's Greek Lexicon was an Oxford enterprise *par excellence*: its authors were undergraduates together, and when Liddell became Dean of Christ Church in 1855, it was only a year before Scott became Master of Balliol. The *Dictionary of National Biography* is another Oxford book, and its supplementary volumes are edited in the city: so far 28 volumes have appeared in all, comprising more than 30,000 biographies, and it was much the most comprehensive thing of its kind until the Italians started producing theirs, taking four volumes to complete the letter A, and planning to go on for 80 more.

The *New English Bible* was partly translated in Oxford, and the Oxford and Cambridge Presses jointly hold its copyright; a committee meets regularly at the Oriental Institute, behind the Ashmolean Museum, to revise its translation even more modernly. The *Oxford Atlas of Britain*, the first national atlas, was prepared by the cartographers of the Press, and Oxford has published vast histories of England, Modern Europe, English Literature and English Art. Oxford dictionaries include dictionaries of nursery rhymes, quotations and place names, and in 1976 work was in hand on a Hebrew Dictionary and a great Latin Dictionary. These are big business by any publishing standards: they sell more or less for ever, and the top Oxford lexicographers can earn very substantial incomes, from the profession that Dr. Johnson defined wryly as harmless drudgery.

Each year the Press brings out a pictorial Almanac, listing the names of University officials for the year, and generally picturing some new University building (though in 1871 a liberal fit overcame the Delegates, and they printed a picture of the new Town Hall). If you go to the shop in High Street which the University Press likes to call its Depository, you may buy back issues of these: and so old is this institution, so bland, and so serenely above the normal urgencies of publishing, that they are quite likely to offer you a few early Victorian examples—neither second-hand nor reprinted, but still in hand from the original stock ('Yes, you're in luck, we do have one or two left of 1836—but they're going very fast now, with Christmas coming on').

Old ladies always say that Cambridge is for science, Oxford for the arts. It has been true in some periods of this University's history, but Oxford's earliest curricula included mathematics and astrology, and you can best trace her intellectual progress by her achievements in the sciences.

The first of her celebrities was certainly a man of science. On a north wall of the car park in St. Ebbe's, well away from the attendant sitting morose in his little glass cubicle, a plaque is set into a remnant of the city ramparts. It commemorates Roger Bacon, 'known as the wonderful doctor, who by the experimental method extended marvellously the realm of science', and who died in 1292 near that spot, in the house of his Franciscan order. Bacon was so clever, and so ahead of his time, that he was suspected of necromancy, and even the Franciscans themselves banished him for a time to Paris. He was interested in everything, from the solar system to the philosopher's stone, and he had a laboratory over the gateway that used to stand on Folly Bridge (giving its name, when it was later grandiosely extended, to the bridge itself). It is said that when some Cambridge savants visited Oxford, Bacon disguised himself as a labourer, and so humiliated the visitors in disputation that they went away thinking even the Oxford peasants were out of their class.

Bacon's great work, the *Opus Majus*, was really a summary of the whole of contemporary human knowledge, and the older annals of Oxford are full of empirical inquiry, regarding the whole of truth as a unity. Astrology and astronomy, for instance, thrived in partnership. On the memorial in the cathedral to Robert Burton, author of the *Anatomy of Melancholy*, there is represented the 'nativity' he cast for himself, and the sixteenth-century mathematician Thomas Allen was supposed to be so skilled in astrology and magic that ghosts were seen 'going up and down his staircase like swarms of bees'. (It was in Oxford, in 1645, that the royal astrologer cast a horoscope predicting that since Mercury, Saturn, Venus, Jupiter, Mars and the Sun were all on the royalist side, Charles I would be 'unexpectedly victorious and successful in all his designs'.) In the Middle Ages Merton was a European centre of astronomy— the zodiacal constellations are superbly represented on the roof of the Fitzjames Gateway, near the hall—and the very first map of the moon, so I learn from a paper communicated to the Soviet Institute for the History of Science, was drawn in Oxford. Aristotle, that universal genius, was the presiding spirit of the mediaeval

University. The teaching friars of Oxford were exponents of speculative philosophy, and until the disputations bogged themselves down in arid abstractions, like the weight of angels or the proportions of sanctity, Oxford learning seems to have been excitingly alive.

Later religion sat upon it, and for centuries Oxford was hagridden by scholasticism. Through the mists of stagnant and sometimes vicious piety periods of scientific adventure break through like sunbeams, and make one wonder how much sooner the electronic age might have reached us, were it not for rivalries between faith and reason. A brilliant group of Oxford men, including the extraordinary young Christopher Wren, played an important part in the beginnings of the Royal Society—soon to have as its President Newton himself. When Robert Boyle devised his law of gas expansion ($PV = P'V'$) in his lodgings in High Street in 1662, he was really giving birth to the age of steam. When Edmund Cartwright, Fellow of Magdalen, invented the power-loom in 1785, he was really launching the Industrial Revolution. The first English aeronaut, James Sadler, took off in a balloon from the Botanical Gardens in 1784, and is buried in St. Peter's in the East. Robert Hooke of Christ Church not only identified the human cell, in the 1660s, but was an eminent pioneer in geology and zoology, experimented in skin grafting, blood transfusion and artificial respiration, and invented the balance-spring for watches.

Halley predicted the return of his comet in Oxford, in 1705—it reappeared in 1758. His personal observatory still stands, in a little shed built on the roof of his house in New College Lane, and up there you will find some pleasant souvenirs of Oxford science—prints, portraits and an old refractor. John Wilkins, Warden of Wadham in Wren's day, wrote two books on how to reach the moon—he thought it might be inhabitable. The eighteenth-century University telescope was the largest ever built in England, except for one made by the same maker for the King of Spain, and lovely old refractors always show in prints of the Radcliffe Observatory in its heyday, when its astronomers looked out at the night sky through its tall windows, or strolled about with hand-glasses on its noble terraces, discussing the meaning of the nebulae.

How delicious it sounds, to pursue such magnificent truths in so beautiful a city! But orthodoxy and classicism lay ever more heavily upon Oxford, until by the first half of the nineteenth century science was almost dead in the University, and the place was, in Geoffrey Faber's phrase, held in the Church's 'death-like grip'. It was then, under the prod of Victorian material success, and the leadership of men like Ruskin, that the modern Oxford scientific renaissance began. When somebody offered a prize for an essay about the fauna of Christ Church meadows Ruskin said it marked a new era in English education: and that moment of release from the old disciplines was deliberately epitomized in the University Museum, the nucleus of today's science area.

It is a memorial to the earnest gusto of the Victorians—an academic building, consciously copying the didactic shape of the old schools, but using the structural techniques of the railway age. With its huge glass roof and its thickets of iron girders, every corner of it was intended to reflect a new awareness of the world about. Each column was made of a different stone, clearly identified at the bottom. Each architrave represented a different flower or plant. It was hoped to add, as one of its progenitors wrote, 'to the wide Philosophical, Historical, Theological life of the old University the means for similar study of the material Universe, considered alike in its Unity and in its special parts'. 'Now, therefore, and now only,' wrote Ruskin, 'the University has become complete in her function as a teacher of the youth of the nation, to which every hour gives wider authority over distant lands.'

You would not think any man of spirit could resist such enthusiasm, or such hopes, but for several decades the fundamentalist rearguard fought on. 'When God made the stones,' John Keble had said, 'he made the fossils in them.' 'Physics without God,' thought Canon Pusey of Christ Church, 'would be but a dull inquiry into certain meaningless phenomenon.' In the end, though, the Museum won, and science became respectable—it was within these walls, as a plaque in the building recalls, that Thomas Huxley confronted 'Soapy Sam' Wilberforce, the fundamentalist Bishop of Oxford, in a famous exchange of asperities on Darwin's theory of evolution.

This occurred at a meeting of the British Association, in 1860. 'Soapy Sam' had sarcastically inquired whether it was through his grandmother or his grandfather that Professor Huxley claimed descent from a monkey, and the reply signalled the triumph of the new sciences in Oxford. He was not ashamed to have an ape for an ancestor, Huxley bitterly replied (at least in one version of the debate), but he would be ashamed to be connected with a man who used his great gifts to obscure the truth—'who, not content with an equivocal success in his own sphere of activity, plunges into scientific questions with which he has no real acquaintance, only to obscure them by an aimless rhetoric'. So devastating was this unscripted retort that a lady in the audience, staggered at the sight of a Bishop so humiliated, fainted on the floor with a clatter, and had to be revived with smelling salts.

Since then the progress of Oxford University has been dominated by science—ever more science students, ever more laboratories, a whole new class and kind of Oxford academic (Sir Cyril Hinshelwood, Dr. Lee's Professor of Chemistry from 1937 to 1964, was President not only of the Royal Society, but also of the Classical Association). All around the Museum, in direct descent to its botanical columns, now stand the scientific departments, served by their own computer laboratory. When Dorothy Hodgkin of Somerville won the Nobel Prize for Chemistry in 1964 she was the first woman to do so since Irène Joliot-Curie, but she was only one of 55 Fellows of the Royal Society then at work in the Oxford laboratories.

Physical chemistry and biochemistry have become Oxford specialities: the chemistry school is the largest and most distinguished in Britain. Important early work on the nuclear bomb was done at the Clarendon Laboratory, beside the Parks—by July 1941 it was so advanced that they were already planning to make three bombs a month, in a factory to be erected by Vickers and Imperial Chemical Industries, and optimistically estimated that the first bomb would be ready by the end of 1943. Some of the first experiments in controlled nuclear reaction were also made at the Clarendon Laboratory, and there, too, in 1959, the lowest temperature ever achieved was attained.

The first Oxford graduate in engineering science died in 1945—there is a memorial to him in Brasenose chapel; but today the new engineering area near Keble has its own nuclear accelerator, and the hefty engineering science block, a mandarin building of glass and concrete, is one of the dominant landmarks of Oxford. The Radcliffe Observatory's 84-inch telescope is in South Africa, where

Oxford astronomers still use it; but solar observations are still made from the domes beside the Parks, and the Savilian Professor of Astronomy makes annual expeditions to clearer heights, in Bolivia or Canada, returning to Oxford to do the paper-work in the mist. (And Oxford money, earned at Cowley and distributed through the Nuffield Foundation, partly paid for the radio-telescope at Jodrell Bank—'Not a project', Nuffield is reported to have said when he was told where the money went, 'that I should have financed.')

Medicine especially has flourished in modern Oxford. The medical traditions of the place are very old. In the Middle Ages there was a hospital, St. John's, on the site of Magdalen: some of its walls are built into the college fabric, and the blocked doorway in the High Street front was once a hospital entrance, with a wicket for the doling out of bread to sick or hungry travellers. The Doctour of Physic in the *Canterbury Tales—in all this world ne was ther noon hym lik, To speke of physic and of surgery*—is thought to have been modelled upon an early Oxford medical graduate, John of Gaddesdon: he was the first English court physician, all his predecessors having been imported, and he once cured Edward I's son of the smallpox by wrapping him in scarlet clothes—just as, some six centuries later, they began treating the same disease by putting the patient under a red light. William Harvey, discoverer of the circulation of the blood, was briefly Warden of Merton in the seventeenth century; among his successors was Dr. Jonathan Goddard, whose secret panacea—Goddard's Drops—was so effective that Charles II paid him £1,500 for the technique of distilling it.

It is only in our own time, though, that the University has supported a clinical teaching hospital. The Radcliffe Infirmary used to be an ordinary county hospital, and if you meander through its shambling purlieus today you may still see how modest were its origins. Its elegant eighteenth-century core has long been embedded in sad accretions of huts, annexes, temporary extensions, furnace blocks and laundries, until the place has become something like a Hollywood shanty-town set, through whose drab corridors there moves with sweet smiles a special corps of Receptionists, their sole duty the reassurance of patients laid low by the environment. It was Lord Nuffield, with a series of benefactions, who turned this hospital into a great centre of teaching and research, and thus put Oxford into a new medical class. The seven Nuffield Professors, plutocrats among doctors because they draw hospital salaries as well as academic stipends, are all based upon the Radcliffe; and the infirmary is the centre of a group of Oxford hospitals offering almost every kind of specialist treatment. Brain surgery, orthopaedics and anaesthetics are all Oxford specialities: sad numbers of undergraduates take their examinations inside the Warneford psychiatric hospital. In Oxford Charles Sherrington first mapped the nervous system, and here the English thalidomide babies came to be taught the use of their artificial limbs.

Though there is a vast new hospital centre at Headington, the centre of all this activity remains the original Radcliffe, at the southern end of the Woodstock Road. It is a fusty old place, with a muscular dryad spouting water in the courtyard fountain, and its own Victorian chapel of St. Luke. I can imagine nothing much more immediately depressing than to be wheeled into this old conglomeration on a stretcher, to feel its thick plastic doors closing behind my head, observe the photographs of English Scenic Beauties that desperately decorate its walls, and see the Receptionist bearing down on me. I would, however, be wrong. That drab decor hides every kind of technical resource, and much enlightened thinking. The Radcliffe was one of the first English hospitals to abolish visiting hours—selected visitors can go when they like, to the chagrin of those patients who would far rather be left alone without any make-up on. And it was here, one day in 1941, that penicillin was first used upon a patient. Research into the medical meaning of the mould had begun in 1938 under Howard Florey, at the Department of Pathology in South Parks Road. During the war the Oxford scientists began producing it in quantity, using every sort of makeshift equipment—milk churns, an ordinary bath, pipes and taps bought from local ironmongers. The rose garden opposite Magdalen commemorates their work, and a small plaque above a bed in Beevers Ward records the first time penicillin was ever used in medicine: but the patient died, for there was not enough of it to save him.

Despite it all, the old ladies are half right still, and the genius of this place remains stubbornly traditionalist. The ancients still have a hold on Oxford—'Greek and Asian Elements in the Origin of the Steam Engine' was the title of a recent lecture, and admirably it seemed to sum up Oxford's old conviction that almost nothing could

be achieved without tradition's sanction. The most famous of the
Oxford faculties remains the School of Literae Humaniores—
'Greats'—which demands a four-year course, instead of the more
usual three, and still attracts many of the cleverest undergraduates—it is said to produce men, as the University Handbook used
to say, 'unrivalled as expositors and judges of any situation or set
of acts placed before them'. The portrait of Bishop Strong in Christ
Church hall, who lived recently enough to have confirmed me,
is supposed to have been painted in its odd oblong shape because
the classical dons who commissioned it could not express the
difference between length and breadth. Once a year the University
Sermon is still preached all in Latin in St. Mary's, to a solemn congregation of gowned academics who follow every subjunctive and
subordinate clause with an attention, I suspect, as much philological
as spiritual.

Classics, theology and philosophy are still deeply ingrained in the
Oxford character, so that even now a common-room discussion
about Stoical doctrines seems to come easier, at least to the
stranger's ear, than any self-conscious mastery of thermodynamics.
The Oxford pedant still prefers to deal in matters long dead or
dusty—as the epigram observes of one local Oxford antiquarian,
'Pox on't!' says Time to Thomas Hearne. 'Whatever I forget you
learn.' My favourite monument in Oxford is the tomb of Dr.
Richard Baylie, a seventeenth-century President of St. John's. He
is dressed in his academicals, and is leaning with one knee cocked
against a pile of books; his forefinger keeps his place in one volume,
and he is looking preoccupied up into the sky, as if his train of
thought has momentarily escaped the argument of the page, and
true to the Oxford method, has soared away to more celestial
syllogisms.

He is the very embodiment of Oxford's scholastic reputation—
cloistered, high-flown, clerical, eclectic. You cannot see the titles
of his books, but I am sure both sides of the case are represented.
A favourite method of Oxford examination has always been the
viva voce, last echo of the disputations, which has survived all academic reforms, and is still used to determine the class of a student
on the brink between a First and a Second. One of the sculpted
panels outside the Examination Schools in High Street shows a *viva*
in progress, four stern examiners grilling one pallid candidate, and

often the very best of Oxford learning shows itself at such a session—sometimes in a clash of formidable brains, sometimes just in ingenuity. F. E. Smith, advised at a *viva* to read more about Real Property, retorted: 'I came here to be examined, not to receive unsolicited advice.' 'With what feelings ought we to regard the Decalogue?' C. S. Calverley the parodist was asked. 'With feelings of devotion,' he at once replied, not being at all sure what the Decalogue was, 'mingled with awe!' ('Quite right, young man,' the Master of Balliol commented, 'a very proper answer.') When Gladstone had his final *viva voce* in 1831, a large crowd accompanied him to the Schools, so towering was his reputation already, and when the examiner, having questioned him searchingly on one aspect of moral philosophy, remarked that they would now leave that topic, Gladstone indignantly interrupted him—'No, if you please, sir, we will not leave it yet'—and went on for another five minutes.

This is the world's image of an Oxford intellectual, and it has survived not only periods of slump in Oxford scholarship, like the notorious eighteenth century, but also the new emphasis on science. When we think of a learned Oxford scholar we still generally see in our mind's eye some high-domed mid-Victorian sage—embroiled without doubt in the doctrinal controversies of the day, brimful of epigrams and learned allusions, easily at home among the profundities, if not the paganisms, of the ancients. This is the figure the old ladies have in mind, and though he grows rarer each year, and more reconciled to the world outside, and readier to believe in the existence of aeroplanes, still his presence lingers powerfully on, perversely more compelling than the physicists and the sociologists, preceded to the pulpit by respectful vergers, or bowed over old commentaries in corners of cold libraries.

His has been a scholarship founded unshakably upon Christian theology and classicism, discreetly laced with a little pure mathematics, and his intellectual demands are well illustrated by a punishment imposed upon a Christ Church undergraduate in the nineteenth century. The youth was told to go away and abridge the whole of Herodotus, master four books of Euclid, write down and work out all the examples in Maclaurin's Algebra, Part One, make notes on all St. Paul's Epistles and the last hundred Psalms in

Hebrew, and translate into Latin both parts of the ninth discourse of the second volume of Sherlock's sermons. We are not told the poor boy's name, but if he really got through all that, he deserves a street too.

13. Vineyard of the Lord

Oxford is a Christian city, built upon the Christian culture—as organically Christian as Bangkok is Buddhist. She has been Christian from the start. The oldest buildings in Oxford are churches: the shadowy old church of St. George within the castle walls, the fortress church of St. Michael guarding the north gate, or the exquisite St. Peter's in the East, now a library belonging to St. Edmund Hall, and which is sometimes said to be the oldest church in England. The oldest door in Oxford is the little wooden priest's door, black with age, in the south flank of St. Thomas's. The oldest glass is the Lily Glass in St. Michael's. On the tower of St. Michael's there used to be a queer little carving of a female figure, which experts have interpreted as a pre-Christian fertility fetish (the vicar prudently keeps it now, locked up in the vestry). Oxford, however, was never a pagan settlement. She was born Christian, grew up Christian, and remains half Christian still.

John Wycliffe once called his Oxford a Vineyard of the Lord. Four big monastic houses dominated the little city—Osney, St. Frideswide's, Rewley and Godstow—and traces of them all remain. St. Frideswide's is built into the cathedral. Godstow is a pretty ruin opposite the Trout Inn, hung about by wild flowers, inhabited by cows, and still approached from the west by a half-buried causeway made of nuns' coffins. All that is left of Rewley is a solitary arch in a garden near the railway station.

As for Osney, its lost splendour has become a legend. Its tower was the third tallest in England, we are told, and is pictured in a stained-glass window in the military chapel of the cathedral, looking very magnificent in the background of a bishop. John Aubrey was so impressed by the ruins, when he was an undergraduate at Trinity in the 1640s, that he had a picture drawn of them—the only other contemporary representation to survive; and when Dr. Johnson saw them, melancholy among the marshes, he walked all the way home to Oxford in silent indignation.

Today all that remains is a fine stone barn with flour sacks in it, to remind you of the times when this great house held sway over all these meadow-lands, levied its charges and tilled its own fields, and so dominated the traffic of the Thames that far away in Windsor the pub called the Six Bells still commemorates the peal of its tower.

Oxford was a city of cults and holy places, with its own familiar anchorites and hermits—some of whom, since they lived in a hermitage on the South Bridge, were handily employed by the city to keep the bridge in repair. Churches of St. Michael, the Defender, stood guard at the north and south gates, churches of St. Peter, the Gatekeeper, at the east and west. Within the walls some lesser saints were honoured. St. Frideswide was, of course, a local celebrity (and was also commemorated, oddly enough, by a village cult in Artois). St. Aldate, on the other hand, whose church stands opposite Christ Church, is unknown to the dictionary of saints, though he is also honoured in Gloucester: at one time or another his Oxford church has been known as St. Eldred's, St. Aldade's, St. Ald's, St. Old's, St. Olave's, St. Oolde's, St. Aldgate's and St. Toll's, but nowadays the experts seem to think that its name merely refers to an Old Gate it stood beside.

There is a church of St. Ebbe, who was a daughter of Aethelfrith, King of Northumbria. There used to be a church of St. Mildred, a pious anchorite from the Island of Thanet, to whom only four other churches have ever been dedicated—Brasenose Lane was its churchyard path. There was once a church of St. Budoc, a singularly obscure Cornish saint. ('If the name had been St. Judoc,' wrote the antiquarian James Parker wistfully in 1885, 'the saint of Brittany who died about 658, it would have been easy to have imagined that some of the Conqueror's followers erected a little church outside the West Gate.' But it wasn't.)

St. Edmund Rich was an Oxford saint. When he once preached a sermon in the churchyard of St. Mary's, it rained everywhere else in Oxford, but not a drop fell on his congregation, and it was inside the church that he placed his ring upon a finger of Our Lady's statue, to signify his own perpetual virginity. The crypt of St. Peter in the East is still called St. Grymald's crypt, after the Saxon saint said to have founded it, and the consecration cross on the south wall of St. Giles is thought to commemorate a visit by St. Hugh, who was Bishop of Lincoln, and was so considerable a person in twelfth-century England that two kings carried his bier to the grave.

There were several places of pilgrimage in mediaeval Oxford. The leper chapel of St. Bartlemas, that Whitstable among Oxford tastes, not only possessed a lifelike statue of St. Bartholomew, once the centre of an idolatrous cult, but also the saint's actual skin, presented by Edward III, a rib of St. Andrew the Apostle, the bones of St. Stephen, and a holy well which only fell into disuse when rumour said it had been poisoned by malicious foreign lepers, bribed by the Saracens. The tomb of the Fair Rosamond, at Godstow, was the shrine of another dubious cult: lamps and candles burnt always about it, and nuns paid perpetual homage to the courtesan's memory, until forbidden to do so by their scandalized bishop.

And down by the river was Binsey, where Frideswide herself had summoned a holy well into existence, and dedicated it to St. Margaret of Antioch. This little well, which lies down some mossy steps behind the village church, has never lost its reputation. Pilgrims first went there, we are told, in the lifetime of the saint herself, and later the fame of the place became so great that at least 20 pilgrim inns are said to have been built in the neighbourhood, and several priests were stationed at Binsey to hear confessions. The water of the well was especially effective for eye and stomach troubles, and for making women fertile, and in the seventeenth century they used to sell it at a guinea a bottle. The first recorded Vicar of Binsey was 'Sir Breakespear'—Nicholas Breakspear, who became Adrian IV, the only English Pope—and to this day the local traditions of sanctity survive, cherished by the quaint remoteness of the place, and the mystery of the well hidden there in the churchyard. Even now women occasionally steal down to the well, when their longing for a child becomes desperate, and the visitors' book in the church sometimes contains grateful thanks to St. Margaret for indigestion eased or eyes comforted.

As for the University of Oxford, it was a religious institution from its inception. Until the Reformation all its scholars were clerks in minor or in holy orders—the academic costumes of Oxford today are remnants of the robes worn by mediaeval ecclesiastics. Some of the liveliest thinkers in early Oxford were teaching friars—

Dominicans, whose first house was in the Jewish quarter, Franciscans, who settled in St. Ebbe's, Carmelites, who were given the old royal palace of Beaumont, Austin Friars, who were particular masters of disputation, Trinitarians, who mostly died in the plague of 1349, Crutched Friars, who were so irritatingly ostentatious in their devotions that they had to be forbidden the use of the church of St. Cross, at Holywell. The University was an ecclesiastic body, under the ultimate control of the Pope. Its early statutes referred to canon, not to civil law, and until the fourteenth century its headquarters was the church of St. Mary, where each faculty used a different chapel.

The colleges, too, were conceived as religious houses. At Worcester you can see how plausibly the college structure may be said to have developed from monasteries, for there the Benedictines, at the end of the thirteenth century, established a college to serve all the abbeys of their southern English province. Fifteen religious houses each maintained their own quarters, many of them in the range of buildings on the south side of the quadrangle that is still called the Mansions. Each had its own doorway and staircase, and some of their crests still stand above the lintels. When Lincoln College was founded in 1427 its anti-Lollard purpose was defined as the defence of 'the mysteries of the sacred page against ignorant laics, who profane its most holy pearls with their swinish snouts'. Magdalen's foundation stone was placed inside the chapel altar, and St. John's original objective was to 'strengthen the orthodox faith, insofar as it is weakened by the damage of time and the malace of men'. A prime purpose of Oxford was the production of divines, and six fourteenth-century Archbishops of Canterbury came from Merton College.

But when Bishop Fox proposed to make his new college of Corpus Christi another Benedictine house he was dissuaded by his friend the Bishop of Exeter—'What, my Lord, shall we build houses and provide livelihoods for a company of bussing monks whose end and fall we may live to see?' This showed prescience, for all this elaborate structure of zeal and orthodoxy was shattered by the dissolution and the Reformation—the bussing monks expelled, the anchorites forgotten, even the nuns of St. Frideswide's convent, we are told, forced to take refuge in the little Nuns' Garden beside Queen's. With them mediaeval Oxford vanished, too. All that was left of the Franciscan house was the name of Paradise Square, in St. Ebbe's, which used to be its 'paradise', or pleasure garden, and all that was left of the Carmelites was Friar's Entry, the little passage that runs beside Debenham's department store. The stones and treasures of the monasteries were dispersed through Oxford. Christ Church's bells came from Osney, together with a good deal of the monastic property. The figure on the west side of the tower of St. Mary Magdalen Church came from Rewley, and the figure of St. Bernard on the gate-tower of St. John's, whose buildings were formerly a Cistercian house, was hastily fixed up with cement hair and a beard, and turned into John the Baptist (until 1915, when he became St. Bernard again). Osney Abbey became a quarry for building material, until Charles I practically exhausted it to build defence works in the Civil War.

Most of the English martyrs beatified by Leo XIII were Oxford men, including Edmund Campion of St. John's, who was hanged, drawn and quartered at Tyburn in 1581; and for three centuries after the Reformation the chief preoccupation of Oxford was the state of the Established Church—expressed sometimes in violence, sometimes in heretical innovation, endlessly in sermons and treatises. When a young lady in *Cranford* asked what a university was, she was told it was 'a place where young clergymen go to be educated'. A very Oxford treasure in the Bodleian is a System of Divinity devised by the Reverend W. Davy at the end of the eighteenth century. Mr. Davy took 12 years to produce this complete exposition of the Correct Way, and I am not surprised, for it runs to 26 devout volumes, and the author printed every word of it himself, two pages at a time.

In the archway that leads from one Balliol quadrangle to the other an old gate hangs upon the wall. It has apparently been blackened by some fierce fire, and it is said to have been scorched by the flames that burnt Archbishop Cranmer in 1556—at a spot in Broad Street, outside the college, that is still marked with an iron cross set in the surface of the road. This was the most terrible of Oxford's spiritual ordeals. Cranmer, the Protestant Archbishop of Canterbury, had been imprisoned by Queen Mary's Catholic régime. He had been a pillar of the English Reformation, and with Bishops Hugh Latimer and Nicholas Ridley he was brought to stand trial for heresy in

Oxford (perhaps because all three were Cambridge men). The prisoners were kept first in the Golden Cross Inn, in rooms which were known for centuries as the Martyrs' Rooms, and stand above the dining-room. Then they were removed to the Bocardo prison, and from there Latimer and Ridley went to the stake. Latimer died quickly, for the powder they hung around his neck soon exploded, and his last gesture was to stroke his own face with the flames. Ridley died agonizingly, for his fire only smouldered damply—'I cannot burn!' he cried. 'Lord have mercy on me—let the fire come to me— I cannot burn!'

But Cranmer was upstairs in the Bocardo still, and had still worse to face, for he was to endure the whole classic horror of an *auto-da-fé* in its most degrading form. Spanish friars argued with him up there, nagging him to recant; some accounts say he was taken to his prison window to see his friends burn; on a rainy day in March 1556 he was led in procession to St. Mary's to make a public recantation of heresy, with the friars singing psalms in antiphony beside him through the streets, and the Mayor and Aldermen processing in front. They had dressed him in a ragged gown and 'an old square cap', and they placed him on a platform built above the pulpit (the sockets cut in the stone for it are still alleged to show). He had signed seven separate recantations, but he was doomed anyway. Dr. Cole the preacher, praising God for the fact of the Archbishop's 'conversion', promised that after his death there should be Dirges, Masses and Funerals for him in all the Oxford churches, and called upon him to 'express the true and undoubted profession of your faith, that all men may understand that you are a Catholic indeed'.

But Cranmer, not always a very noble figure, now did a noble thing. The tears were streaming down his face. He rose to his feet, removed that old square cap, and solemnly withdrew his recantation—'which I now renounce and refuse, as things written with my hand, contrary to the truth which I thought in my heart, and written for fear of death ... and forasmuch as my hand offended, writing contrary to my heart, my hand shall first be punished therefore; for may I come to the fire it shall be first burned'. The congregation was now in uproar. 'Take him away!' screamed Cole, and they dragged the old man from his platform and pushed him out of the church towards the fire, already heaped up on the pavement of Broad Street. Cranmer walked very fast. The friars shouted at him as they went, the priests and the doctors streamed along behind, horrified citizens crowded the pavements. When the fire was kindled Cranmer first placed his right hand into the flame, as he had promised, and then died bravely, 67 years old, dressed in a shirt down to his ankles, with bare feet, bare bald head, and his long thick beard singed down his chest.

Three hundred years later they erected the Martyrs' Memorial in St. Giles, modelled on the Eleanor Crosses set up by Edward I to mark the funeral procession of his wife, and once a favourite pitch for undergraduate climbers. They dedicated the north aisle of St. Mary Magdalen, too, to the Protestant martyrs, and in it they mounted the door of the Bocardo cell in which the bishops had been imprisoned. But by then Oxford was in the throes of another battle, scarcely less vehement, about the validity of the English Church, and had given birth to that phenomenon of Victorian ardour, the Anglo-Catholic Movement.

This was conceived in the common room of Oriel, then the most brilliant intellectual community in Oxford, and its most remarkable leaders were John Keble, Edward Pusey and John Newman. Keble was a gentle and enormously popular clerical poet, whose cycle *The Christian Year* went through 95 editions in his own lifetime. Pusey was Regius Professor of Hebrew at the age of 28, a powerful and cryptic man, identified by a wise woman of Berkshire as the foul frog that was to come out of the dragon's mouth in the Book of Revelations. Newman, vicar of St. Mary's, was a baffling mixture of strength, uncertainty, gall and sweet saintliness—a spellbinder, whose sermons were so mesmeric that even Sir Richard Burton, that godless pornographer, used to be seen entranced at them, his eyes ablaze and his fearful moustaches drooping.

Between them these three men almost split the Church of England in two, and they have profoundly affected its behaviour ever since. The Oxford Movement began as a defence of the Established Church against the supposed interference of the State, but it became a campaign to keep the Church supreme in all national affairs, and to freeze Oxford as an ecclesiastical preserve. Its adherents claimed only to be re-establishing the ancient origins of the English Church, direct in line from the Apostles; its enemies, eyeing its ornate rituals, vestments and sympathies with Roman Catholic dogma, said it was all the thin end of a Papist wedge.

The Movement's views were expressed in a celebrated series of sermons and tracts—hence its nickname, the Tractarian Movement—and the excitement it aroused is almost inconceivable now. St. Mary's was packed every Sunday afternoon for Newman's sermon—as if, so one contemporary observer wrote, 'some Ambrose or Augustine of earlier days had reappeared'. 'Newmania' swept through Oxford, dividing common rooms, enlivening the dullest dinner parties, forcing the more evangelical colleges to change the times of meals and chapel services, to keep undergraduates away from Tractarian meetings. All the instruments of modern politics were brought into play in Victorian Oxford—even down to intimidation, double agents and brainwashing. 'Not to mention the excitement which it caused in England,' Newman later wrote, 'the Movement and its party-names were known to the police of Italy and to the backwoodsmen of America.'

It came to a head with Tract XC, published by Newman in 1841. This was concerned with the Thirty-nine Articles of Faith, which appear still in the Book of Common Prayer, and to which every single member of the University then had to subscribe. Many people in Oxford recognized the hypocrisy of this—the articles cover a very wide range of subjects, from the legality of going to the wars to transubstantiation, works of supererogation and purgatory ('a fond thing vainly invented'). Sir William Hamilton, a violent critic of the system, had actually called Oxford 'a school of perjury', and the Thirty-nine Articles, of course, kept out of Oxford all Catholics, Jews and Nonconformists (poor Jesus College could draw its students only from that small and unrepresentative clique, the Welsh Anglicans).

Even so, when Newman set out to show that the Thirty-nine Articles were not really incompatible with Roman Catholic beliefs—that you could believe almost all the Roman doctrine, and still subscribe to them—he went too far for Oxford, and for England. Several bishops publicly condemned him. Of the heads of colleges, only Dr. Routh at Magdalen supported him. Several Tractarians left Oxford, Pusey was suspended from preaching in his own cathedral, and in October 1845 Newman himself, having resigned from St. Mary's, was received into the Roman Catholic Church. This was a shattering blow, to friends and to enemies. Keble said the spring had gone out of his year. Gladstone described it as an event of 'calamitous importance'. Disraeli said it made the Church of England 'reel'. In the wake of the Tractarians, a wave of liberalism swept in, and Oxford was purged with reforms. Soon the religious tests were abolished, dons no longer had to be clergymen, and the Anglican hold on Oxford was broken for ever.

Newman, though, has never been forgotten in the city, and even has a room named for him in the parish buildings of St. Mary's. Oxford remains a stronghold of Anglo-Catholicism, and many of the city churches are rich in incense and ritual. The church of St. Thomas, near the station, was the first English parish church to re-adopt the use of eucharistic vestments—at a time when a priest could actually go to prison for wearing a cope, for until 1964 the Church of England officially permitted only cassock and surplice. Keble College is a Tractarian memorial, and so is St. Edward's School, and so is Pusey House, a centre of High Anglicanism in St. Giles, with an important theological library and a vast chapel into which, until the 1950s, no woman was allowed. The Anglican order of the Cowley Fathers, founded by Richard Benson in 1865, was the first English monastic community to take root since the Reformation—it still prospers off the Cowley Road, and there are now a dozen other Anglican communities in the Oxford diocese alone.

Since those passionate days the Roman Catholics, too, have happily re-established themselves in the city. Their first church since the Reformation was a Jesuit chapel built in 1794, still standing near the alms-houses in St. Clement's, with a large stone cross on its roof: but Oxford's Catholic revival really began in 1875, when the lavish church of St. Aloysius was built at the north end of St. Giles. Its architect was J. E. Hansom, the inventor of the hansom cab. It has a spectacular semi-circular reredos, crowned with 68 saintly figures, and one of the greatest collections of holy relics in England, housed in a specially built chapel off the north aisle. All over the city modest little Catholic churches have now arisen, none of them grand, all of them neat as two pins, and the friars long ago came back: the Jesuits, the Franciscans and the Benedictines all have their own halls of learning within the University, and the Catholic Chaplaincy is properly housed in the half-timbered palace of Bishop King, iast Abbot of Osney, first Bishop of Oxford.

So these two Oxford trials of faith, both concerned with the integrity of English Christianity, led at last to compromise, and in the new ecumenical movements we may fancy the hatreds of the Cranmers and the Coles, tempered by Newman's vision, settling at last into tolerance. It is not quite reconciliation yet. There are many Oxford Anglicans to whom the 'R.C.s' are still treacherous enemies, and not a few Roman Catholics, no doubt, to whom the shrine of St. Frideswide is still territory usurped. Martyrs and Tractarians look at each other warily across the centuries. The Martyrs' Memorial ostensibly honours Cranmer, Latimer and Ridley, who are described on it as having 'yielded their bodies to be burned bearing witness to the sacred truths which they had affirmed and maintained against the errors of the Church of Rome'. It was really erected, however, as an anti-Tractarian gesture. The Newmanites refused to subscribe to its cost, and for years afterwards it aroused fierce sectarian passions. St. Mary Magdalen's church later became strongly ritualistic itself, and quite forgot about its Martyrs' Memorial Aisle: and the Bocardo door was eventually removed down the road to St. Michael's at the North Gate, where Tract XC never had been popular, and where one nineteenth-century vicar, very much disliking a Papist sort of reredos that had been presented to the church, removed the ivory cross from it in distaste, and buried it beneath the floor.

Altogether new ways of worshipping the Christian Deity, too, have sprung out of Oxford's endless arguments. In the fourteenth century Wycliffe published in Oxford the principles of Lollardism, denying some of the Church's favourite rights and dogmas. In the nineteenth century a ferocious evangelical called H. B. Bulteel founded his own sect, violently at odds with the Established Church and the University, and presided over his own sectarian chapel in St. Ebbe's—now the Deaf Centre in Commercial Road. There was even an Oxford Utopia once: a group of Christ Church men established it in New Zealand, on visionary Anglican principles, and named its principal settlement for their college. It was the Tractarian publishing house of Mowbray's, still active in the city, that invented religious Christmas cards.

When the American Episcopalians found themselves left high and dry by the War of Independence—their Church and their State split from each other—they came to Oxford for advice. Their churches had formed part of the see of London, and they had no bishop of their own, nor any authority to consecrate one. The Archbishop of Canterbury refused to help, arguing that the Established Church of England could scarcely create bishops for foreign States. The Americans thereupon thought of asking the Danes, but their delegates found their way first to Dr. Routh of Magdalen, then only 28, who advised them to apply to the Scottish bishops—disestablished themselves, and therefore free of foreign ties. They did so, and in 1784 Dr. Samuel Seabury was consecrated Bishop of Connecticut in Aberdeen. Seventy years later Dr. Routh sent a message of greeting to a convocation of an American Church that already numbered 40 bishops; and to this day the Presidents of Magdalen like to say that American Episcopalism, now 139 mitres strong, was born inside their college.

The Wesley brothers invented Methodism in Oxford. Charles was an undergraduate, John a don at Lincoln, when they founded the Holy Club, reading the Testaments together, visiting prisoners in the Castle gaol, looking after sick people in country parishes. There were probably never more than 27 members of the club, but Oxford did not like them—it was a scoffing undergraduate of Christ Church who first called them Methodists, which just meant, in effect, prigs. Certainly their piety was sometimes assertive. Wesley was a moving but long-winded preacher—in 1742 a visitor heard him preach for two hours at St. Mary's, 'and having insulted and abus'd all Degrees, from the highest to the lowest, was in a manner hissed out of the Pulpit by the lads'. George Whitefield, the most eminent of the disciples, wore dirty shoes to emphasize his unceasing penitence, and according to his memoirs, *A Short Account of God's Dealings with George Whitefield*, sometimes prayed for two hours at a go, flat on his face in Christ Church meadows. When Dr. Johnson was told that six Calvinistic Methodists had been expelled from the University in 1768, he thoroughly approved: they might be perfectly good beings, indeed, but they were not fit to be in the University of Oxford—'a cow is a very good animal in a field; but we turn her out of a garden'.

Too late did it dawn upon the city what a prodigy it had nurtured. Few converts were made in Oxford, and all the triumphs of Methodism came elsewhere. John Wesley went on to be one of Oxford's few great prophets. Whitefield became so astonishingly vivid a

preacher that when he once described a blind man falling over a
precipice, Lord Chesterfield started from his seat in the congregation, shouting, 'Great God! He's gone!' The Holy Club, swiftly
leaping the Atlantic, eventually grew so phenomenally that by the
1970s the Methodist Church's property in the United States alone
included 79 hospitals, mostly as large as the Radcliffe, and 105 colleges and universities, mostly bigger than Christ Church. Methodism was born in Oxford out of the torpor of the Established Church,
the gulf between the clergy and the new industrial poor, and
Wesley's revolt against the formal religion so characteristic of this
city; but a century later it exactly fitted the moods and needs of
the American frontier, and transplanted with extraordinary ease
from the pulpit of the University Church to the camp chapels and
shack meetings of the Middle West.

In Oxford it is overshadowed still. John Wesley's first sermons
in a non-Anglican building were preached at 33 New Inn Hall
Street, in effect the first of all the meeting houses, but only a plaque
distinguishes it. The Wesley Memorial Church nearby, built in
1878 to celebrate the admission of Nonconformists into the University, is a superb example of Victorian craftsmanship, but is seldom found by tourists. You would not know that this tremendous
religious movement had its origins here. No great tabernacle proclaims the fact, the chapels of the city are still unobtrusive beside
the churches, and all that shows of John Wesley himself is a small
bust in a quadrangle at Lincoln, his presumed rooms there, reno-
vated by the American Methodists, and a kindly portrait in Christ
Church hall.

In 1921 a jovial well-groomed American called Frank Buchman
came to this city, and founded the Oxford Group. Nobody was altogether sure then, just as many are not altogether certain now, what
the Oxford Group was, but its right to use the name was established
in a court action in 1928: and until the movement began to call itself
Moral Rearmament, most people thought of it as one of the Oxford
faiths.

Buchman had been a Lutheran minister, had seen a vision of the
Cross in the Lake District in 1908, and had evolved a First-Century
Christian Fellowship, preaching the 'four absolutes' of honesty,
purity, love and unselfishness. He was 43 when he first appeared

in Oxford, after a year at Cambridge, and his impact on this old and ironic city was unexpected. You would hardly think it fertile ground for a hearty American do-gooder of Swiss descent, especially when Princeton University had already declared his proselytizing methods to be 'dangerous from the medical and psychological standpoints'. In fact he seems to have been a great success, social and evangelical, and conquered Oxford conversationally by his command, as a writer in *The Times* once put it, 'of the remark of such stunning ordinariness that it riveted attention'.

" washed out "

At first he worked privately, inviting undergraduates and dons to discreet house parties at which they 'shared their sins' over coffee. Later his methods became more expansive, and he acquired a strong taste for publicity. Apostles went out to the world at large. The Oxford Group became a registered company. The guests at Buchman's parties became richer, grander and more famous, and began to develop an ideology so towering that it was designed to deal not merely with individuals, but with whole nations—'world-changing through life-changing'.

And so he outgrew Oxford—outgrew her physically, because there was no hall big enough for his mammoth meetings, outgrew her spiritually as he began to tinker with history, thanked Heaven for the existence of Hitler, and realized that much the most useful converts to his cause were those with political power, social influence or bags of money. By the middle 1930s Buchman had done with this city. He established headquarters in Switzerland, Michigan and Berkeley Square, and pursued his absolutes so lavishly that when he mounted a world mission in 1955 the air fares alone cost £40,000—'When God guides,' he used to say, if asked where the money came from, 'he provides.' When an American Admiral once declared that the choice before his country was either Communism or Moral Rearmament, it became clear that Buchmanism was likely to be another of those causes which, alighting briefly in Oxford in search of loftier opportunities, leave scarcely a trace behind.

Not quite a Christian movement, but almost a religion of its own, is the newest and raciest of Oxford's spiritual brotherhoods, Oxfam—the Oxford Committee for Famine Relief. This was founded during the second world war, under the chairmanship of Gilbert Murray the classicist, to send help to children in occupied

Greece—a thoroughly Oxford purpose, conventionally supported by dons and clergymen. At the end of the 1950s, however, it blossomed into an altogether different kind of charitable organization—standing resolutely above class or denomination, professionally run on business lines with a keen eye to competition and publicity, housed in a brand-new building in the Banbury Road that pays for itself by letting its ground floor as shops. This was something quite new to England, where charities had mostly been sectarian in one sense or another. All kinds of people came to work for Oxfam, from retired Army officers to wild-eyed disarmers, and it now states its objectives in almost cosmic terms—'To relieve poverty, distress or suffering in any part of the world, whether it is due to a natural disaster . . . or to lack of resources among the people involved.'

It is possibly the richest charity in Britain, is certainly the bounciest, and early in its career it succeeded in catching the imagination of the young, so that angry adolescents who loathe their Mums and despise Contemporary Morality cheerfully jingle its money-boxes, nearly always returning them to the office at the end of the campaign, and never finding the task an embarrassment. Oxfam brilliantly engaged those forces of idealism which lie below the surface of any people, erupting now and then in religion or war, and it has inspired many imitations. It is really a kind of revivalist movement, though it would hate to say so: it goes with guitars, placards, stalls at fêtes and, somewhere far behind its jazzy façade, Dr. Whitefield's penitence. Dear old clergymen work part-time in its offices, sorting the mail, and clever earnest girls in blouses sometimes make you feel life is treating you too kindly.

By most English standards, I suppose, Oxford is an intensely religious city still. Tithes, advowsons, gifts, livings and peculiars still figure stoutly in the Oxford vocabulary. Obscure problems of ecclesiastical protocol often crop up. They did not have to deconsecrate the new college of St. Antony's, formerly the Tractarian convent of the Holy and Undivided Trinity, because, the chapel being upstairs and the refectory below, it was never consecrated in the first place—you cannot sanctify an upper floor without sanctifying the lower. On the other hand, one of the problems facing the manager of the Mitre Hotel, when he wanted to turn his thirteenth-century cellar into a bar in 1964, was the very real possibility that he would be shaking his cocktails on holy ground. The Church of England can still claim certain prerogatives in the University—the theological professorships are attached to canonries at the cathedral, and most colleges are bound by statute to maintain a chaplain. The Dean of Oxford is *ex officio* the head of Christ Church, or vice versa, and the University Sermon still wanly proclaims an official attachment to the established faith.

Oxford Cathedral is the smallest in England, but Oxford diocese is the largest. There are at least 65 Anglican churches and college chapels in the city, one for every 1,500 inhabitants (in Venice there is a Catholic church for every 2,000). There are about 160 Anglican clergymen 'licensed or permitted to officiate'. There are 50 acres of graveyard: St. Sepulchre's is the most awful of the city cemeteries, the most suggestive is the one beside the railway line, whose chapel stands on the site of Osney Abbey nave, and the most entertaining is Holywell, which is stacked with eminent dead dons, and rich in phrases like 'Died At The Provost's Lodgings', or 'First Waynflete Professor Of Pure Mathematics'. Theological colleges thrive all over the place, and the Romish scholars are back in force again—the Franciscans, the Dominicans and the Benedictines all have their houses here, and the Jesuits are housed in cramped but exceedingly elegant quarters that Edwin Lutyens designed for them on the edge of St. Ebbe's.

An Oxford Sunday, even now, fairly pullulates with devotion. In the cathedral the canons of Christ Church are at Sung Eucharist, sumptuously coped and magnificently hymned. In St. Aldate's across the way the very window-sills are crammed with evangelical undergraduates. In St. Mary Magdalen's a woman has tiptoed in to write her request in the supplication book—'Please pray for a mother, not able to make ends meet', or 'Pray for a family of three, suffering financial hardship owing to an Authority not doing its job properly'. In the chapels of Magdalen and New College the glorious choirs are trilling. In a dozen other colleges two or three are gathered together with chaplain and organist. In St. Mary's the Bampton Lecture is being delivered by some prodigiously learned churchman—like the Right Rev. S. C. Neill, who gave the series in 1964, and was described in the University *Gazette* as M.A. (Cambridge), Hon. D.D. (Trinity College, Toronto), Hon. Th.D. (Hamburg), Hon. Litt.D. (St. Paul's University, Tokyo), Hon. D.D. (Glasgow),

sometime Bishop of Tinnevelly, Professor of Missions and Ecumenical Theology in the University of the Free and Hanseatic City
of Hamburg.

In St. John's, New Hinksey, the vicar ruefully eyes from his
pulpit yet another smashed pane in the bottle-glass windows, an
irresistible target for Saturday night catapults. At St. Peter's, Wolvercote, they are offering a prayer for Meadow Prospect—they pray
for a different parish street each day, except on the thirty-first day
of the month, when they pray for streets *outside* the parish. In the
churchyard at Binsey, perhaps, a man with a bad eye is bathing it
in the holy well, down the steps among the ferns. In St. Philip and
St. James the comfortable families of north Oxford, scrubbed and
white-gloved, are listening to a thoroughly *adult* sort of sermon. In
St. Columba's the Scotsmen, a few of them kilted traditionalists,
are intoning metrical psalms. In St. Aloysius the Spaniards, the Italians and the Irish in their hundreds throng the nave or cluster
around the reliquary. Behind the high walls of Headington Priory,
opposite the Red Lion, the sweet nuns are at Mass. In St. Barnabas,
down in Jericho, incense swirls thickly about the Byzantine frescoes.
In Marston parish church the bell-ringers are flexing their muscles
for a chime.

The Quakers are sitting silent and motionless in their meet-
inghouse in St. Giles—when I went there the day after Kennedy's
death the only prayer offered was on behalf of the assassin. The
Orthodox are assembled with flickering candles and deep voices in
a drawing-room in Canterbury Road. The Jehovah's Witnesses are
bearing testimony in the Kingdom Hall off Cowley Road, looking
for all the world like Tennessee members of the Church of God
With Signs Following After. The Salvation Army sings happily in
its spanking new Citadel near the prison, the Christian Spiritualists
are standing witness next door to the pet shop in Headington, in
modest little chapels from Botley to Barton the Baptists, Methodists
and Congregationalists are quietly at prayer. The two lady readers
at their high desks are quoting Mary Baker Eddy in antiphony in
the Christian Science Church in St. Giles, and in the libraries of
the University, I like to think, a few recalcitrant divines are buried
among the 99 theological journals to which the Faculty of Theology
subscribes.

Every tint of the Christian spectrum is represented here, shining in every category of Christian temple—from the Normanesque grandeur of St. Peter's in the East to the lozenge-shaped church the hopeful Anglicans have erected in the new housing estate of Blackbird Leys. If there is to all this activity a trace of something ineffectual, it is certainly not for want of trying. The Oxford churches are admirably active. This was one of the first English cities to have a branch of the Samaritans, the body set up to help people in immediate and desperate distress—24 hours of every day a member sits on call beside a telephone in a house in Ship Street. St. Aldate's Church runs its own cheerful coffee-shop. St. Mary's offers a baby-sitting service, for those attending the University Sermon. New Anglican parishes are still being created, with every codicil of ecclesiastical legalism: the schedule of the new parish of St. Michael and All Angels, at New Marston, runs in part from the 'southern end of the eastern boundary of the house and premises known as number 18 Eden Drive, then southwards in a straight line across the close numbered 6157 to the eastern end of the northern boundary of the house and premises known as number 98 Stanton Road'.

Yet the new Oxford is scarcely touched—the Oxford of the motor works, the housing estates, the sceptical new generations of dons and undergraduates. Probably not one Cowley worker in a hundred goes to church, except to be baptized, married or buried, and in the University, too, agnostics are probably a majority. 'You must believe in God, my child,' said Jowett once to Margot Asquith, 'despite what the clergymen tell you'—and since his day the doubts have spread and deepened, the theological arguments of Oxford seem to shift ever more uncertainly towards unbelief, and the possibility of an atheist morality even finds its way into the pulpits of the ancient city churches. Oxford looks a Christian city still, and the organs play bravely, and the canons sweep through Tom Quad in their white and crimson, surplices blowing in the breeze: but sometimes I find it easy enough to fancy all these old temples shuttered and neglected, the cathedral a museum, the college chapels lecture rooms, an art gallery in the crypt of St. Peter's and only the faithful Samaritan left, busier than ever, over his telephone in Ship Street.

14. Compact of Ancient Tales

So completely, though, has the Church governed Oxford's affairs in the past that the legendary Oxford characters are nearly always parsons—often in gaiters, sometimes in shovel hats, generally immense old, and sailing perpetually, as Hilaire Belloc said,

> ... in amply ~~bellowing~~ gown
> Enormous through the sacred town.

There is substance to this myth. There used to be no retiring age for dons, and they often seemed almost indestructible—in 400 years there were only 21 Presidents of Trinity, and since 1706 there have only been 10 Presidents of Magdalen. Since they had to be celibate, except for college heads, there was a quick turnover of young dons—the average age of common rooms was lower a century ago than it is now. But a core of clerical bachelors stayed on and on, their long comfortable years in Oxford leading them ever further into idiosyncrasy—sometimes comical, sometimes infuriating, and in the end, as the decades passed them by and they were left with no other home but a college, and no loves but a patient niece or two, and no friends but other aged bachelors—in the end, more often than not, rather pathetic. The undergraduates came and went, in a dazzle of variety, often to become great men of the world; but the celibate dons remained, year after year, making up for their backwater seclusion by growing ever more peculiar, or ever more despotic within their own small corners of their own little kingdoms.

It is a weakness of Oxford to waste too much sentiment on quirks and quiddities. Still, the genius of the place owes much to its rich old characters of the past, and to deny them their place in a book about the city would be like keeping the kings out of a

history of England; for they were, as Belloc saw, regal in their
kind—

> *Dons Admirable! Dons of might!*
> *Uprising on my inward sight*
> *Compact of ancient tales, and port*
> *And asleep—and learning of a sort.*
> *Dons English, worthy of the land;*
> *Dons rooted; Dons that understand.*

Dons Admirable! Nobody more admirable than Martin Routh of
Magdalen, perhaps the most famous of them all, who died in his
hundredth year, still in office, but was called the Venerable Dr.
Routh when he was still in his forties. After middle-age, indeed,
he was hardly ever called anything else—Venerable he is on his
tombstone in Magdalen Chapel, and few Oxford men, however
devoted to his memory, could tell you his Christian name.

Routh was a theologian of European eminence, but he is
remembered chiefly for his personality. He used to sleep in what
is now the drawing-room of the President's Lodgings. This is hung
around with magnificent tapestries—presented to an earlier President, Richard Mayew, when he escorted Katherine of Aragon from
Spain for her wedding to Henry VIII—and nothing is more evocative of the presence of old Dr. Routh than the vision of him sleeping
there with those precious textiles fastened together in the middle
of the room to form a heavy coloured canopy over his bed.

Routh was President for 63 years, and though he died during
the Crimean War, never quite left the eighteenth century. He wore
a wig, had set eyes on Dr. Johnson, and had an aunt who had met
a lady who saw Charles I in Oxford. He was a man of unshakeable
composure. 'A Fellow of the College has killed himself!' he was
once told by a breathless don, but he received the news with
equanimity. 'Pray don't tell me who,' he is supposed to have said.
'Allow me to guess.' John Burgon, later a famous Dean of Chi-
chester, was a fulsome admirer of this old stalwart, and once asked
him for one axiom or precept as a rule of life—'a question', said
Burgon winsomely, 'I have sometimes asked of aged persons, but
never of any so aged and learned as yourself.' The President nodded,
thought for a moment, and then delivered a reply that has gone into
the dictionaries of quotations. 'I think, Sir, since you come for the

advice of an old man, Sir, you will find it a very good practice *always to verify your references, Sir!*'

The Venerable Routh was an Oxford spectacle. J. R. Green the historian described him as 'a mysterious dream of the past'. On Sundays, when he was approaching his centenary, crowds used to assemble inside the gates of Magdalen to see him emerge from his lodgings, a little white crouched figure, stumbling across to chapel in his wig and buckled shoes. When he died he was said to have left behind him 'a vast void, strange and unaccountable', and Charles Daubeny the botanist took one of his wigs to have it petrified in a mineral spring. He was, so everyone seems to have agreed, a dear old man. At 65 he married a woman 35 years his junior, and they lived happily ever after in the President's Lodgings, Mrs. Routh travelling about Oxford in a donkey cart, attended by a hunchback. Routh's last words were 'Don't trouble yourself,' spoken to his housekeeper, and the best-known picture of him shows him in his ninety-ninth year, sitting in his study at Magdalen, bowed over a newspaper beside the fire, in his wig, tabs and gaiters, his legs neatly crossed and his mind, I suspect, deep in the contemplation of the stock prices—for he died in the end, so the memoirist W. Tuckwell affectionately reveals, 'through chagrin at the fall of Russian securities'.

Dons of might! Dr. Richard Jenkyns—'Master Balliol' of the footman's announcement—was a small man physically, but mighty in Oxford memory. He did not go to one of the great English schools, but he had an overpowering admiration for Eton, Harrow and Rugby. He was not a great scholar, but he had an astonishing instinct for spotting clever men. It was Jenkyns who originally offered Balliol scholarships in open competition, the first step towards the later intellectual supremacy of the college. He was one of the dominant college heads of the early nineteenth century, and for generations after his death was known as the Old Master.

He was, though, a born figure of fun—a mincing little man with an archaic accent, made to have comic stories told about him. It was he who was once placed on show for some visitors by the eccentric undergraduate C. S. Calverley—the very one who, on another occasion, so pleased the Old Master by his devotion towards the Decalogue. 'There's the library,' this irrepressible youth told his guests, 'and there's the chapel, and there's the Master's window, and there, for that matter, is the Master'—and as he spoke he threw a stone at the window, bringing the little scholar instantly and irritably into view.

Perceptive though he was, Dr. Jenkyns was scarcely intimidating—Calverley used to call him 'little yellow-belly'. During the Reform Riots of 1832 an angry crowd of townspeople came storming up Broad Street from the western slums, fighting the proctors and bulldogs as they went. The din of it all disturbed Dr. Jenkyns, who was just sitting down to dinner. 'Give me my academicals,' he cried, 'and open the door of this house into the street!' His servants hesitated—it was dangerous out there, they said. 'Give me my academicals,' repeated the Old Master, 'and open the door.' They did so; Dr. Jenkyns stepped bravely on to the doorstep; but he only had time to utter the words 'My deluded friends—' when a large stone hit him in the chest, and he fell back into the arms of his servants. 'Close the door!' he ordered this time, rather hastily, and as he disappeared inside the house again, back to his dinner, so the mob surged past Balliol up the Broad, and the incident was closed.

Dons English! Nobody more proudly or quintessentially English than Jowett of Balliol, 'The Jowler', who wished to 'inoculate England' with his college alumni, and of whom a contemporary undergraduate wrote, as part of the libretto for a college masque:

> *Here come I, my name is Jowett;*
> *There's no knowledge but I know it.*
> *I am the Master of this College.*
> *What I know not isn't knowledge.*

Jowett was the greatest Oxford tutor of his time, with a gift of inspiration that his pupils powerfully felt, but often could not pin down. He was one of the supreme influences of Victorian England, dedicated as he was to the production of a ruling *élite*. He knew everybody—he kept notebooks with the names of his acquaintances listed in them—and he made Balliol the intellectual leader of the University. His house became a focus of Oxford, to which every distinguished visitor found his way. He was worldly, but unexpectedly liberal: in religion he was persecuted as a heretic, in education he was a reformer, in social affairs a champion of middle-class opportunity.

Yet even his fondest biographer cannot make him sound a likeable man, and contemporary stories about him usually portray him as insidiously arrogant—somewhere between niggling and squelching. He was one of those men whose constitutional inability to make small talk forfeits all one's sympathy, and makes one think that social grace is sometimes a moral duty. He was cool to his mother, grumpy to his father, unfeeling towards his sister and often horrid to his undergraduates. Though in later years he kept a notebook full of *bons mots*, to use when important enough occasions demanded them, he is remembered chiefly as a master of the well-turned snub.

It was Jowett who, having walked in absolute silence for a couple of miles with an unhappy pupil, turned on the youth when they returned to college and advised him to 'cultivate the art of conversation'. It was Jowett who once interrupted a doubtful after-dinner story by rising from the table and remarking silkily 'Shall we adjourn this conversation to the drawing-room?' ('Devilish clever that, devilish good,' admitted the raconteur himself, Her Majesty's Ambassador in St. Petersburg, as they left the table to join the ladies.) I strongly sympathize with the 15-year-old girl who once took Jowett for a ride in her dog-cart, and claimed afterwards that she had sustained the conversation by asking him questions, driving him over bumpy patches of the road, and 'joggling the answers out of him'.

Jowett was a cherubic, shrill-voiced, fresh-faced little man—'like a little downy owl', somebody said of him in middle age, and owl-like still are his images in Oxford, looking feathery and goggle-eyed in G. F. Watts's fine portrait at Balliol, or peering unexpectedly out of the shadows, as from a hollow tree, in his bust in the Examination Schools. He had an intimate friendship with Florence Nightingale, but sex apparently did not beguile him, and indeed he did much to set the frigid sexual standards of the Victorians—in his translation of Plato he even managed to imply that when Plato wrote of uninhibited homosexual bliss, he really meant a respectable Christian union between man and wife.

Jowett's queer combination of innocence and ruthlessness exactly fitted the Victorian ethos, and till the end of his life he stood near to the sources of national power—it was his dictum 'Never regret, never explain, never apologize', that governed the life of Admiral 'Jackie' Fisher, and enabled him to build the fleet that won the first world war (Fisher's Uncle John was a Magdalen don in

Jowett's day). But he was kind in many ways, conscientious and often generous, and in Oxford today the sourness has left his memory, and his shade seems more podgy than formidable—his memorial in Balliol shows him very small, almost fragile, lying flat on his back in his academic gown, with a very substantial book in his hand and cherubs all around to joggle the answers out.

Dons rooted! Part of the very matter of Christ Church, as institutional as Tom Tower itself, was Canon Claude Jenkins, who died in 1961. He was a solid, shuffling man with a big face, rather horse-like, who looked much older than he was, and whose white hair was beguilingly curly. His house in Tom Quad was so stacked with books, and so gloriously dishevelled, that sometimes it became actually impossible to open the front door, and the garden behind it, now forming part of the cathedral precincts, was a jungle of weeds and tall grasses.

Dr. Jenkins was shrewd about money, and an indefatigable committee-man—he once claimed to be sitting on 50 different committees at the same time. He consistently opposed the sale of land by the college, and is now seen to have been perfectly right, and he made a thrifty habit of removing small edibles from the common-room table to stock up his own commissary, stuffing them into his clerical pockets and taking them past the cathedral doors to his own house—where, as often as not, they were presently forgotten in the excitement of preparing a sermon, and were left to moulder high and maggoty upon a bookshelf.

Dr. Jenkins smoked a peculiar tobacco of his own mixture—'unknown', as his *Times* obituary put it, 'to the generality of smokers'—and was 'equally hostile to cats and to matrimony'. He arrived for an appointment once looking a trifle distraught, and apologized for being a few minutes late. 'My housekeeper has just died,' he explained, 'but I've propped her on a kitchen chair, and she'll be all right till I return.' In fact he was a much sweeter man than he allowed. He was popularly taken for a misogynist, but when he died he left the first choice of his 40,000 books to St. Anne's, one of the poorer women's colleges (and £100 to his own senior common room to keep it in snuff).

Nobody could deliver a benediction more beautifully, in his quavering but mellifluous old voice—the voice, you would think, of a centenarian—with his hand raised almost timidly in blessing, and his white hair gleaming above his vestments, in a glow of gold plate from the high altar behind him, below the great rose window of the cathedral. Claude Jenkins once baptized a child of mine—the first christening he had conducted for nearly half a century—and at the reception afterwards a friend chanced to see him bending over the cradle. 'Insufficiently prehensile,' the old gentleman was murmuring to himself, trying unsuccessfully to shake the baby's hand, and simultaneously slipping a piece of christening cake beneath his cassock.

'*And when at last*', wrote W. H. Auden in a poem addressed to this beloved character on his eightieth birthday, '*your eager soul shall fly (As do all Canons of the House) on high, May you find all things to your liking there—*

> *Celestial rooms where you may talk with men*
> *Like St. Augustine, Duchesne, Origen,*
> *While Seraphim purvey immortal snuff,*
> *More pungent than our mere sub-lunar stuff,*
> *Baroquish Cherubim cry:—'Glory, Laud,*
> *Eternal Honor to our Dr. Claude!'*

Dons who understand! When Canon William Buckland, a nineteenth-century Oxford geologist, began to disturb the theological convictions of the time by his investigation of fossils, Dr. Shuttleworth (of the port railway at New College) celebrated him with the epigram:

> *Some doubts were once expressed about the Flood:*
> *Buckland arose, and all was clear as mud.*

He was the most lurid of the Oxford eccentrics, and his efforts to understand involved some daring theories—he believed that every day, in the Biblical account of the creation, really meant some immense age of geological time—and some very peculiar experiments. When he visited Sicily on his honeymoon he was shown the relics of St. Rosalia, in her shrine-cave high on the slopes of Monte Pellegrino. 'They are the bones of a goat!' Buckland instantly announced, and the sanctuary doors were closed. In Naples he attended the annual liquefaction of the blood of St. Gennaro, but falling on his knees before the blood-stains, and licking them with his tongue, he pronounced them to be bats' urine.

Buckland claimed to have eaten his way through the entire animal kingdom. At his house in Oxford crocodile was sometimes served to guests, and sometimes mice cooked in batter, while a bear wandered around the dining-room and a monkey occasionally stretched out a hairy hand for the fruit. He once said that the nastiest thing he ever ate was a mole, and the next worse a blue-bottle: but that was before he had gobbled down the heart of a French king, rashly shown him as a precious relic at a neighbouring country house. Buckland's breakfast parties were as famous for their peculiar circumstances as for their eminent guests: one visitor, hearing a munching noise beneath the sofa, was calmly told that it was only the jackal eating some of the guinea-pigs.

Compact of ancient tales, and port! There have been a host of them, mostly immortalized only in an anecdote or two, and resuscitated for strangers after dinner with a certain reluctance, for in Oxford most of their ancient tales have been told to death already. Whately of the diving dog used to stick black plaster to his calves, to save darning the holes in his stockings. Charles Marriott of Oriel, in the 1840s, used to wear a cloak sewn together out of two old M.A. gowns, with a veil over his eyes. Moses Griffith of Merton so disliked undergraduates that he used to spend the whole of each term at Bath, and once, finding an unfortunate student eating in college during a vacation, called for a screen to shut him from view. 'Presence of Mind' Smith, Dean of Christ Church from 1824 to 1831, got his nickname from his account of a boating accident: 'Neither of us could swim, and if I had not with great presence of mind hit him on the head with a boathook, both would have been drowned.' William Spooner, the albino Warden of New College from 1903 to 1924, really did announce the hymn as *Kinquering Kongs Their Tikles Tate*, but probably never referred to Our Queer Dean in a Jubliee service, nor threaten to damn anyone for sewage.

'None whatever, sir', loudly retorted Dr. Lancelot Phelps, Provost of Oriel from 1914 to 1929, when a preacher paused in his account of a Biblical episode, and asked rhetorically what application the tale had to modern times. 'You may go,' said Dr. Edward Hawkins, a nineteenth-century Provost of Oriel, when an undergraduate asked for permission to attend an uncle's funeral, 'but I wish it had been a nearer relation.' A clergyman called Goulburn, preaching in Holywell Church in the 1840s, began his sermon with

the sentence: 'It may be predicated of the Bereans that they permitted no extraneous circumstances to counteract the equipoise of
their equanimity.' 'St. Paul says in one of his Epistles,' Bishop Jackson once observed from the pulpit of the cathedral, 'and I *partly*
agree with him ...'

I have always wondered about Montague B. Bellamy, whose wife
was named Zelpah and whose daughter Mariquita was buried at
St. Sepulchre's in 1892: and I shall never forget visiting W. A. Pan-
tin, Keeper of the University Archives, whose rooms at Oriel uprise
even now upon my inward vision, with their indescribable piles of
books, manuscripts, guides and learned papers, boxes of slides,
parchment scrolls, reference works open on every chair, a microfilm
viewer on a table, a map laid out on the floor—such a wonderful
clutter of loving scholarship that we had to clear a space in it, like
explorers in a jungle, before we could sit down to tea beside the
fire.

A perennial Oxford anecdote tells the tale of two wildly unconven-
tional old dons shaking their heads over the dullness of the times,
and wondering what has become of all the eccentrics. There is no
denying, though, that all too often the Oxford don is a pretty ordinary sort of fellow—clever of course, very likely charming, nearly
always hard-working, but scarcely striking. Heads of houses are
sometimes not academics at all, but return to Oxford, suave and
experienced, after eminent careers in diplomacy or Government.
Fellows generally live unexceptional domestic lives, dining in hall
only once or twice a week, and disciplined by the censure of wives
and over-educated children. The most common idiosyncrasy of the
modern Oxford don is a peculiarly exasperating sort of diffidence,
making table conversation a chore scarcely worth undertaking, and
reducing the pleasantries of the pavement to passing exchanges of
fish-like and apparently insensible glances.

And much more powerful than any Victorian original in his impact on this city was the most colourless of the Oxford characters,
W. R. Morris the engineer—who took his title, Baron Nuffield, from
the village east of Oxford where he had bought a manor house. Nuffield's relationship with Oxford was always equivocal. He was not
born in the city, but he prided himself on his Oxford background,
and was once even heard to remark, in a moment of rare lyricism,

that the High was the most beautiful street in the world. The very first bicycle he ever made, in his shop at 48 High Street, he sold to the vicar of St. Clement's—he later bought it back again, and it stands now in the museum at the Cowley works. The very first backer he had was the Earl of Macclesfield, an undergraduate customer: later Macclesfield offended Nuffield by doubting his unrivalled knowledge of carburettors, and broke with him for ever.

His first big act of philanthropy was a gift of £1,000 to the infant orthopaedic hospital at Headington: he knocked at the door himself, and handed the cheque to the resident surgeon. Most of his famous benefactions were to Oxford institutions—millions of pounds given for medical professorships, hospitals, college extensions, Nuffield College itself. He was fulsomely honoured by the University in return, and was even reconciled in the end, we are assured, to the earnestly progressive sociology of his college, than which it is difficult to imagine an outlook more alien to his own ideals of paternally ruthless free-for-all.

Yet we can hardly doubt that down there among the academics he was never at his ease. He seems to have been, business apart, as unexciting a man as ever walked. He had no interests, except for cars—even his phenomenal wealth hardly seemed to please him, and his lovable wife kept chickens to the last, in case he lost it all. He was a Philistine to the core: and though he was always kind to children, and generally to employees, his vast charitable gifts seem to have been made almost mechanically, without spirit. Childless and hypochondriac, he sounds an arid, sapless sort of man. The only flamboyant gesture ever attributed to him was apocryphal anyway—his purchase of the entire Huntercombe Golf Club, to spite its snooty committee. His only claim to originality appears to have been his gift for spotting an able subordinate, and his skill in cutting prices. For years he had a vicious prejudice against university graduates, sometimes sacking them for no other reason, and against foreigners—*Bonjour, manure*, was a Nuffield witticism. He loathed criticism, and stifled it with threats of libel actions. When he once paid a visit to his own factory during a strike, he walked slowly all down the line of the picket, without a single soul noticing him.

His is a pathetic figure. We are told that his subordinates often worshipped him, but nobody seems able to tell us why. More lastingly than all the Jowetts, Bucklands and Rouths, far more indelibly than Moses Griffith or the man with the cloak made of M.A. gowns, W. R. Morris has left his mark upon Oxford. He created the modern city, and loosed upon the place all the forces of the industrial civilization. Yet today it is difficult to revive a happy memory of this infelicitous millionaire—who died without an heir, without a religion and with few friends. Those who disliked him speak ill of him, and those who were fond of him cannot find anything interesting to say. But of all the dons that Belloc apostrophized, none more absolutely fits his final category—

> Dons perpetual that remain,
> A landmark, walling in the plain.

15. The Ark

In the churchyard of St. Peter's in the East, near the path to the porch, there is buried a lady called Sarah Hounslow. She was the mother of six children; she lived until her thirty-third year; and she died, so her tombstone unmistakably assures us, on February 31st, 1835.

'The least unlikely explanation' of this mystery, as a don of my acquaintance once worded it for me, is that the mason, dazed by the Oxford miasma, merely made a mistake: but my own instinct tells me that the *genius loci* deliberately jogged his elbow. It takes a crooked city to absorb so many human oddities, and Oxford is a very quirky sort of place. Not much about her is symmetrical—though the original Saxon ground plan seems to have been rigidly cruciform, Oxford soon put an end to *that*, fuzzing the outline with tortuous lanes and cul-de-sacs, and making sure that when the city wall was built, it was nothing like a circle. Even eighteenth-century formality found its match here; the great buildings of the period, like Queen's College or the Radcliffe Camera, are nearly all pushed out of true by immovably asymmetrical antiquities all around. When the Botanical Gardens were laid out, the designers so arranged things that if you stand with your back to the urn beside the southern wall, and look down the central pathway to the ornamental gate, over the lily pond, through the ceremonial pillars and across the fountain—if you look down this bower of the Age of Reason, Magdalen Tower is *not* framed in the centre of the great gateway.

It took a foreigner, Arne Jacobsen, to erect the entire college of St. Catherine's in perfect uniformity. Most English architects working in Oxford today avoid the absolute balance as anxiously as a grammarian avoiding a split infinitive, for the irregularity of the Oxford genius is very potent, and casts an intoxicating spell. The thoroughness of German learning, the gift of marshalling vast numbers of facts, tabulating them, comparing them, indexing them and analysing them—all this has been, at least until our own times, alien to Oxford. Even the title 'Professor' came late and reluctantly to this University, from Germany *via* Scotland, and Matthew Arnold said that Oxford, with its easy-going traditions of amateurism,was only a high school compared with the dedicated German universities of the day. Even now you do not often see beneath the imprint of the Clarendon Press those enormous tomes of criticism which rip the hearts out of immortal works of art, or tell us the temperature the water was likely to have been, on the day Shelley was drowned. At heart, perhaps, this University still cares more for the nebulous art of education, the moulding of minds and characters, than it does for the purer kinds of scholarship.

The Oxford style is something peculiarly English. The very structure of this University is illogical—a mass of separate units that seems to have no centre—and Oxford traditionalists have always taken pride in the tangled nature of the thing, its loose ends and innumerable anomalies. Half its charm is its sense of enigma, and even its fondest lovers are often hard put to define the nature of the Oxford spell—

> *Still on her spire the pigeons hover;*
> *Still by her gateway haunts the gown;*
> *Ah, but her secret? You, young lover,*
> *Drumming her old ones forth from town,*
> *Know you the secret none discover?*
> *Tell it when you go down . . .*

The original nucleus of the Ashmolean Museum was Tradescant's Ark of Curiosities, and Oxford herself is freighted deep with singularities. In some ways this is a flaw in her. When Zacharias Conrad von Uffenbach visited St. John's library in 1710, he was rightly contemptuous when they proudly showed him a large bladder-stone in a golden box, bearing the inscription: 'This stone was taken out of the body of Doctor John King, Lord Bishop of London, descended from the ancient Kings of Devon.' Sometimes Oxford people really do seem to care more for their japes and antique novelties than they do for profounder things—just as jolly anecdotes outweigh serious recollection in their memoirs. Often, though, Oxford's love of the off-beat and the back-of-the-hand is only the expression of a deep conviction—the belief that conformity for its own sake is ignoble. When you are shown a unicorn's horn or Guy Fawkes's lantern, or are invited to some preposterous ritual, you are being told in a jester's code that in this city a man may think, act and look as he likes—however ludicrous his tastes or unfashionable his opinions.

And you *will* be shown a unicorn's horn. One is kept in the Muniments Tower at New College—incomplete, because the Earl of Leicester asked to be given it after a visit to the college in 1576: the college protested that it had been 'left us as a speciall Jewell by owr Founder' (which was totally untrue), but Leicester was too powerful an applicant to be refused altogether, so they gave him 16½ inches off the end of it, and he prized it so highly that when they cleaned the portrait of him that hangs in the Warden's Lodgings, they found it clasped between his fingers. You really will see Guy Fawkes's lantern, too. It was presented to the Ashmolean in 1641 by the son of the man who arrested Fawkes, and it stands next door to the iron-lined, bullet-proof hat worn by John Bradshaw when he presided over the trial of Charles I—memorials, so the inscription says, 'one of Popish, the other of Fanatic infamy'.

As for the preposterous ritual, no event in Europe can be much sillier, not the most footling country frolic or pointless Anatolian orgy, than the Ceremony of the Mallard at All Souls—which only takes place, to be sure, once every hundred years, but is vividly remembered in between. It seems that when they were building the college, in the fifteenth century, a mallard duck flapped out of a drain beside the foundations: and this bird has been inexplicably honoured ever since. Twice a year it is serenaded in a famous song, which must never be heard by strangers' ears, and which ends with the following dotty doggerel:

> *Then let us sing and dance a galliard*
> *To the remembrance of the mallard.*
> *And as the mallard goes in pool,*
> *Let's dabble, duck and dive in bowl.*
> *Ho the blood of King Edward, by the blood of*
>   *King Edward*
> *It was a swapping swapping mallard.*

Solemnly the Fellows of the celebrated common room, popularly supposed to be the cleverest men in England, chant this gibberish over their cups: but once every hundred years they go further, and seizing staves and torches, go looking for the shades of that bird, led by a Lord Mallard in a sedan chair, with a dead duck on a pole: first three times round the quadrangle, singing as they go—*Ho the blood of King Edward!*—and then up to the roof in the middle of the night, doubtless as drunk as so many owls by now, their voices thundering across Radcliffe Square, their torches flickering in the sky, until at last they return to their common room in the small hours, drink a final potation laced with duck's blood, and let the bird lie for another century.

Scarcely less exotic ceremonials are offered twice a year by Queen's College, each accompanied by a splendid dinner. In February they have the Ceremony of the Needle and Thread—said to be an obscure pun on the name of the college founder, Robert of Eglesfield, by way of *aiguille et fils.* In the course of it the college bursar presents each guest with a needle and a piece of red thread, exhorting him to thrift. The guest pins it in the lapel of his dinner-jacket, rather like the ribbon of the Legion of Honour, and presently sees advancing down the table towards him an immense fourteenth-century loving cup, made of an aurochs' horn (*au῾rochs, n. Extinct wild ox. OTeut* urus, *etym. dub.,* + ochs *ox*). This is filled with a liquor whose ingredients are known only to the present steward of the college and his nominated successor, and is reputedly so powerful that two henchmen stand ready on each side, in case the unaccustomed guest falls flat on his back with the shock of it.

Then at Christmas they have their Boar's Head dinner, which is supposed to commemorate that resourceful clerk who choked the hog with Aristotle in Bagley Wood. It is preceded, like all dinners at Queen's, by a call on a silver trumpet, and the boar's head is carried into hall to the music of a carol—

> *The Boar's Head as I understand*
> *Is the Bravest dish in all the land*
> *When thus bedeck'd with a gay garland.*

Or as an older and to my mind superior version has it:

> *Hey, hey, hey, hey the boorys hede is array'd gaye;*
> *The borys hede, as I yow say,*

The borys hede ye furst mes.
The borys hede, as I yow say,
He takes his leyfe and gothe his way,
Gone after ye xij twely ffyt day,
          With hey.

This feast used to be held on Christmas Day, in the times when Queen's men from the north of England could not go home for the holiday, because of the state of the roads. It is now combined with a reunion of old members—what Oxford calls a gaudy. These can be boisterous affairs. After the carol the singers are given the embellishments on the boar's head—an orange from its mouth, little paper banners from its chaps, a crown from its forehead: and 'when the ornaments are exhausted,' as one Victorian pamphlet discreetly says, 'the Provost, Fellows and the favoured guests are left to enjoy their dinner'. *With hey.*

Would you prefer to go and see Pocahontas' father's deerskin mantle? It hangs on a wall of the Ashmolean, up the stairs from the gold Bulgarian breastplate bought with the royalties of *Seven Pillars of Wisdom*, and around the corner from the fragment of the dress Lady Hamilton wore for a ball after the Battle of the Nile, printed all over with oak leaves, ivory acorns and Nelson's name. Or would a properly skew-whiff Oxford building amuse you? The tower of St. Giles's church is not aligned with the nave, the north wall is longer than the south, the nave is wider at one end than it is at the other, no two arches in the nave have the same span, and the chancel arch is central neither to the nave nor to the chancel.

A piquant gargoyle? Oxford is full of them, but the most interesting stands on the north-western corner of the Magdalen cloister block, opposite the New Buildings. This was originally carved as a caricature of Dr. Edward Ellerton, senior Fellow of the college in the 1830s. He ordered it to be defaced, so the mason hollowed the cheeks, deepened the eyes and made it unrecognizable: but over the years Dr. Ellerton, looking out from his window nearby, realized with dismay that every term he grew more like that gargoyle anyway, until by the time of his death in 1851 it was the spit image of him. As for the large grotesque figures, called hieroglyphicals, that sit on the cloister buttresses, and which include hippopotami, wrestlers, a jester, a griffin, a greyhound, a camel with an unidentified animal on its back, Moses, a man in a sober hat and seven miscellaneous monsters—as for those flamboyant images, some people think they symbolize a complete pattern of academic discipline, while others think they mean nothing at all.

Copper flames issue, at Christopher Wren's suggestion, from urns on a parapet at Trinity. The Oxford Electric Tramways never had any electric trams. On the seventeenth-century monument to John French, in Wadham chapel, two smiling dolphins jointly carry on their backs a human skull with wings. Turner's picture of Oriel front quadrangle shows a man and a woman above the central steps, but both the figures are really, and unmistakably, kings. The stuffed owl that stands in Binsey Church is there to keep away bats. In the eighteenth century St. Peter's in the East supported a functionary called a Non-Playing Organist.

Nobody knows where the sword came from that hangs in the dining-hall at Oriel. When they completed the University Museum, in 1868, they forgot where they had laid the foundation stone, and it was not found again until 1906, when a Latin inscription was put on it. On the splendid seventeenth-century tomb of the Walter family, in Wolvercote parish church, eight children are recorded in the inscription, but only six are portrayed above, one of them headless. Among all the men pictured in Christ Church hall, the only one in armour is William Penn the pacifist. The grave of Anthony Wood the antiquarian, in Merton Chapel, was dug by Wood himself in 1690, five years before his death—he wanted to make sure, he said, that it was close to the wall. A lane at South Hinksey is called John Peer's Lane at one end, John Piers Lane in the middle, and Barleycott Lane at the other end. At St. John's there is a picture of Charles I made up of minute quotations from the Psalms—phrases for his eyebrows, whole psalms for his moustache and beard. Charles himself, we are told in one of the silliest Oxford stories, so coveted this that he offered the Fellows of St. John's any one wish in return: they dutifully handed it over, and then wished for it back again.

The Ethnological Museum in Oxford is named after General Pitt-Rivers, who was previously known as Colonel Lane Fox, and acquired his interest in the progress of mankind by observing the

gradual evolution of the smooth-bore percussion musket into the
Lee-Enfield rifle. Part of the floor of Hertford Chapel is made of
marble left over when the Greek Government commissioned a bust
of Byron as a present for the British people. At Balliol they have
a candle-stick not very convincingly claimed to be the one Queen
Victoria carried in her hand when she got out of bed at five in the
morning to be told of her accession to the throne. At the Ashmolean
they used to have a curly horn, three inches long, which grew out
of the head of Mary Davis, 'an old woman of Cheshire'.

Enough? Let me end with an extravagance of Brasenose. The
brazen nose of the college title is a door knocker, which hangs above
the high table in the dining-hall. There is another outside the gateway, and a modern replica sails on the prow of the college eight,
but the original was only restored to the college in Victorian times,
after several centuries' absence. It had, so the theory goes, been
taken away to Stamford in Lincolnshire by a fourteenth-century
migration of scholars, and put on the door of a house there. In 1890
this building, then a girl's school, came up for sale. Brasenose
bought the whole property for the sake of the knocker, brought the
trophy triumphantly home to Oxford, and sold the school in 1932
at a substantial profit.

Half Oxford's fascination is this feeling of delicate and deliberate
nonsense. 'We're all mad here', announced the Cheshire Cat, himself an Oxford eccentric, and certainly this city has generally been
proud of its lunatic streak.

The practical jokes mounted by Oxford undergraduates have
mostly been embarrassingly crude—daubing statues with yellow
paint, throwing dead rats across Cornmarket or propping chamber-
pots on fourteenth-century pinnacles. In the nineteenth century
especially the young barbarians often behaved deplorably in their
play—once they destroyed five valuable statues at Christ Church
in a frolic which *The Times* itself called 'the most brutal and sense-
less act of Vandalism that has disgraced our time'. The twelfth Duke
of Hamilton, egged on by the future King Edward VII, once walked
into a grocer's shop, had a pound of treacle poured into his hat,
and then clapped it upon the head of the unfortunate shop assistant—who probably, if I know anything about Oxford, accepted the
outrage with a gurgle of respectful thanks to His Grace.

Occasionally, though, an Oxford rag has just the right touch of genial but deadpan effrontery, and contributes itself to the patina of the city—'Ah,' Jowett used to say, when told of another rag at Balliol, 'the mind of the college is still vigorous—it has been expressing itself.' When Dean Lowe of Christ Church once landed in Christ Church meadows by helicopter, he was greeted by a concourse of undergraduates singing, 'Lo, He Comes in Clouds Descending'. In the 1950s a swan was found loitering elegantly on the pond in the middle of Tom Quad, wearing a black bow tie around its neck. It takes dash to get a flag to the very top of the Radcliffe Camera, up the slippery surface of the dome, and even the chamber-pot joke became fairly funny in 1923, when somebody actually cemented one to the top of the Martyrs' Memorial, so that it had to be shot off with rifle-fire.   ? ?

Soon after the first war, in the early years of psychiatry, a large audience went to the Town Hall to hear an eminent German savant talk about the Freudian system. He was announced as Professor Emil Busch, of Frankfurt University, and he was played with utter sang-froid by a Balliol undergraduate, George Edinger—so successfully that his talk was reported at length in the local Press, and some of his more enthusiastic listeners walked him to his train in earnest converse at the end of the meeting. The Professor's thesis was that the human personality should be seen 'against a mental background yet to be defined, a screen on which the figures of our mental cinema move'. Asked whether the background was something additional to the sum total of the combined personalities, he said he thought on the whole not, it being more in the nature, so to speak, of a *fluid*.

You would think that ghosts would frequent the lore of such a place, but though Oxford is one of the most haunted of cities, her spirits do not often materialize. All the paraphernalia is there, of course—dark old buildings, 50 acres of graveyard, the effluence of history and the creaking of old doors. When Jeremy Bentham came up to Queen's in 1760 his rooms looked across Queen's Lane to the churchyard of St. Peter's in the East, and he lived, so he said, in perpetual fear of spooks. Certainly such phantoms as there are prefer the mediaeval back-alleys. It was in Brasenose Lane, one night in the 1820s, that a Fellow of Brasenose saw an undergraduate, a well-known member of an atheistic society, being hauled out of his ground-floor window by a tall man in a black coat: the don had a not altogether unaccountable feeling of horror, and rushing into the college he found that only a few moments before the under-graduate had burst a blood vessel in the middle of a blasphemous speech, and fallen dead upon the floor.

Across High Street the ghost of a Puritan housemaid lives in a house off Magpie Lane. The house belongs to Barclay's Bank, and is well known to the bank's managers to be haunted, so that new-comers to the job are cheerfully told to keep an eye open for Pru-dence. She is said to have been courted by a Cavalier, and to have died of a broken heart when he deserted her, and there is in fact an entry in the parish register of St. Mary's, opposite, recording the burial of a Prudence Burcote in 1643. Visitors of psychic bent sometimes feel her presence, formidably down-to-earth bankers report odd noises in the house, and though it is not true, as legend says, that there are eternal bloodstains on the cellar steps, I have myself met a lady who once saw Prudence standing there as clear as daylight by the kitchen door—looking, so my informant said, as though she had just delivered the milk.

I disbelieve most of the other Oxford apparitions. I don't think the decapitated Archbishop Laud really potters about the library at St. John's—apparently on his knees, because they have raised the level of the floor since his day. I have never myself noticed the first Duke of Marlborough driving his coach up the Woodstock Road at midnight on New Year's Eve. I very much doubt the psychic origin of the damp patches which, gradually developing on the walls of the cathedral, were said to form a mysteriously accurate profile of Dean Liddell. And I am affectionately sceptical about the most successful of all the Oxford ghosts, the ghosts of *An Adventure*—who were not in Oxford at all, but were at least summoned into human vision by the indigenous fantasy of this place.

In 1901 Charlotte Moberly, Principal of St. Hugh's, and her Vice-Principal-elect, Eleanor Jourdain, went on a holiday visit to Versailles; and there, losing their way in the great park, they had a creepy historical experience. They stumbled into a lost hushed garden, and found themselves talking to a number of people from the time of the French Revolution, including Marie Antoinette her-self with a wide white hat and a sketching pad. The two distin-

guished women published an account of their experiences which
was sensationally received, as one of the most intriguing of all ghost
stories, and made them national celebrities.

An Adventure went through several editions, still reappears now
and then, has inspired more than one critical study, and to this day
always seems to be out, when I look for it at the Oxford City Library.
The two authors were exceedingly annoyed if anyone doubted their
sincerity, and stuck by the tale to the end of their days. Certainly
I cannot imagine Miss Moberly, whose face we have already
flinched before in the hall of her college, pulling the world's leg:
but Eleanor Jourdain sounds more promising, and I have had my
comforting doubts about her ever since I discovered that she once
claimed to have seen a mediaeval gallows, attended by thanes, con-
fessors and executioners, erected beneath the plane trees of north
Oxford.

In some ways Oxford University itself is one gigantic quirk, always
out of step with the times. This infuriates those who prize logic
above independence—just as the emergence of industry in Oxford
offends those who like a city to be all of a piece, all academic or
all commercial, all black or all lily-white. (My inclinations go the
other way: I would like to see Oxford a deep-sea port, too, and
be greeted as I ran down Headington Hill by the derricks and
superstructures of the freighters, moored beside Christ Church
meadows.)

The most notorious symbol of Oxford's syncopation is All Souls,
the all-male graduate college in High Street, which is evil in some
people's minds as a seed-bed of Chamberlain's appeasement, and
despicable in others as an appalling waste of academic resource. All
Souls is theoretically an institute of advanced studies, except that
a substantial minority of its 60 or so Fellows need not actually study.
They need not do anything at all, indeed, though they are mildly
expected to dine in college sometimes, sleep in the bed that awaits
them there, and be looked after by a college scout. Some 40 Fellows
of All Souls are University academics, about a dozen of them actually resident in the college: some are Professors, others young
researchers who have won their place in an atrociously difficult examination. Most of the rest, holding different categories of Fellowship, only appear at weekends, when they come down from London

full of metropolitan gossip, and stocked with the expertise of a dozen professions.

All Souls is rich, and life within its walls is very comfortable, so that its society has become a highly cultivated club—its members clever by definition and often influential by career, its guests picked almost at will from the national roster. In 1976 its Fellows included, besides the academics, three ex-Cabinet Ministers and two former ambassadors: when I dined there once I found within easy spitting distance three men who had, at one time or another, reviewed books of mine, plus my publisher. (Once I also listened to a passionate political declaration by an eminent Fellow of All Souls, who, pausing in his vehement denunciation of some politician or other, suddenly realized what he was saying, broke off in mid-polemic, and turning to me with a disarming solemnity, inserted the awful phrase: *'And I speak, mark you, of a Member of this College!'*)

For myself, I would like to see this place preserving its fastidious privileged character, but packed in every room with eager full-time scholars—the most high-powered, as well as the most sumptuous, of all graduate colleges. The traditional theory is, though, that the give-and-take of thought and controversy, passed week by week across the old oak tables of All Souls, is itself a sort of English lubricant, fructifying the national life, bridging the gaps between professions, and worth preserving in itself as a late survivor of an old, carefree, valeted England.

Oxford University as a whole, to a less pickled degree, preserves this comfortable quality. This is a University still on its own, still half aloof to change. It has tried to adapt an aristocratic tradition to an egalitarian age, and though to the sympathetic observer this generally looks admirable, if a little forlorn, to the critic it is often simply arrogant. Trade unionists, visiting this city for summer conferences, sometimes suggest to outraged college porters that the whole place ought to be blown up, allowing the Ministry of Education to start again from scratch; and the leitmotiv of criticism against Oxford, which never ceases, is the University's sense of antique superiority—the feeling that, for all its enlightened poses, it only caters for the upper half of the nation, and gives its alumni unfair advantages in life.

Most of it, though, is the wrong end of a stick—a misunderstanding of the gravelly evasiveness of the place, which is only a mask for its tolerance and its fine distrust of sameness (exasperating though it is going to be, for anyone living near Radcliffe Square on the night of All Souls' Day, 2001, when the Fellows clamber up there again behind the Lord Mallard, stamping among the chimney-pots and carrying on about that confounded duck).

16. The Argosy

If it is partly an ark, it is partly an argosy. Oxford is like a huge wayward cargo of treasures, shipped home by some eccentric entrepreneur with an eye for a promising talent, plenty of money and stubborn preferences of his own. There is a good deal of expensive trash in Oxford, and the city is cluttered with curios of purely family interest: but there are also superb assemblies of buildings, antiquities, rarities and *objets d'art*—not to speak of books. They may be anywhere in the city. There is a Gainsborough in the Town Hall, and a famous collection of dolls' houses in a private house at Iffley, and the fourteenth-century chalice at Marston church is probably the oldest in use anywhere in England.

This immense accretion of things has taken time. The city's oldest possession is probably that fetish from St. Michael's tower, which has been in local hands for at least 1,000 years, but it is only a few years since the New College was given one of the finest El Grecos in England, and the altarpiece of St Edmund Hall, a painting by Ceri Richards, was bought by the Junior Common Room in 1958. Most of the University's treasures are products of piety, given as acts of homage to God or *alma mater*, and wherever you go in Oxford, you will find grateful lists of benefactors. As early as 1423 the building of the Divinity School was financed by an appeal, and the crests on the bosses of its ceiling are a kind of heraldic subscription list—if the arms of Thomas Kemp, Bishop of London, appear three times, it is only because he gave 1,000 marks towards the cost, or between £40,000 and £50,000 in modern currency.

So most of it has come free. If you have a pint of beer with your lunch in one of the older senior common rooms, you will probably be served it in a splendid silver tankard—perhaps Victorian, perhaps Jacobean, for it used to be a pleasant custom to present a tankard as an admission fee in kind, and thus be tacitly toasted every lunchtime for the next three or four centuries.

When you see her as a whole from the neighbouring heights, Oxford really does sometimes look like a casket of precious things. She has an Ali Baba look then, as though somebody has opened the green lid upon a cache of tall golden incense burners, jewel cases, ivory eggs and reliquaries. Such a view is artificial now, for if you shift your picnic site a hundred yards or so, then the factories and the gasometers show, and bring you sadly home from Baghdad: but the distant prospect of Oxford is still her greatest treasure—one of the supreme townscapes of Europe, and comparable only in my experience with the inland cities of Spain, as you see their castles and campaniles jutting so tremendously above the Sierra. It is a jagged Gothic spectacle down there, and depends for its effect upon its thicket of different shapes and prominences, so that it looks best of all when foreshortened by photography, or when from a circling aircraft you can juggle its perspectives as you please. Now and then they do their best to ruin it, but all in all it is marvellous how inviolate the skyline remains, and how complete and compact old Oxford can still look, if you line up the edge of the fir thicket properly, hold your teacup over your left eye, and wear dark glasses.

The strength of the scene lies in its sense of organic growth. Oxford is not at all a museum. She is a proper working city, and her character has been built up in layers down the centuries, as each street, each building even, has been enlarged, converted or remodelled. Few Oxford colleges survive all of a style for long. Wadham did, until the twentieth century. St. Catherine's and Wolfson probably will, for 50 years or so. Nuffield was a hodge-podge from the start, with a faintly Levantine tower upon a Cotswold Gothic base, and St. Anne's, which only became a college in 1952, already has, delightfully set about its single quadrangle, buildings of four distinct architectural styles, plus a blinding *al fresco* mural.

This is not really an architect's city. Professionals sometimes scoff at its pretensions, I am told, and maintain that these queer heaps and conglomerations are scarcely architecture at all. Many of the best-loved Oxford buildings are by amateurs. Many are by unknown designers, or master-masons, and many more are mere reproductions, or echoes of long-outdated styles. The fan-vaulting of the hall staircase at Christ Church, among the best examples of the *genre*, was erected in 1630—when everybody else had stopped making fan-vaulting at all. Trinity Chapel, built in 1691, was the very first non-Gothic chapel in Oxford—in Oxford the Gothic Revival in the 1830s was a misnomer, for the style had hardly died out anyway. The Ashmolean Museum was based on the Temple of Apollo at Bassae, and the Examination Schools in the High, opened in 1882, were inspired by Kirby Hall, Northamptonshire.

Even so, many of the best English architects have left their mark upon Oxford. Wren built the Sheldonian and Tom Tower, both rather eccentric, both gloriously successful: he also cut the doorway in the north wall of the Divinity School, and the initials CWA, on the canopy outside, stand for Christopher Wren, Architect. John Vanbrugh built a heavy house at 20 St. Michael's Street, occupied by solicitors, Hawksmoor built half All Souls, James Gibbs built the Radcliffe Camera, claimed to be the third largest dome in England (in the Bodleian can be seen Hawksmoor's model for a rival design, deposited there after serving for a century as a doll's house in an Oxfordshire mansion).

John Nash, of the London terraces, advised Exeter on some alterations in 1802: he would accept no fee, but asked instead that his portrait might be hung in the dining-hall—it is still there, was painted by Sir Thomas Lawrence, and cost the college £449. 10s. anyway. James Gwynne, one of the great bridge-builders of his day, designed not only Magdalen Bridge but also the covered market—which turns out to be, if you stand on the opposite side of High Street and relate it to the street façade, quite a monumental piece of design. (Oxford is lucky to have it, for one day in the 1750s Gwynne fell off the dome of St. Paul's, only being saved by a protruding stump of lead.)

Most of the Victorian masters worked in Oxford—William Butterfield at Keble, Benjamin Woodward at the Museum, G. E. Street at St. Philip and St. James, G. F. Bodley at Magdalen. Charles Barry, the architect of the Houses of Parliament, designed the westernmost building of University College, on the High. The only thing Ruskin ever actually designed himself was one window in the Museum. And no one man has invented more of Oxford than T. G. Jackson, that exuberant and unmistakable late Victorian, whose structures here include the vast Examination Schools, half Trinity front quadrangle, the organ case at the Sheldonian, the cricket pavilion in the Parks, and the little chapel, once part of the Cowley Military Academy, which has long since been engulfed in the Morris works.

So down to our own century, to Lutyens, Jacobsen, Powell and Moya, Leslie Martin, James Stirling. What an architectural convention they would all make, if they could be summoned back to compare each other's work, criticize the proportions of the Radcliffe Camera in the moonlight, or hurl execrations towards the biochemistry block from the heights of Elsfield! Between them they could demonstrate to each other every period of English architecture, from the eleventh to the twentieth century, without leaving the central square mile of Oxford.

Two masters in particular might be pithy in their views. Inigo Jones and Augustus Pugin each built one structure in Oxford. When Jones's gateway at Magdalen was pulled down in 1844, Pugin's went up instead: but 40 years later they demolished that too, and today not a pilaster of the one architect, nor a finial of the other, is left in Oxford at all.

Where would they take us, if we were to follow them through Oxford's almanac of architecture? First, perhaps, to brush up on their theory, to the Tower of the Five Orders in the quadrangle of the Bodleian, where the Tuscan, Doric, Ionic, Corinthian and Composite forms are placed one on top of each other, like a refresher course. Then from the Romanesque crypt of St. Peter's in the East, now a library, with its stumpy pillars and its chambers for holy relics, to view the celestial Early English spire of St. Mary's, leaping from its cluster of lesser pinnacles.

To the Divinity School next, one of the best examples of Perpendicular—a marvellously airy structure, so delicately put together that it hardly feels like stone at all, but might be made of alabaster, or aluminium. Along to Tom Quad, for a glimpse of the wealth and magnificence of the Renaissance, with the fountain spouting in its central pool and the huge college flag flying, perhaps, above the corner tower on St. Aldate's. Then back to St. Mary's for a delightful example of the Baroque—the gay twisted pillars of the porch on the High, with the Madonna so cosily graceful above them, and two eroded angels on the roof.

They could visit any of half a dozen college chapels, for standard seventeenth-century work—warm, polished, elaborate, and so alike that almost nobody can remember one from another. They would probably choose Hawksmoor's splendid Queen's College for Palladian Oxford, and for the clash between the Classical and the Gothic revivals, they might go to the top end of Beaumont Street and compare the Greek glory of the Ashmolean on the left with the Gothic push of the Randolph Hotel on the right. Much the most interesting Victorian building to see would be the Museum, which crops up in so many Oxford contexts. Ruskin himself rightly said it smacked of parsimony, Tennyson called it 'perfectly indecent', and there is something distinctly comical to the idea of modelling a chemical laboratory upon the Abbot's Kitchen at Glastonbury: but the whole was built with such fire and dedication that it splendidly represents the conviction of its age—as absolute, in my view, as King James's Magdalen Tower.

I hesitate to suggest where those masters might lead us through the buildings of our own time—'whatever else is said of them,' old Ruskin still whispers caustically in my ear, 'at least it will never be denied that they are beautiful'. In any case, it would probably be technique rather than taste that chiefly interested the tourists, for the challenges that face the architect in Oxford have not much changed down the centuries. They are chiefly demands of scale— in the old days, because building was confined to narrow gravel spits, or within circumscribing city walls, nowadays because the Oxford aesthetic is poised upon so fragile a balance, threatened by so many interests, that one false or selfish proportion can shatter it.

The most beguiling stone treasures in the city, to my mind, are those that have deliberately exploited this jigsaw setting, absorbed the inconsequential panache of the place, and seem to have been notched or levered into Oxford: but these are often the buildings the perambulations ignore, which are unnoticed by the guidebooks, and which you suddenly notice out of the corner of your eye as you pass from one famous spectacle to the next—while the guide prattles on with that particular mixture of hard fact and supposition, spiced with tittle-tattle, which is peculiar to Oxford tourism.

It is not a monumental city. Its grandest streets are wide, but not ceremonial. It is difficult to imagine a military parade down High

Street, or kings following a cortège along St. Giles, and there is not a single equestrian statue in the city. Strangers sometimes wonder at the lack of plinths and laurel-crowned strategists, in a place of so many high-flown memories; but heroic statuary is not in the Oxford style, and anyway undergraduates would soon paint it yellow, or put dustbins over its helmets.

One superbly grandiose figure does stand in the quadrangle of the Bodleian. It shows the third Earl of Pembroke, one of the library's chief benefactors, standing there in full armour in unwavering self-assurance, and was cast by Hubert Le Sueur, the seventeenth-century sculptor, from a portrait by Rubens. 'Solid Velásquez' is how Richard Ford once described the famous equestrian statue of Philip IV opposite the Royal Palace in Madrid, which was taken from a Velásquez painting: but this figure takes the process further, for if Rubens painted its original, when Van Dyck wanted to portray the Earl of Pembroke, he painted a picture of *it*. The statue was given to the Bodleian by Pembroke's greatnephew, who expansively offered it one evening in 1723 to two Oxford guests at dinner. The scholars, fearing their host might change his mind in the morning, are said to have taken the head in advance, as a security, leaving the trunk to come by carrier: certainly head and trunk are separate—you can see the joining line above the ruff—and the head can be moved this way or that, to catch the best light.

Le Sueur also did the handsome effigy of Charles I that stands above the gateway of St. John's. The king looks stylish enough, but when he was taken down during the Civil War, to be offered for sale for the bronze, he turned out to be hollow, and found no buyers. Cecil Rhodes is imperially pompous on the High Street façade of Oriel. Queen Elizabeth II, though almost unrecognizable, certainly looks regal in Christ Church hall—ingeniously illuminated as she is by a beam projected in the same shape as the bust itself, so that no light falls on the wall behind. There are half a dozen fine portrait busts by Jacob Epstein, in one college and another, and I am personally fond of the bust of Brunel the engineer, in the Museum of the History of Science, which shows him stripped of black hat, cravat and even cigar, and wearing only a toga.

But portrait statuary generally fails in Oxford, perhaps because, in the cold elegance of marble or the power of bronze, wrinkles and

laugh-lines do not properly show. The bust of Dr. Pusey the Tractarian, in the cathedral, comes out almost comical, so excruciatingly
Machiavellian is the face of the divine: and the two kings in their
niches at Oriel look as though they are either waiting to strike one
o'clock on a church tower, or are debating which of them is on duty
in an old-fashioned cottage barometer. As for the heads outside the
Sheldonian Theatre, it is a moot point whether they represent philosophers, Roman Emperors, the 12 Apostles or nobody in particular.
They look handsome fellows now, since the sculptor Michael Black
re-made them in the 1970s, but in their previous incarnation they
looked ghostly—so soft was their Headington stone that their
features had long been worn away altogether, till they looked like
mummies' heads, or perhaps players in one of those thrillers that
require a central character to be entirely swathed about with ban-
dages, lest we glimpse the unimaginable warted horror of the face
beneath.

An old snigger of a day in Oxford is a visit to the Shelley
Memorial, which was erected in University College some 80 years
after the college had expelled the poet for refusing to admit his
authorship of an atheist pamphlet. You approach it down a darkish
corridor, past a door loftily labelled The Linen Room, and suddenly
there it is, bathed in a creepy half-light behind an iron grille: a
life-size figure of the drowned poet, stretched out white and realistic
upon a marble bier. It was created by Edward Onslow Ford for
Shelley's grave, but the English Cemetery at Rome declined it, so
in 1894 it was erected here instead, beneath a cupola intended to
recall, we are told, life's 'many-coloured dome'. From the back
the figure is said to look plump-buttocked, supposedly proving that
its model was a girl: from the front, mourned by its supporting
Muse, it looks to me rather beautiful.

It has often been an embarrassment to its owners. So many undergraduates have squeezed through the bars to profane it that traces
of orange paint are irremovably ingrained in the marble, sometimes
flickering when the light is wrong. After the second world war the
college planned to move it, in order to build on the site, but they
could find nowhere else to put it, and the Ashmolean objected
to the paint in its pores. So it stays where it is, and each year
becomes a little less offensive, a little less of a joke, so that only a few
obstinate reactionaries now suggest filling the vault with water,

and allowing tropical fish or alligators to swim bemused about the corpse.

Religious sculpture comes off better. Holy though this city is, and frequently sanctified its purpose, in the ironic Oxford environment saints seem more than usually remote—'This is all, and perhaps rather more than all,' wrote the Oxford historian J. A. Froude in a contribution to Newman's projected *Lives of the English Saints*, 'that is known of the life of the Blessed St. Neot.' Abstract figures of holy persons are therefore all the more acceptable, and Oxford is full of them—figures of bishops, figures of martyrs, figures, I dare say, of St. Budoc or the Blessed St. Neot, looming in dark cloister corners or joyously aloft on bell towers.

You cannot escape them. The Last Judgement itself pursues you from the gate tower of All Souls, placed there, though generally assumed to be as old as Agincourt, in 1939. The effigies that used to stand upon the spire of St. Mary's, before they were removed as dangerous to the passing public, are now distributed between the crypt of the church, the cloisters of New College, and the arcade around the inner quadrangle of All Souls: and there they watchfully await your arrival, battered and blackened with age, suddenly standing before you, crumbled but erect, like watchmen in the shadows. There is an innocuous figure of St. Frideswide on the outside of the pulpit at Binsey: but if you look *inside*, you will be surprised by a far more daring effigy of the saint, carved by Eric Gill, but placed there out of sight because the parish councillors thought it might be too much for the congregation.

In the ante-chapel of New College stands Epstein's tremendous figure of the risen Lazarus, shrouded still for the grave. This is much the most haunting statue in Oxford. It startles you, white and tortured, when you open the chapel door and see it there for the first time. It moves you when you look back from the altar and see it framed beneath the organ. And it looks preternaturally radiant through one of the slits, high on the south wall of the ante-chapel, which enable the Warden of New College to look down from his adjacent Lodgings. From there the risen Lazarus seems to be generating his own ghostly light, shining most strangely far below you. When Nikita Krushchev once saw this great statue, he said the memory of it kept him awake all night.

Beside the Sheldonian stands the building called the Old Ashmolean, itself like an exquisite stone strong-box, and now the Museum
of the History of Science. It contains some of the most covetable
and characteristic of Oxford treasures, for this is a city that has
always been famous for its instruments. It was a sixteenth-century
Oxford mathematician, the Bavarian Nicholas Kratzer, who
designed the dials that show in the foreground of Holbein's *The
Ambassadors*, and Oxford remains a place of pilgrimage for anyone
who likes beautiful, intricate devices for measuring things.

In particular this city seems to have enjoyed measuring time.
Kratzer made several celebrated time-pieces for Oxford, and every
kind of sundial may still be seen here. The mass dial on the wall
of South Hinksey church merely told parishioners when it was time
to go to service. The scratch dial beside it went further, and was
an early device for marking every hour of the day. Living sundials
were a favourite eighteenth-century conceit, and there used to be
an elaborate one at the foot of New College mound, planted in box,
and set around with lovers' knots. There is a sundial painted on
a glass window in the Convocation House, enabling ancient
Registrars, glancing over the Vice-Chancellor's right shoulder, to
know when to advise an adjournment for sack and oysters.

Wren himself designed the magnificent sundial in the inner quadrangle of All Souls: it is said to be exceedingly accurate, and bears
the gloomy motto *Pereunt et imputantur*—'They pass and are
charged for.' John Keble, of all people, once damaged the pillar
sundial in the quadrangle of Corpus Christi, by throwing a bottle
at it (lemonade, no doubt). Nor is the sundial dead in Oxford yet.
There is a new one at Lincoln, put up by the junior common room
as a war memorial, and in the doorway that leads into Brasenose
hall there is a new aluminium panel, as precisely calibrated as a
rocket's pressure gauge, to advise you, if you have a bent for figures,
how to tell the time by the sundial across the quadrangle.

You need not exert yourself, though, for wherever you walk in
Oxford you are sure to find a clock. If you forget to glance at St.
Mary's as you pass up the High, Carfax will soon be in view, with
its two little gilded knights waiting to strike the hour, or there is
the great face of Tom down St. Aldate's, or the clock that shows
through the Broad Street gates of Trinity, or the clock high on the
rubble tower of St. Michael's at the North Gate, or the clock that

you can conveniently consult in Blackwell's bookshop, or the clock that still forlornly stands above the drinking fountain across Magdalen Bridge—erected to celebrate Queen Victoria's Diamond Jubilee, but now slogan-chalked and rubbish-strewn, its taps waterless, its basins cracked, and only the faithful old time-piece above still honouring the occasion. Tickings, whirrings and strikings are fundamental sounds of Oxford: punctuality is, unexpectedly, one of this city's virtues.

And best of all are the instruments laid out for your delight in the Old Ashmolean. The building fairly glows with astrolabes—the finest collection in the world, including that supreme rarity, a spherical Islamic astrolabe, perhaps the only one there is. There are all sorts of orreries, too, some of them presented to Oxford by the Lord Orrery they are named for, and there is a superb silver microscope made, it is thought, for George III, whose lenses are upheld by allegorical figures and chimeras, and embellished with ornamental urns. The Museum also possesses the first searchlight (1872) and the first 'logical machine'—an embryo computer of Victorian vintage, 'capable of exhibiting an answer to any question which may be put to it concerning the possible combinations which form any class'. I love the Museum of the History of Science. I love the superb seventeenth-century lock they lock it with at night, with elaborate jaw-like movements of steel bars and bolts. I relish all its burnished, engraved and venerable devices, with small florid embellishments to set off their precision, and marvellous suggestions of new worlds to be explored. I very much like the fact that its chief modern benefactor was J. A. Billmeir, one of the most enterprising of tramp-ship owners, who made his fortune running the Nationalist blockade in the Spanish Civil War, and proudly sailed with his own ships, when they were detailed for the North Russian convoys.

Some years ago a prisoner in Oxford gaol, looking sadly out of his cell each night, was puzzled by the revolving lights he could see high in the bulk of Nuffield College tower. He wrote to the Warden of Nuffield to ask what they were, and was told they were an illuminated and fanciful kind of orrery, hung in the uppermost room of the tower, and partly designed by John Verney—author of that little masterpiece, *Going to the Wars*. There seemed something pathetic about the inquiry—the prisoner gazing from his

narrow window, while that silvery polished object revolved in the
night outside—and the kind-hearted Warden asked if the convict
might not be allowed across the road to see the orrery more closely.
Permission was refused, however, for the prisoner had a weakness
for instruments of a blunter kind.

Oxford is very proud of her pictures, but they are mostly a fearful
bore. Up and down we dutifully stroll, up one side of the hall and
down the other, and there the enormous portraits hang embedded
in gilt, one after the other in the half-light. Their colours are dim,
their manner is generally forbidding, and they nearly all seem to
be of bishops. Most colleges honour only the most utterly respectable of their graduates. Trinity displays no portrait of Sir Richard
Burton, Worcester none of de Quincey, Magdalen none of Oscar
Wilde, and even University College apparently feels that a marble
corpse is enough for Shelley.

Hidden away among the pious orthodoxy, all the same, are
hundreds of pictures worth seeing—for art or for character. The
Ashmolean is one of the most enjoyable of art galleries—not too
big, elegantly arranged, well lit and guarded by gossipy ladies in
blue overalls reading paper-back romances. It contains the best collection of Raphael drawings in the world, and a superb collection
of Michelangelo drawings too—all once the property of Thomas
Lawrence the portrait painter. It has Uccello's *Hunt in a Forest*,
a roomful of Pre-Raphaelites, lots of Pissarros, and an excellent
series of Samuel Palmer drawings, in which you may see the talent
of that monitory genius fade from mysticism to plump convention.
It also has as good a cross-section of universal art as any English
gallery outside London.

Elsewhere one must hunt the worth-while pictures out—da Vinci
drawings in the lovely modern art gallery at Christ Church, for instance, El Greco's St. James in New College chapel, royal portraits
in the Examination Schools or Holman Hunt's once-celebrated
Light of the World, as good as new in Keble chapel. For myself,
I judge the Oxford portraits more for their faces than for their execution, and here is my own choice of examples: John Locke at
Christ Church, painted by Kneller at 72, looking appallingly cadaverous and fateful, as though he foresees all the bloodshed that will
one day flow from his ideas; Edward VII in the Examination

Schools, painted by John Watson-Gordon as a fresh but calculating undergraduate, running slightly to fat: de Laszlo's Curzon at Balliol, with a formidable curl to the upper lip, half sneer, half dry smile; Millais's Gladstone at Christ Church, for the power of the eagle eye, and Miss Moberly at St. Hugh's, by W. Llewellyn, for the divine right of bishops' daughters; Seth Ward the seventeenth-century astronomer, peering across Wadham hall like a suspicious butcher; Lord Chatham, by an unknown artist, placed between the doors of Trinity hall to give each undergraduate an after-dinner jerk to the ambitions; Cardinal Manning at Balliol, a proper Renaissance face five centuries after its time, painted by Goldborough Anderson and looking at once poisonous and exceedingly good company; and the huge, familiar, swashbuckling portrait of Henry VIII at Christ Church, which is only a copy of Holbein's original, but which looks a proper masterpiece at the end of that great hall, feet apart, arms akimbo, with its eye fixed so equivocally upon you, as you advance tentatively between the tables, that you cannot be sure whether you are going to be given a sheep's head for your dinner, or divorced.

Many of the interesting pictures are in stained glass—for seventeenth-and eighteenth-century glass, especially, Oxford is unrivalled in England. The 'lily glass' in the north aisle of St. Michael's at the North Gate is one of the few surviving examples of a favourite mediaeval motif. It shows a figure of Christ crucified forming the stalk of a lily, with his arms on two of its flower stems—a mystical fancy so repugnant to the Puritans that almost everywhere else they destroyed it. The fifteenth-century glass in All Souls ante-chapel includes a curious assembly of kings, from Constantine to John of Gaunt—who is shown crowned as King of Castile, because of his marriage to the daughter of Pedro the Cruel. Sir Joshua Reynolds created the great west window of the Nativity in the ante-chapel of New College—actually enamelled, not stained, in a queer greenish tint. The shepherd at the top right of the composition is really Thomas Gervais, who did the enamelling, and the one in a saffron smock is Reynolds himself, who was paid 20 guineas apiece for the Seven Virtues at the bottom, but nothing at all for the Nativity group itself.

Inside the chapel proper there is an eighteenth-century window of Adam and Eve, from a cartoon by Biaggio Rebecca, which Victorian restorers dressed up in cloak and leopard skin, for decency's sake. They were the work of a glazier called William Peckett, whose work has had its ups and downs of fortune; though it is highly prized now, it is his forlorn distinction that both here and in Oriel chapel there are windows by him so hacked about, in the course of time and reconstruction, that his signature has been cut in half, and reads merely '*W. Peck Pin.*' Twice mutilated too is St. Thomas à Becket. In St. Lucy's chapel in the cathedral his head was removed by order of Henry VIII, during the King's conflict with the Church, and has been replaced with a blank piece of glass: in Binsey church he has been reduced to palimpsest, and though the torso is unquestionably his, the bottom half is a medley of miscellaneous legs, some of them probably his murderers'.

Two Dutchmen called van Linge were busy in Oxford in the seventeenth century. Sometimes they made their glass on the spot, and the design for the Bernard van Linge window in Wadham chapel is said to have been taken from a book in the college library. I like their work best at University College, where the chapel is gay with Abraham van Linge's colourful pictures, full of ships, distant cities on seashores, camels and turbanned patriarchs. I also enjoy the Victorian stained glass in the chapel of Mansfield College, a Congregationalist body—an astonishing portrait gallery in glass, including pictures of Oliver Cromwell, St. Chrysostom, Abelard, Dr. Livingstone and several college benefactors: to the left of the altar stand Mrs. Sarah Glover and Mr. Henry Manton, to the right are Amos and Plato. In Headington parish church two other celebrities are curiously yoked—Simon de Montfort, 'Founder of English Parliaments', and Vashti, identified in the window as 'Queen of Persia', who has a leopard at her feet, and who looks so stimulatingly heathen that at first the Church authorities were distinctly uneasy about having her there at all.

The old Oxford glass is full of charm, but for plain beauty I admire most of all a modern set of windows. It is surprising to find that Nuffield College has a chapel, so severely progressive is the flavour of the college: but off that Cotswold-pattern quadrangle, up a Gothic-type staircase, you will find one of the sweetest little sanctuaries in Oxford. It is very simple, almost stern, with black and white pews like a New England meeting house, and a reredos of beaten iron: but filling it all with rich colour are John Piper's lovely windows—boldly patterned in black, green and primary colours at the bottom end of the chapel, and looking so spirited and exhilarating in that boring building that it is like opening a tool kit to find a diamond among the wrenches.

If ever they came to sell it all, the books would no doubt go first, quick as a flash across the Atlantic, and the Old Masters next; and the glass would be distributed among missions, youth clubs and churches in new industrial towns; and the portraits would dribble away down the market, leaving a Lawrence in this art gallery, a Henry Lamb in that, until at last the dimmest and most obscure of the ecclesiastics showed up dusty in the corners of junk shops, for the sake of the frames. Up to Sotheby's would pour the astrolabes, and the great silver salt cellars, and the beautiful furniture from Masters' Lodgings, and the Chinese porcelain from the Department of Eastern Art; and the British Museum would intervene, after questions in the House of Commons, to acquire the Minoan, Greek, and Egyptian collections from the Ashmolean; and all the noble old ports would go to the highest bidder, I suppose, extracted cobwebby from college cellars; and the Bodleian's chair made from the timbers of the *Golden Hind* would unquestionably go to San Francisco; and some great State University in the Middle West would acquire from the Bodleian the guitar Shelley gave to Jane Williams:

> *Ariel to Miranda: Take*
> *This slave of music for the sake*
> *Of him who is the slave of thee.*

But I would steal in to the Ashmolean before the sales began, and take for myself my favourite of all the Oxford treasures: Alfred's Jewel, which was found at Athelney in 1693, which is made of a translucent enamel, set in beaten gold, and which shows the old king with one black eye and one grey, looking at you astigmatic out of the marshes.

17. In Art

W hile I was about it, I would also filch from the Museum a large silver crown minted in Oxford during the Civil War. It shows Charles I, wearing his crown, astride a handsome charger, and between the horse's hoofs can be seen the towers of the city, exquisitely stylized. Connoisseurs say it is one of the most beautiful coins ever struck in England: it is also one of the best portrayals of Oxford in art. People never stop picturing Oxford—in expensive picture books, in sentimental water-colours, in television films, in the manifestos of furious critics and the doddery reminiscences of retired proconsuls. It is odd, however, how curiously little appeal this lovely city has had for the great artists and the poets. The malaise of the place is bad for inspiration; the fire splutters with the damp; even the plodding topographer sometimes feels the need to escape, and do his second draft in Wales or Italy.

You would think the distant prospect of Oxford, so successfully exploited by that Master of the King's Mint, would form an irresistible backcloth for painters in the Venetian tradition. Giorgione would surely have loved it, as a distant tranced city behind a silent saint, and Titian might well have had St. Christopher carrying the infant Christ across the Isis. In fact it has rarely happened. Innumerable cities brighten the backgrounds of Oxford's religious pictures—imaginery Florences, visionary Constantinoples, seaports that I instinctively assume to be Smyrna and hill towns that could only be Assisi. Oxford, though, seldom shows.

There is an altarpiece in the Franciscan church in the Iffley Road, which shows St. Francis and St. Agnellus of Pisa, who brought the Order to England, standing at the foot of the Cross on Boar's Hill, a thrush, a magpie and a hawk in attendance. A stained-glass window in the church of St. Mary and St. John at Cowley has the spires of Oxford behind a lovely young St. Frideswide. Among the college portraits, I can think only of the picture of Sir Roger Newdigate, the eighteenth-century donor of the Newdigate Prize, which hangs in University College hall, and shows the entire city basking gratefully in his munificence. As for the comfortable local manor house which is portrayed in that picture of Vashti and Simon Montfort, it has a poignant point: for if you leave the church and seek out the house itself, you find it swamped by a pre-fabricated housing estate, and half deafened by the noise of the northern by-pass.

What Constable would have done with Oxford, with a blurred rainbow forming over Shotover, and the spires encouched in green below! What Kokoschka might have done with her, with her flood of traffic pouring down the exquisite river of the High! As it is, we must make do with some inferior Turners, knocked off apparently in moments of boredom—in 1804 even the Oxford Almanac rejected his picture of Balliol, pointing out that in some parts of it the sun seemed to be shining from the *north-east*. Worcester College has a collection of views by the eighteenth-century water-colourist William Turner of Oxford, whose modest talent hits off the charm, but not the power of the city. Rowlandson vigorously portrayed the fat dons, hussies and coachmen of Oxford life; Ackermann published a meticulous series of architectural pictures; but no great painter, it seems, has found this place an inspiration, and when we think of Oxford visually we tend to think of her in photographs, or in those painstaking prints of college buildings, complete to the black cat on the Provost's wall, which undergraduates often buy as a last and desperate birthday resort.

If any school of art can be said to have flourished in Oxford, it was the Pre-Raphaelite Movement, largely a local product. William Morris and Edward Burne-Jones were undergraduates together at Exeter College, and their friend Dante Gabriel Rossetti often used to visit them from London. There are tapestries, stained-glass windows and paintings by the friends all over Oxford, and it was here that Morris, looking for a model for Guinevere, found one so suitable that he married her in St. Michael's at the North Gate. The most famous Pre-Raphaelite project in Oxford was the decoration of the library of the Oxford Union, the University debating society. Woodward, architect of the Museum, built the library, and Morris, Burne-Jones, Rossetti and other disciples of the Brotherhood painted it with tempera frescoes of Morte d'Arthur. They did not know much about distemper, expert though they were at the stance of a Lancelot or the liquid line of a damsel, and after a few years their ill-mixed materials began to fade. By the 1870s the chivalry could only just be seen, glimmering there above the bookstacks, and there was even talk of covering it with whitewash, to have done with it all.

Fifty years later a restoration specialist was called in to revive it. He spent some months at the task, and eventually announced that the work was done. They threw a party to celebrate the occasion, but when the lights were turned on, so the story goes, and the excited guests looked upward to the ceiling, to mourn the Death of Merlin once more, thrill to the Vision of the Sangrael, and follow Sir Gawaine's fortunes at the Fountain—when the guests looked expectantly upwards to the frescoes, they were just as invisible as they were before. The specialist beamed with pride; the guests shifted their feet; but to this day those pictures, like the Emperor's clothes, exist more colourfully in the imagination than they do *in situ*.

In literature, Oxford has expressed herself best through notices and hymns. *Abide With Me* is not in fact an Oxford hymn, though its author's son once stole several valuable books from Christ Church library, but name almost any other old Anglican favourite, and it probably has an Oxford origin. *Awake, My Soul, Lead Kindly Light, Lo, He Comes, Gentle Jesus Meek and Mild, Hark the Herald Angels Sing, From Greenland's Icy Mountains, Brightest and Best, Holy, Holy, Holy, Ride On, Ride On In Majesty, Praise to the Holiest in the Height*—these are Oxford art *par excellence*, and ring through this city, I like to think, with a special resonant pride.

As for the notices, they are essential to the Oxford flavour, and can hardly be missed. A really well-couched Oxford announcement is a stylist's delight: sardonic, urbane, menacing and rather outrageous—'*Gentlemen coming from homes where Bread throwing at the dinner table is habitual, and finding a difficulty in conforming suddenly to the unfamiliar ways of a higher civilization, will be permitted to continue their domestic pastime, on a payment of 5/- a throw.*' They have not changed much in a hundred years. When a new Dean of Wadham was once rash enough to refer to the junior members of the college as 'students', somebody crossed out the word and substituted 'Undergraduates', and somebody else changed it to 'Gentlemen': for though only Christ Church and University College call their undergraduates 'Mr.', on the little painted notices at the foot of each staircase, still the old *politesse* of the notice board often has its appeal for the most forwardly modernist of reformers.

A notice in Queen's Lane used to announce: *'No Chars-a-Banc Allowed Here'*, and some of the University's admonitions to the public are still paragons of elegance or pedantry. The celebrated nineteenth-century Order at the entrance to Christ Church meadows, for example, tells us that the meadow Keepers and Constables are instructed 'to prevent the entrance into the Meadow of all beggars, all persons in ragged or very dirty clothes, persons of improper character or who are not decent in appearance and behaviour'. A notice in the floor of Rhodes House warns the more erudite class of visitor *ΜΗΔΕΙΣ ΚΑΠΝΟΦΟΡΟΣ ΕΙΣΙΤΩ* — *'Let No Smoke-Bearing Person Enter'*.

Several Oxford buildings are marked with chronograms—inscriptions among whose words the date of construction is whimsically hidden. On the High Street façade of Oriel, built with Rhodes's benefaction in 1911, it says: *e Larga MUnIfICentIa CaeCILII rhoDes*—from which the diligent passer-by may pick up the numerals MDCCCLLVIIIIII. On the Dyson Perrins laboratory, in South Parks Road, is written *baLLIoLensIs feCI hyDatoeCUs o sI MeLIUs*—which means that an architect called Waterhouse (*Hydatoecus*), of Balliol, built it (*Oh that it was better—O Si Melius!*) in MDCCLLLLVVIIIII (1915). The Hebrew inscription beside the entrance to the Botanical Gardens, a memorial to the Oxford Jews whose burial ground it once was, has small arrows above some of its characters, forming a cryptogram of the year 1290, when the Jews were expelled from England.

Oxford epitaphs are often good, too, whether they are terse, like the one the antiquarian Hearne wrote for himself—

> *Here lieth the body of Thomas Hearne AM*
> *Who studied and preserved Antiquities*

—or in the elaborate kind, like the one in the former City Church that commemorates W. Levins Esquire, five times Mayor of Oxford, who died in 1616 in his hundred and first year, and who lies upon his tomb in a sable-fringed cloak, with a ruff and a big sword:

> *What others singly wish, Age, Wisdome, Wealth*
> *Children to propagate our name and blood*
> *Chiefe place in City oft, Unphysicked Health*
> *And (that which seasons all) the name of Good*
> *In Levins all were mixt, yet all are gon,*
> *Only the good name lasts, that looke upon.*

There is a touching eighteenth-century epitaph in South Hinksey church, upon the grave of Jane Cherry:

> *For as't please God I was taken Blind*
> *I no comfort in this world could find*
> *and so to dye I think it best*
> *To live with Christ and Angells bles'd.*

And there is a suitably Stoic strength to the inscription on the tomb in St. Aldate's church of Charlotte Taunton, who died in 1830 aged 22, and of whom we are told that 'her piety and virtues render her removal from this world less the subject of unavailing regret than of patient submission, from the stedfast hope that it has been to a kingdom of unmingled happiness—a change, which may well recompense the premature destruction of fondest endearments, and parental hopes'.

I have my doubts about the John Bull who etched his name so exquisitely beside the door of the Old Ashmolean in 1753, but I feel I know the Oxford craftsman who, instructed to inscribe a pillar of St. Aldate's church, knocked cheerfully off for dinner when he had chiselled:

THESE. PILER

S. WERE. MA

DE. A.D. 1581

Oxford has excelled in the lapidary style—the measured, polished, stately choice of words, such as Walter Pater practised—and the quick apophthegm, sounding as though it has just been invented at the dining table on the spur of the moment—*Procrastination is the thief of time* (Young, All Souls), *Honesty is the best policy*

(Whately, Oriel), *Save O save me from a candid friend* (Canning, Christ Church), or that stinging translation from a Latin original addressed to a seventeenth-century Dean of Christ Church:

> *I do not love thee, Dr. Fell,*
> *The reason why I cannot tell.*
> *This alone I know full well,*
> *I do not love thee, Dr. Fell.*

Somehow, though, in literature as in art, the lyrical vein has not flourished here, and the great poets have rarely taken to the city— it was Southey who, although he first met Coleridge in Oxford, once observed that he never *dreamt* about the place. The Oxford anthologies are rich in addresses from minor practitioners—'*Oxford all hail, delightful seat!*' or '*Hail, Oxford, hail! with filial transport cry!*'—but scarcely a phrase of them remains alive today, and the name of Oxford is surprisingly rare in the dictionaries of quotations.

Keats, indeed, thought this the most beautiful city he had ever seen, but he celebrated it only with a series of lumpish nonsense rhymes:

> *The Gothic looks solemn,*
> *The plain Doric column*
> *Supports an old Bishop and Crosier;*
> *The mouldering arch,*
> *Shaded o'er by a larch,*
> *Stands next door to Wilson the Hosier.*

Shelley spent a year in Oxford without writing one poem about the place. A. E. Housman was at St. John's, T. S. Eliot at Merton, but *An Oxfordshire Lad* was never written, and Eliot only saw one of his contemporaries ever again, so little was he enthralled by the Oxford college spirit. Yeats lived in the Broad for years, and most of the famous British poets of our century have been Oxford graduates: but the city itself seldom fired them, and the only immortal sonnet about Oxford ('*The stream-like wanderings of that glorious street*') was written by a Cambridge man, Wordsworth.

Nor, for her part, has Oxford much welcomed the writers. Oscar Wilde got a double-first, and wrote one or two adolescent paeans to the city: but among those who, for one reason or another, failed to get their degrees at Oxford were Sir Philip Sidney, Vaughan, Davenant, John Evelyn, Gibbon, Steele, Beaumont, John Aubrey, Otway, Shelley, Swinburne and Max Beerbohm. De Quincey, who took to opium at Oxford after trying laudanum for a toothache, simply gave up in the middle of his final examination, and left the city for ever. Walter Savage Landor was sent down from Trinity for discharging a shotgun at a neighbour's window, and childishly refusing to admit it. James Shirley the dramatist was told by Archbishop Laud, then President of St. John's, that because of a large mole on his left cheek he was unfit to take Holy Orders: he went to Cambridge instead, and became a priest anyway.

All this is partly, no doubt, because the artist neither needs a degree, nor generally responds to communal living: but it is partly because there is something cloying and possessive to Oxford's liberal genius, a feeling that you may spread your wings as ostentatiously as you like, providing you don't fly too far. It is significant that the one great poet Oxford can really call her own was an educationalist through and through—son of a great headmaster, Inspector of Schools, college tutor and professor. Matthew Arnold's inspiration naturally dried up when he became Professor of Poetry, but by then he had already distilled, once and for all, the lush fascination of this city, the haunted green idyll of its surrounding hills, its sense of calm and elegy: and in one famous passage he enshrined the nostalgic grandeur that has eluded so many lesser artists since:

> Beautiful city! so venerable, so lovely,
> so unravaged by the fierce intellectual life
> of our century, so serene!
>   'There are our young barbarians, all
>   at play!'
> And yet, steeped in sentiment as she lies,
> spreading her gardens to the moonlight, and
> whispering from her towers the last enchantments
> of the Middle Ages, who will deny that Oxford,
> by her ineffable charm, keeps ever calling
> us nearer to the true goal of all of us,
> to the ideal, to perfection,—to beauty in
> a word, which is only truth seen from

another side.... Adorable dreamer, whose heart
has been so romantic! who has given thyself
so prodigally, given thyself to sides and
heroes not mine, only never to the Philistines!
home of lost causes, and forsaken beliefs, and
unpopular names, and impossible loyalties!

Of course every undergraduate writes poetry, or so at least convention says. Even Blackstone, whose legal commentaries were later to become standard works on both sides of the Atlantic, wrote verse when he was up at Corpus Christi in the 1730s—*The Lawyer's Farewell to His Muse* formally marked his change of aspiration. Even Jeremy Bentham, when he was at Queen's, wrote an ode on the death of George II, which Dr. Johnson admired, but which Bentham himself later described as 'a mediocre performance on a trumpery subject, written by a miserable child'. Often the muses are serenaded in the old way, with long hair and midnight oil. Edward Young of the *Night Thoughts*, who was a Fellow of All Souls, used to seal up all his windows when he was writing, lighting candles in the middle of the day, and strewing his table with human bones. Richard Barham, the author of *The Ingoldsby Legends*, used to excuse himself from Brasenose morning chapel, at 7 A.M., because, he airily said, his regular poetic habits prevented his attendance— he normally went to bed at five in the morning, and if he stayed up for chapel he would be *utterly* unfit for work later in the day.

The best-known lines in Reginald Heber's poem *Palestine* came in one of those flashes of instant inspiration that we so often read about in old-fashioned lives of poets. In his rooms at Brasenose, beside the chestnut in Brasenose Lane, Heber was reading a draft of the poem to Sir Walter Scott. When he reached a passage about King Solomon's Temple, Scott broke in to recall the statement, in the First Book of Kings, that the building had been erected entirely without tools. Instantly the flame of genius fired. Heber thought for a moment, clasped his hand (I think we may reasonably assume) to his high forehead, and in a moment extemporized the couplet:

No workman's steel, no ponderous axes rung,
Like some tall palm the noiseless fabric sprung.

An even more famous Oxford line was construed by even more
traditional means: it was apparently stolen. *A rose-red city—half
as old as Time* comes, so the reference books mostly say, from John
Burgon's poem *Petra*, which he wrote when he was an undergraduate at Worcester. It was much the best line in the poem, was recognized at the time as a supremely smooth and evocative phrase, and
is all that we now remember of the piece. Alas, before very long
doubts crept in. When the poem was reprinted Burgon, without
explanation, put the phrase in quotation marks. Then people
remarked that there was a line suspiciously like it—*'by many a temple
half as old as Time'*—in Samuel Rogers's *Italy*: and in 1964 somebody else looked at a satirical essay about Burke, published in 1791,
and found the couplet

> *Ensigns armoured, pedigrees sublime,*
> *And wax and parchments half as old as time.*

Most of the images in this satire were taken from the writings
of Burke himself, and we are thus squeezed towards the unhappy
conclusion that what Burgon took for poetic inspiration was only
sublimated politics—but then it was another 30 years before
the poet, having consulted so many aged persons, was advised by
Dr. Routh to verify his references (and another few generations
before William Plomer carried the line a caustic stage further, and
described some ageing exquisite as a 'rose-red cissy half as old as
Time').

*Harold
Nicolson*

How rarely the most prominent student versifiers actually
become poets you may see from the lists of winners of the Newdigate
Prize. This is the chief Oxford poetry award, and has been awarded
annually since 1806 for a poem on a set subject, sometimes stark,
sometimes soaring—*The Sandwich Islands* (1841), *Alfred the Great
Contemplating Oxford University at the Present Day* (1856), or *The
Man in the Moon* (1937). The winner reads part of it aloud at the
presentation of honorary degrees at the Sheldonian, and it is probably the only English university prize that the great public vaguely
feels it has heard the name of somewhere.

Most Oxford prize poems are pretty embarrassing. When Heber
won the Newdigate with *Palestine*, and stood up in the Sheldonian
to recite it, he was disconcerted to recognize two young Jewesses

in the audience: but the Temple couplet had exhausted him, and
for the life of him he couldn't extemporize any more verses to replace

> Israel's sons, by scorpion curses driven,
> Outcasts of earth, and reprobate of heaven,
> Through the wide world in friendless exile stray,
> Remorse or shame sole comrades of the way,
> With dumb despair their country's wrongs behold,
> And, dead to glory, only burn for gold.

We are not told how the poor girls responded to these dreadful lines,
but the poem was rapturously received by the audience at large—
so rapturously that Heber's father, who was present, actually died
of joy.

Here, in an annotated prize entry, the Nymph Inoculation
addresses the Fallen Tyrant, Plague:

> 'By me protected shall they now deride
> 'Thy baffled fury and thy vanquish'd pride:
> 'Sacred to me, near Thames' level mead,
> 'A beauteous Temple* rears its rev'rend head.'

> *Small Pox Hospital

Here Dr. Livingstone is rescued at last in the bowels of Africa:

> Death's outstretched hand half grasped the
>   feeble prey:—
> Stanley appeared:—the spectre shrank away.

And here we succinctly pursue the career of General Gordon:

> When winter came again we find this man
> Made Governor-General of the whole Sudan.

Proper poets have sometimes tried for the Newdigate, and sometimes even won it—among them Oscar Wilde, Matthew Arnold,
John Addington Symonds, John Buchan and Laurence Binyon.
Swinburne entered and failed. Ruskin tried twice and won the
second time. Burgon failed three times, and won the fourth. Mostly,
though, the winners are soon deserted by their muse, move on to

politics, schoolmastering or the higher civil service, and never strum a lyre again.

If lyricism pines, fantasy exuberates. Dr. Johnson, it was once observed, would not step upon the cracks between the paving-stones of University College quadrangle—what Oxford schoolchildren call 'walking on the old man's toes': something in the Oxford air plays upon such fancies, encourages *jeux d'esprit* and talking to oneself, and sometimes elevates nonsense into art. From Thomas Coryat to Kingsley Amis, from Brandon Thomas's *Charley's Aunt* to Laurel and Hardy in *A Chump at Oxford*, Oxford has always favoured the gift of the light fantastic.

The Wind in the Willows was mostly written in the form of letters to Kenneth Grahame's only child Alastair, who was killed by a train near Oxford in 1920, when he was an undergraduate at Christ Church. Grahame himself is buried in Holywell cemetery—where his epitaph says that he 'passed the river on the 6th of July 1932, leaving Childhood and Literature through him the more blest for all time'. The whole world of the hobbits, that amiable race of beings that lives somewhere beyond the Sea of Mere, was invented by J. R. R. Tolkien in Oxford. *Zuleika Dobson* begins on the down platform of Oxford railway station and ends with the entire undergraduate population throwing itself desparingly into the Isis. At Merton they have a little collection of Beerbohm relics, pictures and manuscripts and funny drawings, from which you may see how easily Max's urbanely quixotic humour fitted into the Oxford setting: in the Randolph Hotel Osbert Lancaster has exuberantly illustrated the *Zuleika* saga in a series of jolly paintings.

The thrillers and detective stories that have streamed out of Oxford's common rooms in the last few decades have mostly been of the serio-comic kind, full of dream-like improbabilities—shops that disappear, country houses commandeered by secret brotherhoods, presidents of colleges wheeled dead in invalid chairs through quadrangles. Imaginary colleges have been invented by writers as varied as Ronald Knox, J. C. Masterman and J. I. M. Stewart, and Lord Peter Wimsey, in Dorothy Sayers's *Gaudy Night*, proposed to his girl friend in New College Lane with the immaculate academic inquiry: *Placetne, domina?*

And out of it all, out of the donnish joke and the absurdity, has

come one great work of art—*Alice*. Lewis Carroll was the complete
Oxonian. He was born in a Christ Church rectory in Lincolnshire,
was an undergraduate at Christ Church, was ordained by 'Soapy
Sam' Wilberforce, became a tutor of his college, spent all his working life teaching mathematics, and is honoured in a posthumous portrait, looking sad and ill, that hangs immediately to the right of the
door in Christ Church hall. He first told the tale of Alice rowing
past Port Meadow, and he wrote it in his college rooms.

He was the most donnish of dons. He loved mathematical jokes,
controversies, small decorative girls and portrait photography, and
he wrote not very funny satirical rhymes about local issues of the
day. Like most famous academics, he was neither satisfied nor sated
by worldly success—though even he, from the impregnably phleg-
matic citadel of Christ Church, must have been taken aback by the
stupendous popularity of his inventions. Already the respected
author of 'The enunciations of the propositions and corollaries
together with questions on the definitions, postulates, axioms etc
in Euclid Books I and II', he now found himself the master of
a very different audience—just as the modern don, graduating
from the Welsh Campaigns of Edward I to a television panel
game, suddenly finds himself flattered by perfect strangers in
trains.

Carroll defined the writing of *Alice* as 'a task where nothing of
reward is hoped for but a little child's whispered thanks, and the
airy touch of a little child's pure lips'. Within a few years, however,
nursery gratitude had materialized into editions in most European
languages, plus Esperanto, Braille and Pitman's shorthand, and
Alice has since passed into most of the Asiatic tongues too—even
ending up, in 1964, in Latin. The English editions alone have been
illustrated, at one time or another, by 21 different artists, including
Dodgson himself, Mabel Lucy Atwell, Arthur Rackham and Harry
Rountree. Walt Disney made a cartoon of *Alice*; when Paramount
filmed it in 1933 W. C. Fields played Humpty Dumpty, Cary Grant
the Mock Turtle and Gary Cooper the White Knight; the best-
known German translation of *Jabberwocky* was made by Scott of
Liddell and Scott—

> *Es brillig war. Die schlicten Toven*
> *Wirrten und wimmelten im Waben.*

In his day Lewis Carroll was one of the lions of Oxford, a sight in the same category as Dr. Routh or the Radcliffe Camera: today visitors who have known his books since childhood are sometimes surprised to be told, half-way through their Oxford tour, that this is where he wrote them. In fact there are reminders of Alice wherever you look: not just the garden where Carroll first met the original Alice, or the stretch of river they rowed along that changeable Independence Day, but things that were transposed out of Oxford into the books themselves, and thus given a back-of-the-hand kind of glory.

The dodo in the Museum achieved this kind of apotheosis, and so I like to think did Cooper's Oxford Marmalade, for it could surely only be a two-pound pot of Vintage that Alice failed to grasp half-way down the well. The chess-board pattern of Looking-Glass Land is said to have been inspired by the chequered ditches of Otmoor, north of the city. The original of the old sheep's shop is popularly supposed to be the confectioner's called Alice's Shop in St. Aldate's: certainly Tenniel's picture fits it, except that he conscientiously portrayed it back to front, looking-glass style.

The Dormouse, an animal now very rare in these parts, may owe something to an Oxford character called James Mozley, who was always going to sleep in the middle of dinner. 'Pray what do *you* think, sir?' dear old Dr. Routh would mischievously ask him, having noticed in the middle of a discourse that Mozley was asleep again. 'Did you not hear what I said?'—and somebody else would always say, just as the Hatter said of the Dormouse, 'No, Sir, he did not. He is fast asleep.' The Mad Hatter himself is said to have been modelled, at least visually, upon a local inventor, Theophilus Carter, whose revolutionary 'alarm clock bed' (it threw you out at reveille) was exhibited at the Great Exhibition in 1851. The White Knight, balanced so precariously upon his charger, would do very well as the Sheriff of Oxford, hilariously horseback at the annual Port Meadow roundup, and it was, of course, a standard Oxford tutorial of the more alarming kind that the Caterpillar gave Alice from the top of his mushroom.

The dedicatory poem at the beginning of Carroll's other nonsense book, *The Hunting of the Snark*, was once described by Newman as being 'so entirely of the School of Keble, that I think it could not have been written, had *The Christian Year* never made its appearance'. Is there not, though, something naggingly familiar to the style of the verses Newman himself addressed to his friend Pusey, 10 years before the poetical début of Humpty Dumpty?

I saw thee once, and naught discerned
For stranger to admire;
A serious aspect, but it burned
With no unearthly fire.

Again I saw, and I confessed
Thy speech was rare and high;
And yet it vexed my burdened heart,
And scared, I know not why.

'It was', said the Dormouse, after taking a minute or two to think about it, 'a treacle well.' Perhaps the gig was passing Binsey as this fancy came to Carroll's mind; for there, so an old Oxford country joke has it, treacle mines are worked. This derives from the presence in the village of St. Frideswide's holy well—'treacle' meaning, in its mediaeval sense, a healing fluid, as in the Treacle Bible, or the Venetian panacea called *teriaca*, or the *tiryak* that the Emir Mohammed demanded of Doughty at Hayil. They are treacle mines, though, in the local joke, and sometimes people turn up in Binsey and ask the way to the shafts. Not long ago a visitor arrived with a permit to view them—given him, he said, by a friendly official of the treacle company he had met in Oxford. He did not know this helpful fellow's name, but it would not surprise me to learn that he had a sad, rather ill-looking face, and talked a lot about little girls, double equations and photography.

Carroll's books have been interpreted in many ways—as Freudian self-revelations, as mathematical caprices, as political allegories, even as an elaborate allegory of the Oxford Movement—the Jabberwock, suggested Shane Leslie slyly in 1933, 'can only be a fearsome representation of the British view of the Papacy'. I once met a psychiatrist who attributed their more nightmarish effects to the Oxford climate. Carroll, he said, suffered from migraine, brought on by the lowering dampness of the city, and one of the hallucinations of that condition makes your head feel grotesquely swollen and your body uncannily long—just as Alice, nibbling her cake and sipping her bottle, found herself now a giantess, now a dwarf. I know the sensation, and certainly Carroll's own pictures for the original draft of *Alice* exactly reflect it, and make you feel a little queer looking at them.

My own opinion, though, is that Carroll's gay but eerie stories, like most of Oxford's fantasies, represent an escape into some wider, freer world, where the traditions are not so solemn, the conventions are not so subtle, where the horizons are as wide as imagination can make them, and pedantry only intrudes in fun. There is to Oxford, if you spend too long beneath her powerful influence, a closeted power of oppression, which every now and then goads men of intellect into leaping all the barriers of logic, and breaking into nonsense. Half Oxford is deadeningly introspective, and writes stuffy stanzas about its own over-praised beauties: but the other half springs flamboyantly out of itself, and saunters up Boar's Hill to watch the ships sail by.

18. Right of Way

It is an island city. Cross-currents always swirl through Oxford—plans or discoveries leaving these shores to be marketed through the world, men and ideas coming in from abroad, goods to sustain the islanders, cars or books going out to pay the bill. Five minutes in the shopping centre of Oxford will demonstrate the point. Here an American clergyman buys half a pound of Roquefort cheese, here a French hitch-hiker queues for salami at Mrs. Palm's delicatessen, and here a don just back from a semester at Sydney slaps you on the back and calls you sport. There are tomatoes from Spain, oranges from South Africa, bananas from Jamaica, Belgian grapes, American nuts, melons from Cyprus, canned pineapples from Hawaii, Australian peaches and ginger in glass pots from Hong Kong. Sometimes a sari glides sinuously by. Three little Jamaican girls in hair ribbons chase each other round a pillar-box. A crocodile of elderly Scandinavian ladies strides through from Carfax to the Broad, led by a guide with a goatee. There is a sudden fragrance of foreign tobacco, and an Italian waiter you know says good morning and asks after the children. You must be a resolute reactionary indeed, to remain an isolationist in Cornmarket.

From earliest times foreigners have frequented this city. It is not true, as my *New Oxford Guide, Or Companion Through the University*, suggests, that the Romans knew the city as Bellositum, for the Romans did not know the city at all: but if you have any doubts that the Norman seigneur Robert d'Oilley built the castle, take a look at the Oxford telephone directory, and you will find that 14 Deeleys are still farming around Oxford. Strangers from all parts have always passed this way. The Welsh herdsmen used to lope through Oxford with their animals, on their way to London—they are said to have had a legal right of way through Merton College, and the pub called the Welsh Pony is a memory of their trade. Some of the rowdiest Oxford residents of the Middle Ages were the Irish beggar-students called Chamberdekyns, who evaded a fifteenth-century ban on Irishmen by signing on at the University, and became a frightful nuisance.

A Cretan introduced coffee to Oxford (and a plaque in the Co-operative grocery store in the High marks the site of the first coffee-house in England). A German was the first Oxford printer. The first gardener at the Botanical Gardens was a Hanoverian, Jacob Bobart, who used to go for walks with a goat: a madman once seized hold of this worthy's beard, in which he used to hang little pieces of silver on festive occasions, and shouted to the passers-by that Bobart had swallowed a horse, and that its tail was hanging out of his mouth.

Foreign savants of every kind have spent their times in Oxford, from Erasmus to Einstein, and every year others arrive as visiting professors, exchange lecturers, research students or honorands. Nuffield's first designer was a Norwegian, a Swede made some of his first engines, Oxford's most famous modern brain surgeon was an American, her most eminent orthopaedic surgeon a Spaniard. An Oxford M.A. was originally a licence to teach in any European university, and though that grand ideal has sadly withered since, still in 1978 about one in eight of the student body came from abroad.

From time to time, driven by persecution or profit, alien communities have settled in the city for good, and permanently coloured its fabric. These small pockets of foreign settlement help to raise Oxford far above the provincial awareness you would expect for her from the map. The wealth of a Cotswold market town first brought such immigrants to Oxford; later the semi-royal status of the city attracted them here, and the growing fame of the University; today the immigrants gravitate here, I suppose, not exactly out of choice, but *faute de mieux*.

A plaque on the wall of the central public library, in St. Aldate's, tells us where Oxford's mediaeval Jewry stood. This was never large, but it included members of some distinguished Jewish families, and enjoyed intermittent periods of prosperity and freedom. The Jews had their own cemetery, beside the Cherwell—it is said that Dead Man's Walk, the path along the north side of Christ Church meadows, is so called because the Jewish funerals passed along it.

They had a synagogue almost on the site of Tom Tower, and they were economically influential, on and off: in 1209 the D'Oilley of the day, the greatest local landowner, borrowed money from an Oxford Jew, and the site of Merton College, founded in 1264, was bought from Jacob of Oxford—the existing muniment room, over the entrance to Mob Quad, is thought to have been his counting-house.

Later in the thirteenth century the state of the Oxford Jews sadly worsened. They were remorselessly taxed, the Dominicans tried to convert them, rumours of ritual and child-burning surrounded them. Once students attacked the Jewry, and the Jews were repeatedly accused of clipping the coinage, spitting at Crucifixes and charging unfair interest (more than 40 per cent, that is). In the barn that is the sole relic of Osney Abbey a plaque records the story of an apostate deacon who became a Jew, married a Jewess, and adopted the name Haggai: he was accused of desecrating the Host, tried within the walls of the Abbey, and burnt alive by the Sheriff. When, in 1290, the Jews of England were expelled *en masse*, having been taxed out of usefulness, the Oxford Jewry was only a pitiable relic of its great days—a hundred souls or so, who were then scattered through the Continent, and left scarcely a trace behind.

A few returned in the eighteenth century, but the first professing Jew did not graduate from Oxford University until 1862, and even then his name was Sackville Davis. Hardly any Jews lived in the city until our own times. Elderly Oxford citizens, casting their memories back to the Oxford of the 1900s, paint a forlorn picture of the local Jews in Edwardian days—'old Freedson the hunchback watchmaker, I remember, and the wardrobe dealer in George Street, and that's about all'. Samuel Alexander the philosopher was the first Jewish Fellow of an Oxford college—at Lincoln from 1882 to 1893: there was not another until the 1930s. It is really since the second world war that the Oxford Jews have come into their own—helped by the influx of refugees from Nazi Germany and blitzed London, and the Jews who have since become famous figures of the University.

Today there are always Jewish undergraduates at Oxford—elegant sporting ones at Christ Church, clever disputatious ones at Balliol, or tough idealistic ones who spend their long vacations on kibbutzim in Israel. St. Catherine's offers a scholarship exclusively for boys from the Jewish public school, Carmel College, at Wallingford. Jews bring bite to the Wednesday market, with their Cockney repartee and their competitive prices, and Jews have been among the greatest modern benefactors of the University.

The Oxford Jews are buried nowadays in Wolvercote cemetery, and they have a modern synagogue in Nelson Street, on the edge of Jericho. Though its architecture is engagingly modest, a service there can still evocatively suggest the old separateness of Jewishness, its shuttered pride and its oriental origins. On a Saturday morning the streets of Jericho are usually cheerfully animated—family men in shirt-sleeves polishing cars, youths in leather jackets comparing motor-bikes, women in aprons gossiping at front doors and children kicking balls about in car parks. There is a snort of engines from the railway yards across the canal, and the milkman trundles up and down on his little electric trolley.

Through all this homely activity the Jews pass in their dark suits: and through the doors of the synagogue they go, bowing to their friends and murmuring Sabbath greetings: and there inside the grand irrepressible rites of Judaism are performed, the ancient chants are chanted once more, the scrolls are gravely processed, and hunched beside the prayer-desk, like officers pondering a tricky navigational problem, the courteous young men worry their way through the sacred texts.

It feels strange and foreign still, and older by far than any Saxon fetish or Norman crypt: but Oxford is a mart of the cultures, and if you look at the title-page of the Hebrew Testament in your seat, you will find that it was printed at the Clarendon Press, 100 yards away across Jericho.

The Russians have been in Oxford since the Revolution: seldom more than 20 now, but endlessly ebullient. Until the 1940s they had their own Orthodox priest—the Archimandrite Nicholas Gibbs, an Englishman who had been a tutor to the Romanoff family. His little house in Marston Road, off the Cowley Road, is still sometimes used for services, and if you peer through its downstairs window from the pavement you may see the back of an ikon inside, dim and incongruous in that prosaic English setting, and make out through the dust the name of its framer—A. Gecele, 45 Rue aux Pois, St. Petersburg.

Nowadays a priest comes down from London, under the authority of the Moscow Patriarchate, to take Sunday services in the Chapel of the Annunciation in Canterbury Road—the drawing-room of a comfortable north Oxford house, looking across a trim north Oxford lawn, where you may hear the sweet music of the Orthodox ritual any Sunday morning, and glimpse the gorgeous vestments of the priest at his altar in the bay window.

This little church, with its ancillary hostel of St. Gregory and St. Macrina, was founded with the help of well-wishers all over the world—the list in the hall includes names from Chios, the Lebanon, New York, Tiflis, Cairo and Budleigh Salterton—and though its aims are ecumenical, the congregation that fills it on Sundays has scarcely been Anglicized at all, but looks as though it might just have come jostling in from Red Square, stamping the snow from its galoshes.

There are Serbs in Oxford, too, refugees from the first world war, and several hundred Poles, refugees from the second. There are Cypriot or Spanish waiters in half the city's restaurants, and German or Scandinavian *au pair* girls all over the suburbs. Four or five Chinese eating-places flourish, and three Indian restaurants. In the quaint little country shopping-street called North Parade Avenue, with its homely pub and its village grocer, a restaurant has been done up with fishing nets and check tablecloths to reproduce a café in Capri. They serve *gazpacho* in the half-timbered restaurant called The Elizabeth, and *tagliatelle* in the old country pub, on the road to Wantage, called the Noah's Ark.

The West Indians and the Pakistanis mostly live along the western side of the city, buying their *Jamaican Gleaner* at the neighbourhood news-stands, attending occasional Muslim prayer meetings at an Indian restaurant in Walton Street. The Irish prefer Cowley, and can pick up the *Irish Independent* or the *Cork Weekly Examiner* in the porch of almost any Catholic church. The Welsh, very often Cowley workers, have been totally integrated in this English city, only emerging now and then with a soulful song in a pub corner or a service in Welsh in Jesus College chapel.

The Scandinavians have an annual Christmas service in St. Michael's at the North Gate, with familiar old hymns in three languages—*Et Barn er født i Bethlehem*, or *O bli hos mig! Nu er det aftentid*. The saddest and loneliest grave in Oxford is the grave of Abdulillah Azzam Abdullah Saleh al Mohdar, who died in 1963.

aged 15: he is buried high in the cemetery at Headington, overlooking the towers of this Christian city, with his feet pointing to the
east indeed, and the epitaph 'God Bless Him', but 3,000 miles
between him and Mecca.

In modern Oxford you always know you are in Europe. This is a
welcome retrogression, for until the 1960s the European comity
seemed far away, and the old links with Paris or Padua were
apparently severed for ever. The University, though, vigorously
supported British entry to the Common Market; and when in 1975
a national referendum was held to determine the issue once and for
all, among the deciding factors may well have been the debate on
the subject at the Oxford Union, addressed by passionate political
leaders of both factions, televised nationally in a three-hour
marathon programme, and ending with an overwhelming vote for
Europeanness.

But America, too, is still inescapable in this city. Romantics like
to say that Oxford was actually responsible for its discovery, on the
grounds that a paragraph from Roger Bacon's *Opus Majus* first gave
Columbus the idea of a westward passage to India. Certainly it was
the ecclesiastical policy of Archbishop Laud, formerly President of
St. John's and later Chancellor of the University, that led to the
founding of the New England colonies, and when it came to the
settling of the eastern seaboard, Oxford men were always there. The
founders of Georgia, Maryland, New Hampshire and Pennsylvania
were all educated at this University, and so was Lord North, who
lost it all. John White, 'the Father of Massachusettes', was born
at Stanton St. John, four miles out. The first President of the United
States had a great-grandfather at Brasenose, and the second President had a grandfather there. If it had not been for a six-to-one
preponderance of Cambridge men on the Great and General Court,
Harvard might well have christened its attendant town Oxford,
Massachusetts: as it was, one of the original nine students later
became an Oxford Fellow—he was Henry Saltonstall, the first of
10 generations of Harvard Saltonstalls.

Charles? When they built Dunster House beside the _Cambridge_ River, in
1926, they modelled its campanile upon Tom Tower—or so the
guidebooks maintain, though I must say the inspiration seems fairly
distant to me. At Chicago they have built a complete replica of

Christ Church hall, and at Princeton the unwarned English visitor
may rub his eyes to find Magdalen Tower rising unmistakable above
the white frame houses. The college system, which has survived
in Europe only at Oxford and Cambridge, was at first discarded
by the Americans: but in the 1920s both Harvard and Yale adopted
it after all, and even the vast University of California, alarmed by
its own scale and scope, has divided one of its campuses into college
units. The Cowley Fathers have a flourishing house in Massachusetts, where recruits for their Order are easier to find than they are
at home. The Oxford University Press Inc., of Madison Avenue,
is one of the great American publishing houses: *'Gifts that reflect
knowing taste'*, ran one of its recent Christmas advertisements—
'books from OXFORD.'

In return for all this America has poured money, skill and initia-
tive into Oxford. I sometimes wonder how the University would
have survived at all, were it not for the American link, and so eager
has Oxford been to attract American scholars that the very degree
of Doctor of Philosophy was instituted to induce them away from
the Continental universities. (It took many years to acclimatize. In
1964 Dr. Lee's Professor of Experimental Philosophy received a letter addressed to D. Phil, Esq., MA, FRS.) Two American idealists,
Walter Vrooman and Charles A. Beard, founded Ruskin College,
and two-thirds of the cost of the New Bodleian was borne by the
Rockefeller Foundation. Almost any issue of the University *Gazette*
shows how much of Oxford's research is backed by American
money—from Government departments, armed forces, business
firms or great foundations—and the pallid idiom of the mid-Atlantic
intellectual is familiar to every senior common room. A recent
American Master of University College, being a millionaire both
in pounds and in dollars, cheerfully gave his college an entire new
quadrangle—in which, in his retirement, he very sensibly kept a
flat.

Americans are the mainstay of Oxford tourism: they place this
city, polls tell us, fourth in their list of English Sights—after London, Stratford, and Scenic Beauty. Ever since the second world war
there have been American bases in the Oxford countryside: in the
days before the Prostitution Act, when the English whores were still
on the streets, U.S. airmen were much their favourite customers.
The Pressed Steel Company, half American by origin, still

exchanges technical ideas with a firm in Philadelphia. In 1926 General Motors of Detroit offered to buy out Morris, offering him £11,000,000 for his business (he refused without a moment's thought, and they bought Vauxhall's instead). The very first buildings you see in Oxford, when you drive in from London, are the premises of an American office management company, and the heaviest man in the Oxford eight usually seems to be an American. Whenever I take Americans around the city, they seem to know it better than I do myself—besides being, by and large, far less interested.

Oxford University was not always so universal. In the middle nineteenth century especially it was not even a properly national university, but was almost monopolized by the English privileged classes: if it is the English social revolution that has broken down its façade of caste, it was Cecil Rhodes the imperialist who re-opened it to the world outside. His scholarships bring scores of Americans, Australians, Canadians, South Africans, New Zealanders, Rhodesians, West Indians, Maltese and Pakistanis to Oxford each year. Henry James, with a convert's bigotry, said they would ruin the place: in fact they have proved one of the best things that ever happened to Oxford.

They were conceived as part of Rhodes's childish secret-society view of history. He was at Oriel himself, University College having rejected him ('all the colleges send me their failures', grumbled the President of Oriel at his admission, but when he died he left them £100,000, and they put that statue of him on their High Street wall). All his life he retained a passionate love for Oxford. He was already a successful financier when he went up, and so often had to return to Africa to look after his mines that it took him eight years to scrape through to a degree: but nothing could shake his conviction that an Oxford education was one of the greatest of privileges. ('I'll send you to Oxford!' he once beamed at a small boy in the Cape. 'Oh no you won't,' the child replied, hastily leaving the room.)

This devotion persuaded him that if he could impregnate the ruling forces of the world with Oxford's values, history could be manipulated in the right direction: and the Rhodes Scholarships were intended to put Oxford men in positions of control in the three commanding societies of the earth—the British Empire, the United

States and Germany. Under the terms of Rhodes's will, young men carefully selected as 'the best men for the world's fight' were to be given three years at Oxford, pumped full of its confidence, panache and sportsmanship, and sent back home to rule the earth.

The colossal arrogance of the idea has not, oddly enough, prevented its working. Its underlying racialism has mercifully gone by the board—it was not prejudice that separated the first American Negro scholar (1907) from the next (1963). The existence of German Rhodes Scholarships certainly did not prevent the world wars, and they have now unhappily been abandoned, but in their time they did nothing but good. Under Rhodes's will the Kaiser himself chose the German scholars, and he became an enthusiast for Oxford—'My felicitations to you and your gallant crew' he once cabled the German Professor of Comparative Philology, Max Müller, after Oxford had won the boat race. The committee that replaced the All-Highest, between the wars, was one of the few organizations in Germany to escape Nazification, and when the second world war came most of those German Rhodes Scholars who were abroad refused to go home. Two were actually killed by the Nazis: Adam von Trott zu Solz, of Balliol, took part in the bomb plot against Hitler, one of the supreme tests of courage in our time, and one that chills me to think of still when I visualize the few years of the man's life that separated the pleasures of Oxford from the mad court that sentenced him to death, after torturing him almost to insanity, and compelling him to stand in degradation before the cameras with nothing to hold his trousers up but his own shaking hands.

Rhodes Scholars have been the supreme exemplars of the Anglo-American culture, of the special relationship that has, often against the odds and sometimes against the national inclinations, linked the destinies of Britain and the United States. Some of the most loyal of Oxonians are Americans: when, in 1940, a group of Rhodes Scholars had to return home without taking their finals, they were allowed to sit for them at Swarthmore College instead—and solemnly dressed up in *sub fusc* for the occasion, several thousand miles from the nearest proctor. So successful have the American Rhodes Scholarships been that the Harkness, Guggenheim, and Fulbright scholarships, American institutions themselves, are all recognizably based upon the Rhodes model. The climax of this

prestige came in the early 1960s, when President Kennedy's administration was in its tragic fullness. Two Associate Justices of the
Supreme Court were then Rhodes Scholars, including Byron R.
White, who was known in his youth as Whizzer White, and arrived
at Oxford a term late because he was playing professional football
for Pittsburgh. The chairman of the Senate Foreign Relations Committee was a Scholar, and the administration itself included 16 more,
headed by the Secretary of State and the Secretary of the Army.

You cannot carry a secret society much higher, and Loyola himself, one of Rhodes's heroes, would surely have been satisfied.
Oxford's highest values, though, are not those of political power:
and perhaps the old imperialist, gazing down from whatever
dubious Valhalla he eventually achieved, gets more pleasure after
all from the Balliol war memorial, where the name of von Trott
zu Solz nobly reminds us that the fittest men for the world's fight
do not necessarily win.

Oxford is too big for her environment—just as England is too big
for her islands. When Thomas Bodley dedicated his library it was
not to English scholarship alone, but to the whole 'republic of letters'. Today a quarter of the books acquired by the Bodleian Library
are published abroad, and Oxford depends more than ever, for her
vivacity, her style and her prosperity, upon the wide horizons. She
depends upon Canary bananas, visiting professors, the market for
MGs in Florida, Jamaican bus conductors, Swedish mothers' helps
and the insatiable wanderlust of tourists ('Please Do Not Feed the
Animals', an undergraduate notice once warned the sight-seers in
Tom Quad). The worst thing that could happen to this city would
be a withdrawal into national pride or self-sufficiency, reducing it
to the level of a Salamanca—once among the great intellectual
centres of Europe, now merely an historic spectacle. Oxford is not
only the Welshmen's, but the world's right of way.

19. Distant Trumpets

The Indian Institute is an Indian Institute no longer, but has been converted into a library. It is the drab brown building that stands at the end of Broad Street, peering frumpishly between the Clarendon Building and the New Bodleian, like the rump of a railway terminus. Just inside its porch, however, there is affixed a huge brass plate, inscribed in Sanskrit and English, which tells us that the High-Minded Heir Apparent Albert Edward, Son of the Empress of India, inaugurated the building on Wednesday, the 10th lunar day of the dark half of the month of Vaisakha, in the Sambat year 1939—May 2, 1833, of the Christian era. 'By the favour of God may the learning and literature of India be ever held in honour; and may the mutual friendship of India and England constantly increase.' Sanskrit scholars no longer frequent the building, but this lofty plaque is polished like a mirror still, as though turbanned bearers rub it each morning, before laying the fires of juniper wood: for though Oxford is not an heroic city, sometimes she reflects a glint of the heroic style, down there among her water-meadows.

The brief but dazzling phenomenon of the Raj has left its traces here, to remind us how the flare of the nabobs came home with the tea-chests. Sometimes they make Oxford herself seem a niggling sort of place. In King Edward Street, off the High, there is a small uninspired plaque recording the fact that Rhodes lodged there as an undergraduate: whenever I pass it, I think of the dull time he seems to have spent at Oxford, compared with all the flamboyances to come. Oxford honoured Rhodes warmly enough—even now the official handbook to Rhodes House still respectfully calls him 'Mr. Rhodes'; but she was never in sympathy with the piratical streak in him, and even in the act of giving him a degree, in 1899, the Public Orator could not resist making one sly reference to the fiasco of the Jameson Raid—'Ah! let not excessive love of country drive to rashness, and do not resort more than is proper to alliances, stratagems and plots!' Oxford was not made for derring-do, and does not readily respond to historical *coups de théâtre*.

The imperial idea, I suspect, never really fired this place. Oxford was famous before the Union Jack defied a single sunset, and has survived the loss of a couple of empires far more calmly than she endured the Oxford Movement. Kipling resigned from the Rhodes Trust when they appointed the Liberal Philip Kerr as General Secretary, and the least successful car they ever made at Cowley was a 1934 model called the Empire, of which they sold *two*.

Rhodes called this University 'the energizing source of Empire', but the role was accidental. Half the Viceroys of India were Oxford men: but for most of them it seems to have been no more than another appointment of English State, such as comes naturally enough to an eminent Oxford graduate in the course of a conscientious political lifetime.

Many Oxford people died in the service of this distant cause, and their memorials remain, mostly forgotten and generally ignored, in the churches and college chapels of the city. Unless you actually searched for them, you would not know of all the small imperial tragedies re-enacted on these walls—the drownings at sea off the Cape, the lonely deaths on the long voyage home, the fearful epidemics of typhoid or cholera, the long-forgotten frontier skirmishes. A stranger would not guess, for instance, that the little brass plate in the chancel of St. Ebbe's commemorates anyone as memorable as Bishop Thomas French, once rector of the church, who founded Lahore Cathedral, and at the end of a long life went to die all alone among the Muslims of Muscat. Only the most pertinacious of tourists notices that the stations of the Cross in St. Thomas's church were erected in memory of an adjutant of the 35th Sikhs, killed at Shahi Tangi 'while bravely leading his men against the Mamunds on the Frontier of India', or that the dining-hall at St. Peter's College is a tribute to James Hannington, first Bishop of Equatorial Africa, 'killed by savages in 1855'.

Merton library possesses the last diary of Andrew Irvine, who died on Everest with Mallory in 1924, still an undergraduate, in the days when the Himalaya was part of the imperial preserve, and even the monks of the Rongbuk Glacier knew the Raj by sight. In University College chapel there is a superb memorial, by John Flaxman, to the orientalist William Jones, who codified the laws of India, and thus built the administrative foundations of the Raj: this was originally intended for Calcutta Cathedral, and it is Anglo-India at its most tremendous—a large white marble frieze of the Law-Giver at work, on his lap the tablets and the pens, at his feet the subject sages, Muslim and Hindu, squatting meditatively in his shadow.

And for me the most telling of Oxford's imperial traces, the relic that brings the far-flung vision most vividly into focus, is a memorial in Holywell cemetery to a young man called John Blagrove, who died as a private in the Australian infantry in 1917. His home was Brewarrima, New South Wales; one imagines him a lean, lanky, hard-riding, dinkum sport of an Aussie; he was a great-nephew of the Venerable Routh.

Of course the wealth of the Empire seeped through to Oxford, and put an extra lick of gilding, here and there, upon the treasure-chest. The Sibthorpian Professorship of Rural Economy was endowed from the fortune made by a seventeenth-century British Consul in Smyrna, in the great days of the Levant Company, and the Codrington Library at All Souls was paid for by an eighteenth-century Barbados sugar magnate, Christopher Codrington, who had collected some 12,000 books while he was still an undergraduate, and now stands in the middle of his library dressed, all in white marble, as a Roman grandee.

Nineteenth-century order books at Salters, the boatbuilders, give some inkling of the Empire's economic meaning to such an English city. In the 1890s this old firm, as an infinitesimal cog in the imperial machinery, exported boats to Canada, Rajputana, Rangoon, Demerara, Hyderabad, Cawnpore, Cuddalore, Cuttack, Hong Kong, Poona, Lucknow, Adelaide, Madras, and Natal—not to speak of purchasers in places like Heidelberg, Oporto, Canton and Boston who stood, so to speak, on the sidelines of power. They must have been boom times for this little concern, and though the imperial phase does not seem crucial to the University of Oxford, it clearly helped to restore the confidence of the City, cherishing it with new wealth, and preparing the markets that were one day to make all its people prosperous.

What is left now, of the great adventure? Portraits in college halls, of proconsuls and imperial judges; tarnished brass slabs in corners of churches; Rhodes Scholars from Geelong, Durban or McGill; two leprosy clinics, run by the Oxford Mission in the slums of Calcutta; those strands of Empire that still link the universities of the Commonwealth, offering jobs for dons in Sydney, Accra or Dacca, and enabling the University Press to maintain profitable offices in Canada, India, Pakistan, South Africa, Ghana, Zambia, Malaysia, Tanzania, Kenya, New Zealand, Australia, Hong Kong and Nigeria.

St. Antony's original collection of books on Persia was presented by the British Petroleum Company, who no longer needed them, I suppose, after the loss of Abadan. Rhodes House, in South Parks Road, was designed by Herbert Baker—Rhodes's favourite architect, whose imperial works still stand at Pretoria and New Delhi: it has a Zimbabwe bird on the top of its rotunda, and diverse imperial symbolisms inside. The University's Department of Forestry is financed partly by Commonwealth Governments, and its building was partly paid for by the White Rajah of Sarawak. In 1964 an Australian became Vice-Chancellor of the University: he is portrayed in a drip-stop, on the south-west corner of the Bodleian, overlooking Exeter Fellows' Garden, supported by an emu and a kangaroo.

There are still signs in the streets that this has been an imperial city in its time. Tibetan lamas are sometimes to be seen, dhotis and African togas are common, most of the bus conductors come from former subject lands far away, and not long ago, opposite that burnished plaque at the entrance to the Indian Institute, I found a second notice on the wall. 'The Indo-Pak Welfare Film Society', it said, 'proudly presents Amar Singh Rathor—A Hit Programme Full of Songs and Dances': and pleasantly did this perpetuate, I thought, the original purpose of the Institute—'to improve among Englishmen, and even among Indians, a proper appreciation of the arts and literature of India'.

Oxford is anything but martial. I have tried to muster her great fighting men, and have recruited only Sir Walter Raleigh, Admiral

Blake (who was refused a Magdalen Fellowship, it is said, because he looked so ugly), Earl Haig, T. E. Lawrence and General Fridolin von Senger, who commanded the German forces at Monte Cassino. Several wars, all the same, have scarred her. There were prehistoric battles in these parts, if we are to go by the weapons sometimes found in the Thames, and Oxford's strategic position in the middle of England obviously made her important in the early wars of the English. The first big defeat the Danish invaders suffered was in a battle for Oxford in 871, when Alfred trounced them, and some theorists believe that the city only fell to the Normans after a long and cruel siege—the Domesday Book records that more than half the city's houses were then in ruins.

More than most country towns, Oxford therefore grew up with war in mind, and many of her older buildings stand in a fierce defensive posture. The old castle tower, though used as a prison since Henry III's day, still commands the river approaches, with its ancillary mound beside it, and the crypt of St. George's chapel still at its feet. The city walls, built by Henry III, still potter shakily but resolutely among the buildings, with a bastion here and a battlement there, now redoubtable beside a college garden, now tucked away behind an ironmonger. The open space behind the Sheldonian Theatre is the remains of the 'royal way', the gap behind the walls that was left clear for the movement of troops and supplies, and the quaint cluttered houses around the Turf Tavern stand in the hollow of the city ditch.

New College itself formed part of the civic defences. Its founder, William of Wykeham, was a royal surveyor of castles as well as Bishop of Winchester: he had a hand in the design of Windsor Castle, and built his college like a fortified monastery. Its north wall is the city rampart—which the college has been obliged to keep in good repair ever since. Its bell-tower replaced one of the bastions, and is itself a sturdy watch-post. The cloister forms a breastwork for the vulnerable west windows of the chapel, and the south façade of the college, on Queen's Lane, still looks like a fortress wall.

They were prepared for the worst, and they knew well enough what war meant. All Souls was founded as a war memorial—to honour the victors of Agincourt, and to provide a chantry where masses could ever afterwards be offered for their souls. Among the kings, archbishops, apostles, dukes, earls and Latin Fathers portrayed on the chapel reredos, one anonymous figure respectfully stands. He is an archer of Agincourt, and he keeps his thumbs down the rivets of his greaves because he knows that to this day, among the great county families of Oxfordshire are the Stonors, descended from the commander of the English left wing at Agincourt, and quite likely to look in to see if there are any complaints.

The two battered angels on the porch of St. Mary's were not war casualties, but are merely the victims of time and climate: the Madonna that stands below them was an early target of the Parliamentarians in the English Civil War. They occupied the city first, mutilated that image in the name of Puritanism, burnt some books and pictures, confiscated some plate, warned the University to keep out of things, and after six weeks left Oxford to be King Charles's headquarters. The Royalist Government of England moved in. The city became an armed camp and a royal court. The King lived in Christ Church, the Queen lived in Merton, and you can still see the door in Corpus Christi garden cut to enable them to visit each other without disturbing the porters.

For four years Oxford stood *cap-à-pie*. The earthworks survive, here and there, and cracks in the walls of Keble Chapel are blamed upon a defensive ditch dug beneath its site. The University Parks got their name because the royal artillery was parked there. Magdalen Bridge was turned into a drawbridge, Magdalen Tower became the city's eastern watch-post, and the New Cut, connecting the Cherwell with the Thames east of Christ Church meadows, was made to strengthen the defences on the London side. Munitions were stored in New College tower. The royal mint was established in New Inn Hall Street. They sharpened swords on the Godstow millstones. Prisoners were kept half-starved in the castle, and others were locked up in the church of St. Thomas à Becket where, having a particular aversion to that martyr, they took the opportunity of breaking the windows and burning the seats.

Life in the city was colourful, crowded and sometimes exciting. Troops of horses came clattering in, from Gloucester, Bristol, or the circuit of fortresses that formed Oxford's outer defences. The shouts of the sentries echoed through the night. Bonfires celebrated the King's victories, and occasionally word went round that another Parliamentary spy, slipping through the lines on the edge of

Otmoor, had been caught sneaking into the city from the north. Sometimes Prince Rupert, pennants flying, led a swift foray through the earthworks. Sometimes foreign ambassadors arrived from London for an audience of King Charles. The warlike portraits of Royalist officers painted in the city by William Dobson opened a new phase in English portraiture, so sternly virile was the style of his art as of his sitters.

Swank and dash abounded, it appears. There were gay dangerous visits to the fortified country houses still in Royalist hands: at Blechingdon House Oliver Cromwell himself surprised a party of officers and their ladies at dinner—the colonel in command, who escaped to Oxford, paid for his hospitality by being shot for negligence. In 1644, when the war was going badly for the Royalists, the King himself decided to launch some audacious counter-blows in the west, and secretly withdrew from Oxford. With an army of 5,500 men he slipped out at night across Port Meadow, by a route that local antiquarians have followed to the last cart-rut: off he stormed into the West Country, winning victories all the way, and by this brilliant manœuvre he staved off defeat for another two years, returning triumphantly to Oxford five months later.

When Oxford fell at last, in June 1646, it meant the end of the war, so symbolic had the city become of the Royalist cause. Its fall was an anti-climax. The Battle of Oxford was never fought. There were skirmishes on the fringes of the city—North and South Parades, in north Oxford, are said to mark the front lines of the two armies, and popular legend says that Shotover Hill got its name because Cromwell fired his musket over it. But as Lord Fairfax remarked, 'this was no place to be taken by a running pull, but was likely rather to prove a business of time hazard and industry'. One by one the ring of fortresses around Oxford fell, and when Bristol was lost the city was cut off from its supplies from the Continent. The King left Oxford once again—less dashingly this time, disguised as a servant over Magdalen Bridge—and within two months the isolated city gave in.

The surrender was negotiated in the manor house at Marston, now called Cromwell's House, and the articles were signed in Christ Church hall. The city was hardly scratched. A shell hit Christ Church hall, the church tower at North Hinksey was knocked down, and a flat tombstone in the graveyard of St. Giles, now used as a bird-table, is pointed out by fond traditionalists as the place where one indomitable Royalist escaped his Cromwellian pursuers. Oxford Castle was 'slighted' by the occupying army, reducing it to its present hang-dog state. The surrender was altogether orderly, the Cavaliers marching over Magdalen Bridge with flags flying and drums beating, only to disperse forlornly to their homes when they were out of the city: and half the Royalist veterans who died during the siege, and whose record is recalled in the Oxford churches, seem to have been the victims of old age or disappointment—'*Reader, look to thy feet*,' says one memorial, in the church at North Hinksey. '*There lies Wm. Fynmore ... who in the year of our Ld 1646, when loyalty and ye Church fainted, lay down and died.*'

The regimental museum of the former Oxfordshire and Buckinghamshire Light Infantry is housed in a military complex called Slade Park, at Headington—along the road from the nuclear warfare headquarters of the Royal Observer Corps, with a roof made out of 2,000 tons of concrete. All the English county regiments have such collections, and they are a reminder how deep the military tradition goes in even the most peaceable part of this normally gentle country. The Headington museum contains all sorts of intriguing mementos—shakos and mess crockery, old red tunics, souvenirs of the Maori Wars, medals and guns and maps and pictures. There is a cullender looted from the regimental mess during the Indian Mutiny, and found in the 1920s on sale in a Calcutta bazaar. There are the very shroud straps used to lower Sir John Moore, the regiment's most celebrated officer, into his grave upon the ramparts of Corunna (*We carved not a line, and we raised not a stone—But we left him alone with his glory*).

It is largely a collection from the days when battles were picturesque, gentlemanly, half-amateur, sometimes fun—when officers were country gentlemen, sergeant-majors stalwart yeomen, private soldiers scum. The wars of those times, it seems, fired their salvoes at Oxford from very long range indeed, and scarcely interfered with the more urgent controversies of the day, like Bulteelism, or whether dons should marry. Such traces as they have left in Oxford only make one feel what a perfect waste of time and sacrifice they were. A plaque on Carfax Tower, at the site of Penniless Bench, records the city's gratitude at the peace of 1814—but within a year Napoleon was back from Elba and the war had started again. A Boer War memorial in the cathedral records 25 deaths—but 12 were from disease. An obelisk at the corner of New Inn Hall Street commemorates the dead of the Tirah War, and ends with the names of three small dead buglers, A. J. Betts, T. Bull, C. Cox—but today not one Englishman in a thousand could tell you where the Tirah War was fought, or when, or why A. J. Betts, T. Bull and C. Cox had to die out there at all.

Until 1914, one feels, Oxford scarcely knew the weight of tragedy: since then she has never altogether shaken it off. In Oxford retrospect the second world war, though the stakes were probably higher, and the issues more fearful, seems only an aftermath of the first. The undergraduates went off to fight, of course. There was a German prisoner-of-war camp in the Hinksey hills. Beside the western by-pass there is a little war cemetery, with the graves of airmen killed in training, or unable to land their crippled bombers safely after raids on Germany: Australians, Canadians, New Zealanders, Italians, Belgians, Poles, Germans, a Ukrainian, a Greek and a Dutchman—every year a wreath arrives through the Red Cross for the grave of a German who died in captivity in 1944. Oxford people still remember looking out of their windows to see the soldiers stumbling home from Dunkirk, and Trinity College still remembers the college boat crew of 1939, which was Head of the River in the Eights Week races: it was stroked by Richard Hillary of *The Last Enemy*, and six of its eight members were killed in the war.

The War Office filled Keble College with girl secretaries and cipher clerks, and I am assured that on Friday nights, when there was fire practice, a girl called Elsie used to serve dinner at High Table wearing a big brass helmet. The Ministry of Food took over St. John's, and there is an elegant Latin inscription above a staircase there, deploring those 'six years of barbarian tribulation'. Part of the D-Day operation was planned by the Admiralty Intelligence services in the vaults of the New Bodleian, all among the Tibetan scrolls and the municipal charters.

But Hitler never bombed Oxford—he is said to have coveted the place too dearly—and the distant bugles whose echoes one still hears in this city call to us from the poppy-fields of Flanders. I sometimes feel the full impact of the Great War only fell upon Oxford fifty years later, like the cruel after-effect of some terrible wound, when the numbness has worn off, and the victim finds how crippled he is. When they speak of the lost English generation of 1914, Oxford and Cambridge come first of all to mind—so pitiably willing were those young men to fight in what seemed, for the first two years of it, so glorious a cause. At a time when the undergraduate population never exceeded 3,000, nearly 2,700 members of the University were killed in that war. In almost every Oxford graveyard there lies some soldier brought home from France, beneath the standard stone War Graves cross, or even a wooden one shipped back from Flanders with him.

More than 6,000 men, mostly local people, died with the Ox and Bucks: but it is the sad lists of the dead outside the college chapels that bring home the tragedy most terribly. New College's memorial is a vast and beautiful slab in the ante-chapel, 30 feet long, containing 263 names. Christ Church lost 256 men. Keble, then scarcely half a century old, lost 163—the college enrolment was less than 200. Sometimes they never even had a chance to matriculate, but were only members of a college by acceptance, though they went on to command ships or battalions before they died. Often, though they bore famous old names, they died as troopers. The very records of their service, preserved in the University Roll of Honour, are keys to a vanished England—like H. G. C. Perry-Scough, for example, Master of Arts of St. Alban's Hall, Captain in the 4th Connaught Rangers, holder of the Order of the Excellent Crop (6th Class), wounded and missing, believed killed, in a battle at Yooge in 1915. Julian Grenfell's war poem *Into Battle* appeared in *The Times* on the day he was killed in action. The one college acquaintance T. S. Eliot retained from his years at Merton was killed on his very first day in the trenches.

At every level of War Oxford was represented, from Field-Marshal Haig (Brasenose) to the enlisted college servants who made the best of all batmen. A Merton don invented the standard British gas mask, and when Lawrence first mooted his adventure in Arabia, his most influential support came from D. G. Hogarth, Keeper of the Ashmolean, who was then director of the Arab Bureau in Cairo. Eight Presidents of the Oxford Union were killed, and 120 members of the Diocesan Society of Bell-Ringers.

Sixteen Oxford men won V.C.s in the first world war, and pre-eminent among the heroes was the astonishing Noel Chavasse, whose wooden cross from Brandhock Cemetery, near Ypres, stands now in the chapel of St. Peter's College, which his father founded. At school this prodigy played rugger in the first XV, and was the best runner at almost any distance; at Oxford he not only got a first, but also ran and played lacrosse for the University; as a medical student he represented Great Britain in the Olympic Games of 1908; as an Army doctor he won the M.C. in 1915, the V.C. in 1916, and a second, posthumous, V.C. in 1917. On November 2, 1914, the All Souls betting book tells us, Pollard bet Hulton 2s. 6d. that the war would have ended before February 1916: but it was in November 1916 that Hulton was killed in action.

All these sadnesses are hammered home to you, brass by brass, name by name, as you wander around Oxford today, and for the first time you see this happy place as an elegiac city—so many hopes denied, so much wasted bravery, so many disillusionments. 'In Memory of Our Chums', says the wreath from the Old Contemptibles Association placed before the city cenotaph on Armistice Day—and there are little bunches of carnations still, for young men killed so long ago at Arras, Kut or Jutland. They are the ghosts of 1914 that chiefly haunt this haunted city, for to many of these soldiers Oxford represented the one altogether happy period of their lives—perhaps the one great emotional experience, or the one ecstasy.

> *Clad in beauty of dreams begotten,*
> *Strange old city for ever young,*
> *Keep the dreams that we have forgotten,*
> *Keep the songs we have never sung.*

So wrote one of them on leave in 1915, in that strange mood of exalted sentimentality in which his generation went to war: and it is easy to believe that if ever his shade strays from the silent battle-fields, it comes home to Oxford. Sometimes, it is said, a young man in a stiff white collar appears at Merton, looking very scrubbed and fresh, holding an old-fashioned notebook as if he is asking freshmen whether they would care to join the Cycling Club; and sometimes in old lodging-rooms above Duckers the bootmaker in the Turl, there appears for a moment or two, no more, a worn old wicker chair, such as an undergraduate might have loved for its homely friendliness, when he drank mulled claret with his friends up

there, or wrote to his sisters about the arrangements for Eights
Week.

It was not all golden glory. Grenfell used to delight in cracking a
stock-whip at the alien Philip Sassoon, when they were undergraduates together, and Oxford is probably a more truly civilized
city today than she was 50 years ago. After the first world war there
was angry resentment when New College erected a memorial to
three of its members who had died on the enemy side—'In memory
of the men of this College', says the slab in the ante-chapel, 'who
coming from a Foreign Land entered into the inheritance of this
place and Returning fought and died for their country.' After the
second war, when several colleges did the same, nobody thought
it wrong, or strange.

To many survivors of the holocaust, nevertheless, the real
Oxford, like the real England, died with those young men in the
Great War, and even now it is their standards that this city, half
regretfully, half mockingly, still fitfully aspires to: their fair frank
forms we instinctively look for, and fail to find, on the cross-benches
of the Union: their particular culture which is only now disappearing from the Oxford scene, like the smile of the Cheshire Cat—
the substance mostly gone, the shadow now dissolving, until soon
there will only be a wicker chair in an upstairs room, or 30 feet of
names on a college memorial, to remind us what it was.

20. The Heart of Things

One of the mediaeval chroniclers called Oxford the navel of the kingdom, and anatomically the metaphor is not far wrong. She has never been far from the heart of things. If you walk out of 10 Downing Street and turn left into Whitehall, ten brisk minutes will take you to Oxford Circus: and from there, in the very centre of the English capital, Oxford Street sets off for Magdalen Bridge and Carfax. Oxford and London feel even closer than they are. Smart undergraduates nip up to the night clubs in the twinkling of a headlight, and scarcely an evening train pulls into Oxford station without its quota of limp dons—home from a commission of inquiry, a television programme, a recording session, lunch at the *Times Literary Supplement* or a seminar on Slavonic Philology somewhere in Bloomsbury. Brasenose once actually owned an inn in the Strand, with rooms permanently reserved for its Fellows, and today many prosperous business people commute from London to Oxford every day.

There was a time, to judge by the language of the Anglo-Saxon Chronicle, when Oxford and London were more or less equals—in 912 Edward the Elder, we are told, 'took to himself Lundenbyrg and Oxnaford and all the lands that were obedient thereto'. In some ways Oxford was better placed to be a national capital, and the growth of a metropolis here might have prevented the awkward ill-balance of modern England, with its concentration of things richest, liveliest and nastiest in the south-east. As it is, Oxford has often been a kind of prod to the capital—feeding it with ideas, sometimes mocking its pretensions, always looking over its shoulder. Every cause has had its partisans here—'No Bombs', say the layered slogans on the Oxford walls, 'No War', 'No Franco', 'No Yanks' ('No Peel', hammered in nails into a door below Christ Church hall, refers to Peel's advocacy of Catholic emancipation, but 'No Popery', a familiar slogan of the 1880s, was only aimed at an unpopular proctor, R. W. M. Pope).

Oxford has a foot in most English doors: not merely because in almost any executive of the State there is sure to be a moiety of Oxford graduates, but also because whenever academic brain-power is needed, to sort out a social ratio, analyse an election result or examine an historical parallel, somebody dials Oxford on the telephone.

Kings and Oxford go together, as Mrs. Miriam Freeborn demonstrated in 1953, when she wrote a book about the connection at the age of 94. The Lord Mayor of Oxford is an Assistant Butler at the coronations of the English monarchs, and three of the Oxford colleges boast as their Visitor, so the University Calendar tells us in capital letters, H.M. THE QUEEN.

It is said that St. Frideswide laid a curse on royalty, after her unhappy experience with Prince Algar, and in fact the place has not always been lucky for monarchs. The blurred King Mephric was eaten by wolves at Wolvercote, Edmund Ironside is supposed to have been murdered in Oxford, Harold Harefoot died in the city, it was a *gemot* at Oxford which, by forcing King Harold to march northwards and crush a rebellion in 1066, left his southern flank open to William the Conqueror.

Later the curse wore off, and Oxford became a favourite city of the English sovereigns. In the grounds of No. 302 Woodstock Road, now a school, you may see a crumbling masonry arch, surrounded by a wooden picket and half-smothered with ivy. It is all that is left of Beaumont Palace, which Henry I built for himself at what is now the western end of Beaumont Street—where a plaque on the wall commemorates it. So lavish was this palace that in 1595 St. John's College bought its remains just for the sake of the materials, and took 1,000 wagon-loads of stone and timber to build the college library. King John was probably born inside its walls, and so was the most toweringly romantic of all Oxford's sons, Richard the Lion-Heart.

Do you dimly remember, from the schoolroom wall, that picture of the Empress Matilda, swathed in white, stealing across a frozen river escorted by a knight in chain-mail? It was Oxford that stood mistily in the background, and it was from the rubble walls of

Oxford castle that Matilda, besieged there by Stephen, was lowered by rope one night in the winter of 1143, to escape up the ice-bound Thames to Wallingford. Henry III, who built the walls of Oxford, regularly gave clothes and firewood to the anchoress who lived in a cell by Iffley church. Henry V is said to have been an undergraduate at Queen's, where he presumably learnt the 'damnable iteration' that Falstaff admired—'the art indeed able to corrupt a saint'. The only authority for the birthdate of Henry VII is an entry in a fourteenth-century Psalter in Exeter College library, which the Tudors used as a family record, and in which Katherine of Aragon was later to write, with a bride's satisfaction:

Thys book ys myn
Katherine the qwene

Poor Katherine must have had mixed feelings about Oxford. When Henry VIII wished to marry her, it was an Oxford don who went to Spain to escort her to England. When he wanted her to bear a son, it was to the fertility well at Binsey that he took her in pilgrimage. When he wanted to divorce her, he asked the advice of the Oxford lawyers, who said it would be illegal. And she could not know that one day Archbishop Cranmer, one of her tormentors, would have her ills revenged upon him in this very city.

Queen Elizabeth I seems to have had a high old time in Oxford. She came twice, and was feasted, orated to in Greek and Latin, entertained with comedies, tragedies, a pack of hounds in Christ Church hall, disputations and several kinds of 'academicall exercises'. The walls of St. Mary's, All Souls and University College were hung with sheets of verses in her honour, and the Bishop of Hereford delivered a speech so interminably loyal that the Queen sent word to him to cut it short. (Another welcoming address was read by Edmund Campion, who much impressed the Queen, but 15 years later was to be tortured in the Tower and hanged at Tyburn as a Catholic.) Elizabeth was an enormous success in Oxford. She replied in Greek and Latin herself, and was escorted to the top of Shotover Hill by the Chancellor, Doctors and Masters of the University, leaving behind her, in 1566, a valediction that is still quoted: 'Farewell, farewell, dear Oxford: God bless thee and increase thy sons in number, holiness and virtue.'

For the Stuarts, Oxford was frequently a reserve capital. They sometimes shifted their Parliaments here, even in peacetime, and Oxford has never quite lost her sympathy for them. James II, indeed, is not this city's favourite character, and when William of Orange was offered a vast banquet at the Sheldonian in 1695 he refused to eat a single thing for fear of being poisoned: he spent only an hour in Oxford, leaving all the food to be scrambled for by the town louts, who poured in through the theatre doors, like Arabs after a sheikhly feast, the moment the last of the courtiers had disappeared. James I, though, sits comfortably above the Bodleian quadrangle, handing out copies of his own works to Fame and to the University: and the two Charleses, who clearly enjoyed themselves in Oxford, are remembered affectionately in return. Charles II and his Queen used to stay at Merton: during their visits the college garden became such a scene of fashionable dalliance that it has been closed to the public ever since, and Lady Castlemaine once actually bore a son to the King within the college precincts, just around the quadrangle from the Queen. As for Charles I, in whose life Oxford played so fateful a part, candles burn before his portrait in the church of St. Mary Magdalen, and once a year a large Anglican congregation assembles there to honour his martyred memory.

The early Hanoverians preferred Cambridge, and Wadham, traditionally a Whig college, was almost alone in welcoming them to the throne: over the hall staircase there is a figure of James I, placed there at the college's foundation, but the Stuart arms above it have been altered to the Hanoverian. 'How d'ye do, marm?' said the Mayor of Oxford casually when Queen Adelaide came down in 1835. 'How's the King?' Queen Victoria disliked Oxford on principle, it is said—perhaps because the first attempt on her life was made by a madman called Edward Oxford: but the Prince Consort visited the city several times, once translating Marshal Blücher's speech for him during a banquet at Christ Church—'omitting only,' we are told, 'with that exquisite taste which distinguished him, those parts which were complimentary to himself'. Once Victoria came down herself, to visit her son. At Magdalen a chorister pushed a friend of his into the Queen's arms as she passed, but Her Majesty was not in the least put out, and simply pushed him back again.

Edward VII was an undergraduate at Christ Church, in a manner of speaking—he matriculated, that is to say, he was forbidden to smoke cigars, and he saw his first fox killed on the eastern heights, but he never lived in college, having at his disposal the whole of Frewen Hall, beside the Oxford Union, where his tutors dutifully came to educate him. George V was once found on his knees beside the fire at St. John's, sticking stamps into a huge album with the President. Edward VIII was an undergraduate at Magdalen, where he occupied the set of rooms traditionally reserved for royalty, beneath the Founder's Tower, and drove around in an enormous open Daimler. It was George VI in whose hand that key broke at the opening of the New Bodleian; when Queen Elizabeth the Queen Mother dined formally in Christ Church in 1946, she was the first woman to do so since Queen Elizabeth I.

You cannot actually learn kingship at Oxford, except by the study of your predecessors, but there is probably nowhere on earth where so many men have learnt how to be politicians. The most famous of political nurseries is the Oxford Union, the debating society of the University, which is a House of Commons in epitome—often as pompous as Westminster, sometimes as boorish, and frequently just as far-sighted. The Union Society is a club, physically the most depressing I know, with a gloomy bar and a restaurant like an indigent church vestry. The core of it, though, is the debating hall, a humped red-brick structure at the bottom of the garden. Here each Thursday evening the members, reinforced by a few eminent guests, meet in debate to all the protocol of Parliament—interruptions on points of order, references to the Honourable Gentlemen on the other side of the House, invitations to the Honourable the ex-Treasurer to take the chair, Tellers for the Ayes and Noes, hoity-toity references to the rules and angry interventions by young men with beards who want to know why the President had the heartless effrontery to say good morning to the South African Ambassador during his recent offensive visit to the city.

Around them there meditate, long hardened to it all, busts of distinguished predecessors—Gladstone, Asquith, Curzon, F. E. Smith, Macmillan. They represent a predominantly patrician past, but today the elected officers of the Union more faithfully represent the social spectrum. The President may be a Socialist from a Bradford secondary school, the secretary the son of a Scottish duke, the treasurer a Bengali in white trousers, the librarian the jolly decent son of a former colonial Civil Servant. They debate most of the obvious political issues of the day, helped along by visiting Ministers of the Crown, Opposition leaders, journalists and miscellaneous experts, except in the farewell debate of the term, when the motion is usually funny—'That this Union be Consummated', for instance—and the guests are likely to be erudite comedians.

Visiting foreigners often like to attend a Union debate, to see how decadent the young English are these days, and often the affairs of this society get into the newspapers. When the famous 'King and Country' motion was carried in 1933—'That this House will on no account fight for its King and Country'—it was interpreted as proof that England had gone soft at last (though it was really a reflection of the confused idealism, part pacifist, part Communist, then aflame in the English universities). Public opinion was severely shocked by it, and though *The Times* tried to shrug it off with an editorial headed 'Children's Hour', Winston Churchill called it disquieting, disgusting, squalid, shameless and abject, all in one speech—'one can almost feel', said he, 'the curl of contempt upon the lips of the manhood of Germany, Italy and France'. The curl faded in time, and for once *The Times* was probably wiser than Winston, but in the days when the privileged classes ruled England, and Oxford educated the privileged classes, the Union could usefully be watched as a political weather-gauge, to show how things were likely to go when the young gentlemen graduated from St. Michael's Street, and took the train to Parliament Square.

It is not so seminal now, because English politicians are drawn from a much wider background, and 25 new universities have been founded in the past half-century. Nowadays an evening at the Union is only a convincing, and sometimes alarming, demonstration of the fragile artificiality of the English democracy—quivering always on the edge of anarchy, and apparently at the mercy of strong characters. Sometimes you feel, when the president seems to be losing control, that the whole evening is going to break up in abuse and violence. Sometimes you can see how a swift and graceful stroke of repartee can dissolve an ugly situation in a trice, and instantly restore the discipline of the debate. Sometimes, when the tough in the hairy jacket persists in his interruptions, ignoring the instructions of the chair and loudly supported by cronies at his side—sometimes you may imagine how easily a forceful demagogue may break down the whole structure of democracy. Sometimes a supercilious lisp from the other side of the house, languidly suggesting that if the *spluttering* is to continue, the house might perhaps be provided with what one must assume the Honourable Gentleman opposite would call *serviettes*, reminds us how recently the caste system controlled this country, and how long it takes an English prejudice to die.

Like the city itself, the Union is always poised in a tricky balance—ready, you would think, to be pushed into chaos by a shove from any ill-wisher. It has been debating now, however, for more than a century, and visiting Cassandras are repeatedly surprised to find that when all the shouting is over, the obstreperous revolutionary has sat down at last, the insufferable true-blue has been hissed into silence, and the impossible pedant has been briskly squashed—'You are out of order yourself, you silly little man'—when the time for a division comes, the house carries the motion with orderly restraint, and does not even trip each other up, as it files out through the glazed doors into the Oxford night.

It is an incomparable school of politics. The groups of old committees that hang all over the corridors of the Society contain many familiar faces—not yet puffed or jowled by success, but recognizably a Foreign Secretary in his salad days, old Lord Thingummybob before he grew that awful moustache, or even a Prime Minister in hopeful embryo (for they nearly all have, even so early in their careers, a look of forbidding ambition). To have succeeded in Oxford politics is still a strong claim to a parliamentary nomination: at the Union you can get the feel, learn the language, acquire the thick skin of politics.

The whole atmosphere of Oxford is highly political. The University is run by inner politics, the shuffling of arguments and the alignment of forces, and the city's affairs have sometimes been a key to the state of the nation—which means that in the past they could be fearfully corrupt. In 1786 the Mayor and 10 others were arraigned before the House of Commons for corruption—they had offered to fix the election of two rich parliamentary candidates in return for some cash towards the settlement of the civic debt. 'A more enormous Crime you could not well commit,' said the Speaker (but all they got was four days in Newgate).

'An almost universal system of treating and bribery', is how a Commission of Inquiry described the municipal elections of 1832, and throughout the nineteenth century Oxford's parliamentary elections were notoriously crooked. Three times the elected member was unseated, because of corruption: when Thackeray stood unsuccessfully in a by-election in 1857 he said afterwards that he had 'gone down into Jericho and fallen among thieves'. The polling booths were rumbustious places in those days, with agents distributing beer and cash, dazed inmates of the workhouse pressed in as hustings-fodder, drunks everywhere and the Deputy Town Clerk busily handing out orders to draw liquor—'the mode of electing corporate officers in Oxford', as the 1832 Commission fastidiously observed, 'is peculiar'. As recently as 1924 a Liberal Member of Parliament for Oxford, Frank Gray, was unseated on petition because he had failed to keep proper election accounts—he was the first non-Conservative to be elected since 1885, and there wasn't another for 40 years.

This civic worldliness, coupled with the brain-power of the University, means that Oxford's political campaigns are often fought on a plane at once more ruthless and more sophisticated than most. The Oxford by-election of October 1938, the first in England after the Munich settlement, crystallized the nation's viciously mixed feelings about Neville Chamberlain's foreign policy. It was fought on the issue of national unity—for or against appeasement—and seldom can so many clever men have been involved in a single provincial election. The Conservative candidate was Quintin Hogg, Fellow of All Souls, who described Munich as a step towards 'a glorious goal'; his opponent was A. D. Lindsay, Master of Balliol, who saw Chamberlain's policy as 'vacillating, indecisive, fumbling and drifting', and who was actively supported by Roy Harrod the economist, Patrick Gordon-Walker, then a Christ Church don, R. H. S. Crossman, of New College and the City Labour Party, and the heads of six colleges. In the Union an organ scholar of Balliol, Edward Heath, accused Chamberlain of securing 'the peace which passeth all understanding': in the Town Hall Captain Harold Macmillan, himself a Conservative M.P., passionately supported the anti-Conservative candidate. A. P. Herbert, one of the University Members of Parliament, warned the electorate that Hogg's defeat would 'strike a dagger labelled "Oxford" into the heart of the Prime

Minister of our country at a perilous moment in our country's history'.

Hogg won, but Oxford's dagger struck home in the end—two years later, when Chamberlain was removed from office at last, and Quintin Hogg himself was one of those who voted against him. The episode sharply illustrated Oxford's special place in politics. On the one hand we have a highly coherent, prosperous, politically active municipality, important to any Party. On the other we have the University's powerful external links and influences, which often have international meaning. One of the incalculables of recent statesmanship was the incidence of Rhodes Scholars in Kennedy's administration: in Chicago in 1963 the British, German and French Consul-Generals were all Oxford graduates (though the Governor of Illinois, as it happened, was at Cambridge). In recent years Prime Ministers of Ceylon, Malta and Jamaica have all been Oxford men. General de Gaulle's daughter was at Lady Margaret Hall. The King of Norway was at Balliol. For 16 years President Radhakrishnan of India was Spalding Professor of Eastern Religions and Ethics. Felix Frankfurter, the most celebrated U.S. Supreme Court judge of our day, spent a year as Eastman Visiting Professor at Oxford—he called it the 'fullest, amplest and most civilized' year of his life. There is seldom a time when the University is not without some future Head of State, whether it be an African intellectual soon to thrust his way to the Presidency, or some plutocrat princeling of Arabia.

Almost half the English Prime Ministers have been Oxford men—since the second world war Churchill and James Callaghan have been the only exceptions, and Churchill was born at Blenheim, eight miles out. Attlee and his brother were both at this University, and the brother became vicar of Holywell church, where there is a memorial to his memory: the politician's name was Clement, but the clergyman was christened Bravery. Eden read Oriental Languages at Christ Church, Macmillan was a scholar of Balliol, and would have been President of the Union if it had not been for the first world war. Harold Wilson was an undergraduate at Jesus, where he won all kinds of prizes, and a Fellow of University, and he was married in Mansfield chapel in the presence of Amos and Mrs. Glover.

Traditionalists were disconcerted to discover, when the Labour Government took over from the Conservatives in 1964, that there were more Oxonians in the Socialist Cabinet than there had been in the Tory, including at least three dons. One of the perennial complaints of the English reformers is this dominance of Oxford in the affairs of the kingdom—Oxford bishops, Oxford politicians, Oxford publicists, Oxford lawyers: but it is likely to last, for there is no city in England where a young man may better get the feel of the State, tread in the footsteps of so many leaders, or more easily slip up the road to picket the party headquarters.

On warm summer nights I have sometimes parked my Volkswagen bus in Radcliffe Square, unrolled my sleeping bag and gone to bed in the shadow of the Bodleian. This is like sleeping in some private inner chamber of the city, where old letters are bundled, locks of hair are kept in envelopes, and the air is thick with memories. Very early in the morning I look through my open roof to see the top of Radcliffe's dome, and the comical pinnacles of All Souls, and the pink-grey sky above it all: and being of a romantic turn, and half-asleep too, I sometimes imagine I hear voices mingling with the first birds and bells of the morning.

I hear old Latimer in the flames—*'Be of Good Cheer, Master Ridley, and play the man!'*—and James II's angry voice at Magdalen—*'Get you gone! I am King!'*—and the Venerable Routh's last thoughtful murmur—*'Don't trouble yourself'*—and the tinny singsong of the Headington children—*'Who's ate all the bread and cheese? Us too, Quarry hogs!'* Gladstone, I fancy, has not quite ended his *viva voce*, and Newman's sweet oratory is still enthralling Richard Burton in St. Mary's across the square. Shelley argues on in his rooms at Univ., almost in my ear Heber is trying out that extra couplet on Sir Walter Scott; and there are scientific murmurings over by the Parks, and snatches of philosophical quibble from the Bodleian quadrangle; and somewhere in the Turl a young voice is singing, to the tune of *Armentières* or *Tipperary*, a sad soliloquy to the city.

And far in the background, beyond Magdalen Bridge and Shotover, I think I hear a constant solemn *basso profondo*, confused but commanding: the voices of all those men who have gone out from this city of the English provinces to guide or govern the world—with Hindus at their feet or Russians across the conference table, and Oxford always at the backs of their minds.

FIVE

*Ring roads surround Oxford, and allow the traveller
to give the city a long last circular inspection—to sympathize with its problems from one viewpoint, mock
its pretensions somewhere else, wonder how long its
character can survive, and draw some suitably in-
conclusive conclusions. Oxford inspires both love and
loathing: and in this, as in so much else, she is not
just a city, but a civilization, too.*

21. Gone Away!

By-passes encircle Oxford, throwing the traffic northward to Banbury and Birmingham, westward to Stratford and South Wales, southward to Southampton or eastward over the hills to London. Along them you can drive clean around the city, delayed only by odd moulds of suburbia—sometimes with the spires shining across the meadows at your side, sometimes with only the idea of Oxford there, like a glow in a night sky.

She looks different each time you catch sight of her, as the towers group and re-group themselves, and the foreground shifts. From the west she may look yellowish and desolate, with the railway lines investing her and the electric pylons skulking up Hinksey Hill. From the east she is lushly embedded in greenery, not a building in sight but some sort of masterpiece, not a harsh line to her composition—'cuckoo-echoing, bell-swarmed, lark-charmed, river-rounded'. Changing in this way, as you speed around her perimeter, she gives a proper impression of aged restlessness: the components always the same, the whole constantly altering. I recommend a run around the ring roads, with one eye on those distant buildings and one on the family motorists, as an epilogue to a study of this moody city—counting ten, like the testy citizens down the road, before you decide not to reach any decision at all.

Headington roundabout, and all is *ordinary*: not even hideous, only humdrum—a row of 1930-ish shops, a mock-Tudor pub, a few skimpy trees on the bump in the middle of the roundabout, a service station and a housing estate. 'Never to the Philistines!' cried Matthew Arnold: and as you swing through these unexciting purlieus, and take the northern by-pass past the A.A. box, Oxford down the road still feels a bastion against cheap and threadbare values, still sticking it out at the foot of Headington Hill.

She stands for the right to be special, and to be alone. The ring roads give form to this determination, binding within their periphery all her activities—the factories, the housing estates, the University at the centre. They are like a city wall in mediaeval days, and already the burghers are trying to cross them, to build their bungalows and warehouses on the other side, as the freemen of the Middle Ages broke up the pattern of the ancient city by building outside the gates. The character of Oxford lies largely in her suddenness—suddenly there, in all her richness, surrounded by damp countryside—but only unshakeable hostility to the Philistines will keep her so, and prevent suburbia from blurring her outlines and her style.

The times demand expansion, logic and majority rule. The specialness of Oxford, physical and spiritual, depends upon restraint, idiosyncrasy and the taste of a minority. By letting the city grow and grow, you could probably make it more prosperous still: but you would sacrifice its scale and temper, and perhaps reduce it in the end to the ranks of those unhappy English cities—Gloucester, Worcester, Exeter—that have been ruined by progress once and for all. By abolishing the college system you might make Oxford University more efficient; but you would lose half its fertile variety, and tacitly abandon its noble struggle for the privilege of being private.

There she is now, away to the left, with a flicker of Magdalen Tower across the fields. Turn up to Elsfield for a moment, on the ridge above the by-pass. John Buchan, Lord Tweedsmuir, is buried in the graveyard of the village church (a Christ Church living), and close beside him is the tomb of his faithful manservant—'Twenty Years', says his epitaph, 'A Friend of Lord Tweedsmuir.' From here, in one of the most famous of the city views, Oxford looks almost sickly in her perfection—with that Scottish gentleman and his loyal retainer lying so peaceful beside the church, and the sun on the fresh meadows, and perhaps, if you listen hard through the rumble of the traffic, a distant peal of Wadham Bob from the belfry of Marston church.

Why do people hate Oxford so? Chiefly because she so often

presents this picture of nostalgic idyll, of privileged persons enjoying outmoded delights, attended by servants to the sound of bells. For all the factories, for all the prosperity of the place, Oxford still stands for privilege. 'Where the lords go?' exclaims the miner's son in *The Corn Is Green*, when told he is to sit for a scholarship to Oxford: and if you tell a foreigner you are an Oxford man, he is likely either to shift his feet a little, and apologize for the soup, or laugh a steely sarcastic laugh—'Jove, old boy, you from the old *alma mater*? How's the jolly old school tie, what?' Almost every social reformer thumbs his nose at Oxford. State schoolmasters do not even bother to enter their pupils for admission, so unfairly do they feel the odds are weighted against them, so reluctant are parents to have their children humiliated among the toffs. They tell me that at Coventry workers from the local car factories are often to be seen dining in the best restaurants, but seldom indeed do Cowley families run the social gauntlet of such an evening in Oxford.

This is a dreary legacy of history. It is based on half-truths. The proportion of rich men's sons at Oxford is still unfairly high— because for so long the fee-paying schools have been geared to the Oxford system, and because old social habits take a few generations to break down. But it is largely insensibility. Oxford is not half so grand as her reputation. Listen to the accents of the student body, as it talks over its coffee in the cellars of the Union, and you will find that every class and every region is represented. Not since the first world war has Oxford been a preserve of the governing classes—and even then it was only a hang-over from the Victorian era, for traditionally the University was open to all comers, and in mediaeval days was the poor boy's surest route to great office.

But Oxford lacks the gift of persuasion, and until a few years ago, at least, abided still by old Jowett's dictum—'never explain, never apologize'. The more her colleges were criticized, the more loftily they withdrew into their halls of tradition, mumbling Latin aphorisms. Rude porters, diffident dons, gardens closed to the public, needless obscurantism—all unpleasantly tarnish Oxford's image: the façade this University offers to the world remains falsely snooty, as though it is by heredity a cut above the rest, and entitled by virtue of its Aluredian foundation to ignore the opinion of the helots outside.

It is changing fast—many of the dons I meet nowadays seem

almost abjectly sensitive to criticism, and there is even a University Information Officer: but from Elsfield the irritating side of Oxford shows. You feel like putting your tongue out at her.

Pray do so, and rejoin the highway—past the road that leads to the site of the Cuttleslowe Walls, until you reach the cluster of round-abouts in the north-west. Oxford is invisible now, and for a moment or two the environment feels more American than English. There are rows of middling, comfortable, house-proud villas, each with its car in a garage; and gas stations with Toilets where Agency Cards are accepted; and a couple of motels where they probably serve chicken-in-the-basket and cole slaw. It looks lively and rather gay, with striped umbrellas beside the motel swimming pools, but it feels an altogether different culture from those old grey spires down the Woodstock Road.

Oxford is at heart an intensely English city. The only foreign place she reminds me of is Kyoto. Like Kyoto, she is old, and private, and embeds her beauties in gardens behind high walls. The English tradition she embodies is, like the Japanese tradition, peculiar to the island—and as in Kyoto, it is only heightened by the fact that this is a provincial city, removed from the pressures of the capital. In both cities you feel that a manner of thought is stubbornly defying all that the world can do to humiliate it; and you feel too that not so long ago the tradition over-reached itself—in Kyoto, at the moment of Pearl Harbour, in Oxford, when the young man in the wicker chair went off to Flanders. In both cities an ancient religion infuses every wall and every custom. In Kyoto the students burn prayer-sticks at a Shinto shrine before taking their examinations: in Oxford the students used to pray in the hexagonal chapel of St. Catherine's, on the corner of New College Lane, before they crossed Catte Street for their disputations in the Schools.

They are both cities that reached their heydays in the era of the nation-States, and that era is now passing. Till now Oxford has, with the ease of a virile and confident culture, absorbed all the flow of foreign ideas, but remained absolutely her English self. Today the alien grafts show more. The undergraduates do not look so incorrigibly English as they used to look. The young workmen have a Latin air. A new, American kind of bourgeoisie is perceptibly emerging from the Cowley factories—rootless, classless, freed from many old inhibitions of caste or guild, devoid of craftsmanship, prepared to go wherever the money calls. The old English resistance to innovation has been replaced by an eager yearning for foreign notions. There is much more colour in the city than there used to be, and the old symptoms of stiff upper lip and modest reticence are fading. Oxford is once again becoming, as she was in the days of Catholic Europe, part of a wider comity: and if she felt somehow out of tune with the British Empire, the new groupings of States by cultures, civilizations even, is much more in her style.

Over the Thames now, and there is the paper mill at Godstow, and the Trout Inn beside the weir, and beyond Port Meadow the spires are ringed in Victorian red brick. To your right Wytham Wood looks like a mound of virgin woodland, haunted by deer and basket-makers, but it is not: it is part of the University's Experimental Farm, and all along that western ridge hidden villas are sprinkled, theological colleges look down upon the valley, and happy house-holders are fencing in their lawns with larchwood panels and wrought iron.

What about those crayfish, I can hear the reader expostulating, and eating moor-hens, and the tug-of-war across the river, and all that about casting lots for hayfields with cherrywood balls? It is true still, and the survival of that horny old rural society, within a mile or two of Oxford, adds piquancy to this city's flavour, and sets its sophistication into a sharper relief. It cannot last, though. Already the Cowley factories have cast their shadows across the villages, and before very long this rural island in the middle of England will be an island no more. The industrial complexes on each side are gradually extending their limits, like great landowners silently buying, year by year, smallholdings on the marches of their estates. Already High Wycombe, inside the Chilterns, feels like an appendage of London, and Banbury is fast becoming a colony of the industrial Midlands.

Slowly, as the English accept the truth that theirs is an urban society, the towns will doubtless coalesce, the suburbs will reach out to marry one another, and the agricultural land that remains will lose its earthiness. Oxford will no longer be the node of Middle England. The countryside will look to newer centres for its loyalties, its used cars and its cheeses. Already the traffic to South Wales,

which had travelled this way since Saxon times, passes by motorway
further to the south, across the Berkshire Downs and over the
Severn Bridge. Today's paradoxical juxtaposition of a curiously
rooted countryside and an exceptionally worldly county town is losing its punch—and its point.

For that other world, of huge urban masses, one town running
into the next, is not far away. More than once the smoke has come
right through the Goring Gap, and drifted up the Thames to Oxford
herself. There was London smoke over the city during the Great
Fire of 1666; people claimed to smell it during the bombing of the
capital in 1941; and if you cannot see it now, smudging the skies
over Iffley, it is only because computers have no chimneys.

Drive slowly now if you please, past North Hinksey where Ruskin
built his bumpy road, past South Hinksey where the archbishop
was born in the cottage opposite the pub, and the lane evolves so
cheerfully from Piers to Barleycott; and when you can find somewhere to park the car, nip through the hedge into the gravel pit
at the bottom of Chalgrove lane. This is where gypsies sometimes
stop, with their gleaming caravans and their Sunday television, and
with luck two or three cheerfully grubby children will come running
down to look at you, while Mr. Lee inspects the state of your tyres.

From here, among these genial nomads (half-gypsy, half-
mumper, some ferociously blonde, some as dark as sin itself) you
may look back across the ring road for the last time, and see Oxford
in a last perspective. There stand her buildings beyond the railway
lines, seen in flashes between the passing cars. *Wham*—there's the
spire of St. Philip and St. James, and the engineering block like
a white fortress—*swoosh*—and the noble central complex, dome and
spire and clustered pinnacles—*zoom*—that's Magdalen Tower at
the eastern gate, all alone among the trees—*slam*—and there are the
Cowley factories, huddled beneath Shotover: and so, between the
ding-dong of the cars, the noise hammering in your ears and the
pressure thudding in waves through the gap in the hedge, you can
intermittently see the whole of her.

And what you cannot see, you now remember—all the accumu-
lated experience of this famous city, all the wisdom, nonsense and
complexity, the sound of old pianos in college quadrangles and the
smell of the paint in the Morris paint-shop. It is as though a separate

little world exists over there, with its own private time-scale, and in a way this is true: for the Oxford we have been inspecting represents a civilization that is almost gone. Try though you may to see this city as a whole, still the factories and the housing estates feel like intruders upon some ancient preserve. All that is most re-markable about Oxford, setting her apart from other towns, or from other universities, comes from the lost order of the English—essen-tially a patrician society, stable, tolerant, amateur, confident enough to embrace an infinite variety within a rigid framework. The English gentleman dominates Oxford: not in the flesh, for he has almost vanished from the scene, but in the lingering spirit of the place.

Another England has emerged now, and Oxford is adapting to it, learning to live with the motor plants and the traffic, trying to keep up with the times. There is nothing pathetic to this city—'never regret', said Jowett—and the new Oxford will doubtless be just as self-satisfied as the old. But as you stand there in the gravel pit, with the cars thudding across your field of view, and a tangled imp in a long red frock tugging at your coat-sleeve, it is as though you are watching the envoi to a majestic play. The great trees planted in the heyday of the English landscape gardeners are now past their prime, and will soon be toppling, and the island character of the English is waning, too, as the wider civilization of the West takes over. Soon it will survive only in the history books: but we are not too late, and Oxford stands there still to remind us of its faults and virtues—courageous, arrogant, generous, ornate, pungent, smug and funny.

So you cross the river for the last time, and lurch through the Cow-ley factories (six men in a car in a traffic jam at the roundabout, as the afternoon shift goes home). Presently you complete the circle at Headington again, turn east towards the Chilterns, and are away. Middle England is behind your back. London and the great world enfolds you, and all the pageantry of Oxford fades and weakens in your memory, till you can no longer hear Buckland's jackal crunch-ing the guinea-pigs beneath the sofa, nor even see the midnight march of the proctors, so stately, so antique, past the quarrelsome Irish scaffolders in the doorway of the Old Tom.

Index